Who Is the Client?

The Ethics of Psychological Intervention in the Criminal Justice System

Edited by

John Monahan
School of Law, University of Virginia

American Psychological Association
Washington, D.C.

Library of Congress Cataloging in Publication Data
Main entry under title:

Who is the client?

  Bibliography: p. 154
    1. Psychologists—Professional ethics.   2. Criminal
justice, Administration of—United States.
I. Monahan, John, 1946–
BF76.4.W48   174′.9364   80-14101
ISBN 0-912704-14-4

Published by the American Psychological Association, Inc.
1200 Seventeenth Street, N.W., Washington, D.C. 20036
Copyright © 1980 by the American Psychological Association.
All rights reserved.

Contents

Foreword

Who is the Client? is the complete report of the American Psychological Association's Task Force on the Role of Psychology in the Criminal Justice System. It contains the conclusions published in the *American Psychologist* in December 1978 and, published for the first time, the five complete background papers commissioned by the task force.

The task force was created in late 1975 by APA's Board of Social and Ethical Responsibility for Psychology to consider the ways in which psychologists interacted with the criminal justice system and the ethical issues such interaction created. The recommendations of the task force were to serve as the basis for future APA policy in the area of criminal justice. The National Science Foundation's Ethical and Human Value Implications of Science and Technology Program provided funding (Grant OSS 76-15832) for a group of 12 persons, with numerous consultants, to meet periodically over two years to identify and articulate the ethical issues most salient in criminal justice work.

Although the report of the task force was approved by APA's Board of Social and Ethical Responsibility for Psychology in March 1978, it does not represent the official policy of the American Psychological Association. Likewise, the opinions, findings, conclusions, and recommendations expressed herein are those of the authors and do not necessarily reflect the views of the National Science Foundation.

The task force began by undertaking a survey of every psychologist whose primary employment setting was an agency of the criminal or juvenile justice system. Next, it commissioned comprehensive background papers on the ethical issues confronting psychologists in four areas of the criminal justice system: the police, the courts, correctional institutions, and the juvenile justice system. Each background paper was then used as a stimulus for discussion and debate at a national workshop. At these workshops, task force members and invited guests discussed the ethical issues involved in the particular areas, suggested revisions to the background papers, and contributed to the conclusions formulated in the final report.

The task force wishes to acknowledge the many people who have assisted us during the two years of our deliberations. Richard Boone, as a member of the Board of Social and Ethical Responsibility for Psychology, was instrumental in forming the task force. Frank Ochberg served as a member of the group during its initial phase, and Fred Strassburger and Serena Stier provided APA staff assistance. The authors of the commissioned background papers provided an excellent framing of the issues in their various areas. These papers were skillfully critiqued by the participants at our national workshops: Morton Bard, Terry Eisenberg, Patrick Murphy, Martin Reiser, Jerome Skolnick, Paul Lipsitt, Elizabeth Loftus, Richard Millstein, Paul Nejelski, Bruce Sales, Saleem Shah, Carolyn Suber, John Boone, Robert Levinson, and Jane Knitzer.

As chair of the task force, I would like personally to thank the task force members for their dedication and insight. I learned an enormous amount from them about psychology, ethics, and criminal justice. I hope and believe that the reader will be as stimulated by this book as I was by their dialogue.

John Monahan
February 1980

1
Report of the Task Force on the Role of Psychology in the Criminal Justice System

Psychologists are involved in virtually every facet of the criminal justice system. When a person is arrested, it may well be by a police officer who was screened by a psychologist before being hired and trained by other psychologists in ways of handling such potentially hazardous situations as an arrest. Should the police officer use undue force or poor judgment in effecting the arrest, the officer may be sent to the department's psychologist for treatment.

The defendant may then be evaluated by a psychologist to determine whether he or she is competent to stand trial before a jury that other psychologists are in the process of selecting. If competent, the defendant may be examined by a psychologist to determine whether he or she was insane at the time of the offense and so should be sent to a mental hospital for psychological treatment. At the trial, eyewitnesses to the crime may have their perceptions and memories challenged by a psychological expert. The fate of the convicted offender may rest in part on what a psychologist recommends to the judge in a presentence evaluation.

Should the offender be sent to prison, he or she may be classified by one psychologist for the purpose of being treated by another, and the treatment may not end until a third psy-

chologist predicts that the offender can be released into society without risk of recidivism. Remaining free on parole may be contingent upon attendance at outpatient psychotherapy.

Encouraged by presidential commissions and supported by federal and foundation funds, a substantial increase in the involvement of psychologists in criminal justice work has occurred in the past decade along with an equally substantial increase in criminal justice and law as topics of interest for psychological research. Numerous recent works have chronicled and conceptualized the burgeoning interactions between the two areas (Brodsky, 1973; Konečni & Ebbesen, in press; Lipsitt & Sales, 1980; Meehl, 1970; Monahan, 1976; Sales, 1977a, 1977b; Sarbin, 1979; Tapp, 1976; Tapp & Levine, 1977; Toch, 1979).

The Task Force

In late 1975, the Board of Social and Ethical Responsibility for Psychology was confronted with requests that it recommend official positions for the American Psychological Association on matters of criminal justice policy involving psychology. Rather than attempting to evaluate each proposal on an ad hoc basis, the Board commissioned a Task Force on the Role of Psychology in the Criminal Justice System to investigate comprehensively the complex ways in which psychologists are involved in

Reprinted from the *American Psychologist*, 1978, *33*, 1099-1113. Revised and updated for publication in this book.

the criminal justice system and the ethical issues raised by this involvement.

The task force was composed of 12 members representing psychology and other disciplines having varying perspectives on the criminal justice system and the roles of psychologists in it—law, criminology, social work, corrections, and philosophy—as well as a prisoners' union representative.[1] The National Science Foundation's Ethics and Values in Science and Technology Program provided support for four meetings between February 1977 and January 1978 at which the task force members plus invited groups of psychologists and others working in police, court, correctional, and juvenile justice agencies considered prepared background papers (Chapters 2–5 of this book). In order to guide the selection of topics for debate and to present case material, a survey, (see Chapter 6) had been conducted of the 349 psychologists who responded on the 1975 APA Manpower Survey that the criminal justice system was their primary employment setting.

What follows is our attempt to isolate the key ethical issues for psychologists in criminal justice work and to present recommendations on the ethical course that psychology, as a profession, should set in this area. A detailed summary of the roles occupied by psychologists in the various agencies of the criminal justice system and the myriad ethical quandaries encountered in performing is beyond the scope of this report. The reader is urged to consult the comprehensive background reports commissioned by the task force (Chapters 2 through 6 of this book).

A Preliminary Consideration

Before addressing ethical issues related to the role of the psychologist in the criminal justice system, we would like to stress a conclusion that became evident early in our deliberations: Many of the ethical issues facing psychologists in the criminal justice system are shared with psychologists working in any other organizational setting.

A principal role conflict and ethical dilemma of psychologists in criminal justice—to help the client, to further the "system," or to serve what they perceive to be the interests of society—is also a principal conflict of psychologists in educational, health, industrial, and governmental settings. The confidentiality of psychologists' records in prisons is no more, and no less, an ethical concern than the confidentiality of psychologists' records in schools, mental health agencies, insurance companies, and the military. The ethical questions of professional competence that arise when psychologists offer their services to screen police candidates are the same as those occasioned by the screening of applicants for the airlines or the Peace Corps.

However, there is a special urgency to address ethical problems in dealing with the criminal justice system, since that system has such a profound impact on the fundamental liberties of the people within its grasp. While other institutions, such as mental hospitals, also restrict individual freedom, the criminal justice system is the principal locus of legitimate force in American society. The consequences of its misapplication may be severe and irreversible. An additional reason for placing a high priority on ethical concerns in criminal justice is that the people processed by that system are likely to be poor or minorities and thus to have little access to conventional means for redressing their grievances.

What psychology appears to lack at the present time is an effective way to differentiate obligations owed to organizational as opposed to individual clients, of which dilemmas in criminal justice work are only one example. Most of the ethical norms of the profession derive from situations in which an individual client freely contracts for services with a

---

[1] While the large majority of the task force members had experience in working with the criminal justice system, most were primarily employed in academic settings. In retrospect, we would recommend that APA boards strive to achieve a greater balance between "academics" and "practitioners" in the appointment of future panels.

psychologist in private practice or voluntarily enters an experimenter-subject relationship. While such arrangements do indeed engender ethical difficulties, principally regarding the best interests of the client versus the broader social good, they fail to reflect the complexities that arise when an organizational third party makes competing claims on the psychologist's loyalty.

Consider the simple example of the psychologist in private practice whose client, in the course of therapy, reveals racist attitudes or behavior. The psychologist, depending upon his or her ethical convictions concerning the relevance of such attitudes or behavior to the appropriateness of continuing therapy with the client, may choose to ignore such attitudes or behavior as irrelevant to therapy, may attempt to alter them, or may, if he or she feels strongly enough, choose to terminate treatment or refer the client elsewhere. But under no conceivable circumstances would it be considered appropriate professional ethics if the psychologist—in furtherance of his or her view of the interests of society—informed the client's employer or wrote an exposé on the client's racism for the local newspaper.

Consider an alternate example. A psychologist working as a consultant to a law enforcement or educational organization discovers, in the course of his or her work, racist organizational policies—perhaps a pattern of discriminatory hiring or a biased application of sanctions. As in the previous example, the psychologist, depending upon his or her ethical convictions, may choose to ignore such behavior as irrelevant to the consultation, may attempt to alter it, or may, if he or she feels strongly enough, choose to terminate the consultation or refer the organization elsewhere. But would it *always* be inappropriate professional ethics for the psychologist to inform the organization's employer (e.g., the city council) or to write an exposé on the organization's racism for the local paper, as it would in the case of the individual client? Might there not be some limited number of severe cases

where, all else failing, a "whistle-blowing" breach of confidentiality is the *only* appropriate ethical response, even though a "clear and imminent danger" of physical violence is not present?

We are not suggesting that psychologists should avoid serving in imperfect organizations, only that the perennial debate concerning whether it is better to work from the inside to achieve gradual change or to leave the organization and apply pressure from the outside for reform (Levinson, Note 1) is common to all organizational structures, not just justice system ones, and that such debates are not always enlightened by recourse to analogies based on the ethics of clinical practice. What is right for the psychologist's work with an individual may be wrong for the psychologist's work with an organization—any organization—and vice versa. The question in dealing with organizations is not, on reflection, so much "*Who* is the client?" but rather "*What* is a client?"—What ethical obligations are owed to an organizational, as opposed to an individual, purchaser of psychological services? It is a reflection on ethical issues such as these—how to differentiate the kinds of obligations owed to organizational and to individual clients and how to relate these obligations to the broader concern for human welfare—that the field of psychology currently lacks. Since it is our strong belief that psychologists in criminal justice settings are, as a whole, no less "ethical" than psychologists in other organizational settings (such as universities), we have no desire to single out criminal justice psychologists as scapegoats for the profession's ethical quandaries in dealing with organizations.

The Ethics of Psychology or the Ethics of Criminal Justice?

The charge of the task force was to consider the ethical issues that arise when psychologists work in the criminal justice system. It quickly became evident in our discussions that two re-

3

lated but clearly separable questions were being asked: What are the ethical issues confronting psychologists who work in criminal justice settings, and what are the ethical issues created for the criminal justice system by the presence of psychologists and the ideology that fosters their participation? Despite repeated attempts to remain focused on the former question, the task force found it impossible to consider the ethical dilemmas of the psychologist without repeated reference to the ethical dilemmas of the system in which they work. While recognizing that to address only the larger ethical questions of criminal justice would be insufficient at best and likely ill-advised, since psychologists have no special claim to be the arbiters of ethical issues in criminal justice, the task force concluded that to fail to address at least some of the broader social and ethical issues raised by the presence of psychologists in the criminal justice system would be an even worse failing. It would be to accept blindly the criminal justice system as it is presented to us—to accept without question the goals and nature of that system and their implications for the roles psychologists might be provided. We have chosen, therefore, not to accept such a "take it or leave it" dilemma in regard to the system. The fact that the roles currently open to psychologists in criminal justice are sanctioned by society and therefore "legal" is of only mild consolation, since it is obvious that what is legal can be immoral (e.g., human salvery was at one time legal in the United States) and what is illegal can be moral (e.g., helping persons who were slaves escape to freedom was at one time illegal in the United States) (Wasserstrom, 1963). Bittner (1970) has put it well in the context of the police:

> The formulation of criteria for judging any kind of institutional practice, including the police, rather obviously calls for the solution of a logically prior problem. Clearly it is necessary that it be known *what* needs to be done before anyone can venture to say *how* it is to be done well. In the case of the police,

this sets up the requirement of specifying the police role in society. (p. 2)

For psychologists to fail to consider the social context that frames their perceived ethical alternatives, we believe, unnecessarily limits the scope of ethical discourse and restricts the range of ethical response. To accept the criminal and juvenile justice systems on their own terms may be to settle for "first order," or cosmetic, change rather than "second order," or more fundamental, improvement in how we conceptualize the roles and ethics of psychologists (Watzlawick, Weakland & Fisch, 1974; also see Chapter 5 of this book).

We have, therefore, attempted to consider both the ethical issues that the criminal justice system creates for those psychologists who work in it as well as the ethical issues created for the criminal justice system by the assumptions that lead it to hire psychologists and employ them in certain roles. We intend our ethical recommendations to be interpreted not as immutable commandments but rather as guides to action and stimuli to provoke self-searching. Circumstances may arise that would justify exceptions from the general principles we offer. While none of us, for example, believes it ethically justifiable to kill political leaders with whom we disagree, just because we disagree with them, if we were colonels in the German Army in 1944, we hope we would have had the courage and the moral judgment to join in the plot to put an end to Hitler. Hard cases do not make good law. In criminal justice, as elsewhere, an entire constellation of relevant factors must be taken into account before implementing a generally sound ethical principle in any given situation. We recognize that many dilemmas faced by psychologists in the criminal justice system involve clashes of values for which no completely satisfactory solution is possible. In such situations, people of equal integrity and commitment to moral values may arrive at conflicting courses of action. While wishing to promote intensive dialogue and debate on ethical issues, we urge that the self-righteous condemnation that sometimes passes for moral reasoning in this area be avoided.

Ethical Issues the Criminal Justice System Creates for Psychologists

Questions of Loyalty

Recommendation 1: *Psychologists in criminal justice settings, as elsewhere, should inform all parties to a given service of the level of confidentiality that applies and should specify any circumstances that would constitute an exception to confidentiality, This should be done in advance of the service, preferably in writing.*

Recommendation 2: *The ideal level of confidentiality of therapeutic services in criminal justice settings should be the same as the level of confidentiality that exists in voluntary noninstitutional settings.*

No question arises more frequently in discussions of the ethics of psychological intervention in the criminal justice system than "Who is the client?" Often the question is asked rhetorically, for any attempt to answer it is dismissed as a "value preference." Since questioning someone's values is viewed as akin to questioning his or her religion, the discussion often ends there. When psychologists do try seriously to articulate who their client is—where their loyalties are to be given—in criminal justice, they sometimes appear to be under the impression that they are constrained to a multiple-choice answer, with the alternatives being (a) the "system" (or "society") and (b) the offender (or police officer or defendant, as the case may be).

It appears to us that there is no need for psychologists to impale themselves on the horns of this dilemma, since "Who is the client?" is not a multiple-choice question. It requires an essay answer.

To us, *both* the offender (or the police officer, etc.) and the criminal justice system may be the clients of the psychologist working in the criminal justice system, but *in different roles and with varying priorities*. There are surely situations in which the psychologist cannot serve two masters, but it does not follow that allegiances must be invariant and that one must always have priority over the other.

In the role of a therapist providing treatment for an offender or a police officer who wants to change his or her behavior, the psychologist, we believe, primarily must be the agent of the individual. This would mean the therapy should only be given on a truly voluntary basis and that it should not be used as a means to pursue administrative ends, such as release or promotion decisions. This is a question of priority rather than an absolute prescription, since in a limited number of defined situations, allegiances may be reordered, such as when information is presented in therapy that a life-threatening act is imminent.

There are other roles in which the criminal justice system may be the psychologist's primary client. Psychological assessments performed for the purpose of selecting police officers and prison guards are the clearest examples. The psychologist's primary goal here is not to assure that applicants achieve their greatest life potential, but rather to help the system improve its odds in choosing those candidates with the highest probability of being able to fulfill job demands.

One psychologist, for example, who works with a large metropolitan police department maintains strict confidentiality concerning the content of therapy sessions with police officers when they themselves initiate the request for help. The psychologist, in this situation, takes the individual officer as his primary client. If, however, an officer is referred by the administration of the police department for treatment of a problem interfering with his or her job, and the department inquires about the progress of treatment, the psychologist may reveal information gained in therapy. In these situations, the psychologist takes the agency as his primary client. Further, the psychologist clearly informs the officer when each of these contingencies apply (Reiser, 1972).

Likewise, a recent report commissioned by the Federal Bureau of Prisons' Executive Staff is generally supportive of a high degree of confidentiality in the limited situations in which it is believed appropriate for psychologists to conduct psychotherapy with prison staff members. Yet the report clearly specifies that there is one situation in which the priorities of allegiance can be reversed: "The responsibility [of psychologists] to keep the Warden advised of staff problems which may affect the overall security of the institution must override keeping staff statements confidential" (Federal Bureau of Prisons, Note 2).

As these two examples indicate, the question of where the psychologist's loyalties lie centers most often on concerns for the confidentiality of information obtained by the psychologist. Fully three out of four of the criminal justice psychologists surveyed by the task force reported that one of the major ethical issues they face concerned confidentiality (see Chapter 6).

While confidentiality dilemmas—which we see as only one manifestation of the larger issue of the psychologist's loyalties—are acute in the criminal justice system, they appear to be a growing concern to all psychologists who engage in treatment. In a far-reaching and bitterly contested decision, the California Supreme Court recently ruled that

> public policy favoring protection of the confidential character of patient-psychotherapeutic communication must yield in instances in which disclosure is essential to avert danger to others. The protective privilege ends where the public peril begins.[2]

---

[2] Tarasoff v. Regents of the University of California, Sup. 131 Cal. Rptr. 14 (1976).

Some psychologists have interpreted this decision as driving a stake into the heart of psychology. Siegel (1977), for example, has argued that there are no circumstances that ethically can justify the breaking of confidentiality:

> When we agree to "exceptional circumstances" under which the confidentiality of information about individuals is waived, we not only violate the civil rights of children and adults, but we violate our essential role as psychologists. (p. 2)

Shah (1977), on the other hand, while agreeing with the importance of confidentiality in psychological practice, does not view specific exceptions to it as necessarily lethal to psychology:

> Some clinicians are utterly convinced that therapeutic confidentiality must remain an *absolute* and paramount value over all other societal interests. Such ethnocentric zeal seems to demand that the entire society should accept the value and ideologies of psychotherapists. In other words, what is good for psychotherapists is good for society! (p. 2, emphasis in original)

The view of the task force is closer to that of Shah (1977) than to that of Siegel (1977). We would note that the APA *Ethical Standards of Psychologists* (1963) have always allowed for an exception to confidentiality "when there is clear and imminent danger to an individual or to society" (Principle 6, p. 3). Surely the psychological assessment of candidates for police and prison work would be meaningless without some "feedback" to the potential employer. In the case of psychological treatment undertaken in criminal justice contexts (whether with prisoner or staff), we would take as a goal that the same standards of confidentiality should apply in criminal justice settings as apply in "free-world," privately contracted therapy—no less, but no more. This would mean that information obtained in treatment not be released without client consent (as a privately contracting client can request to have information revealed to an insurance company). It would also mean that the same specific exceptions to confidentiality in "free-world" settings can apply to confidentiality in criminal justice settings, namely, when knowledge of a "clear and imminent danger" (e.g., a prison riot) is volunteered.

One crucial point in addressing confidentiality, as in addressing other dilemmas of the psychologist's loyalty, is that all parties with a claim on the psychologist's loyalty be fully informed in advance of the existence of confidentiality, or lack of it, and of any circumstances that may trigger an exception to the agreed-upon priorities. The individual being evaluated or treated then has the option of deciding what information to reveal and what risks to confidentiality he or she wishes to bear.

We recognize that many psychologists feel strongly that absolute confidentiality is a prerequisite to the provision of ethical and effective psychological treatment, and at the same time that the pressures to violate confidentiality are extreme and constant in many criminal justice settings. Given the intensity of these feelings regarding confidentiality on the part of many psychologists and the strength of the opposing pressures on the part of the criminal justice system, psychologists would do well to make themselves aware of and come to terms with agency policies on confidentiality before accepting employment in a criminal justice setting.

In a basic sense, confidentiality is a right not so much of the psychologist but of the client. As with release of information to third parties, the pressure to violate the client's "right to know" what is being said about him or her is great in the criminal justice system. While the issue of client access to psychological records is a complex one that is raised in many settings, we believe that, as a minimum, there should be a general presumption that formal psychological reports made to criminal justice agencies be available to the individuals who are subjects of the reports.

Recommendation 3: *Other than for legitimate research purposes, psychological assessments of offenders should be performed only when the psychologist has a reasonable expectation that such assessments will serve a useful therapeutic or dispositional function.*

At the risk of appearing naive, the task force believes that there may be situations in criminal justice work in which the above kinds of conflict among priorities of loyalty do not arise. The psychologist sometimes may be able to serve several masters without slighting any. Training police officers in psychological techniques for nonviolent conflict resolution (Bard, 1969; Driscoll, Meyer, & Schanie, 1973; Novaco, 1977) may be one such situation. To the extent that the techniques are effective, all "clients" of the psychologist—the police officers, the police agency, and the larger society—are better off.

Unfortunately, there is another category of situations where conflicts of loyalty do not arise. Here, however, it is not because the psychologist is serving many masters but because he or she is serving none. The survey conducted by the task force revealed a substantial number of psychologists who were dismayed by their assignment to administer endless batteries of tests to prisoners to assess their suitability for treatment programs, when in fact no treatment programs existed or were likely to. As Corsini (1956) has noted,

> correctional psychology is in a chronic state of stagnation, well illustrated by excessive overemphasis on psychological testing—most of which is either not used or misused. The operation of testing becomes an end in itself: numbers go into folders and there are decently interred. (p.22)

Brodsky (Chapter 4), 20 years later, similarly has observed,

When they exist for their own sake, such psychological assessments can be ritualistic and pointless. In [prison] reception and diagnostic centers, these assessments have been described as boring, repetitive and frustrating to the staff, an Edsel-like flop for the system and a disservice and waste of resources for all involved. (p. 65)

Such assessment-without-disposition functions, when not done for legitimate research purposes (see Recommendation 8), constitute an unethical intrusion into the lives of offenders and an unprofessional squandering of limited psychological resources and limited public funds. Perhaps most objectionably, they give the illusion that psychological services are being provided to offenders and thus serve to legitimate aspects of the criminal justice system that are in serious need of reform.

The answer to the question of where the loyalties of the psychologist in the criminal justice system should be placed, therefore, is a complex one. It depends upon the specific role of the psychologist under consideration, and specified situations may arise within each role that can reorder priorities. It is the precise delineation of these roles and situations, and their unambiguous communication in advance to the various "clients" of the psychologist in the criminal justice system, that is the thrust of our ethical recommendations.

Questions of Competence

Recommendation 4: *Psychologists who work in the criminal justice system, as elsewhere, have an ethical obligation to educate themselves in the concepts and operations of the system in which they work.*

"Psychologists," according to the 1979 APA *Ethical Standards of Psychologists*, "recognize the boundaries of their competence and the limitations of their techniques" (p. 2). This is essentially a consumer-protection principle with which it is difficult to take issue. As with other products, it is in establishing the precise boundaries and limitations of a psychologist's service that disagreements arise.

"Competence" is not so much a characteristic of the psychologist, in the sense of having the appropriate degrees or license, but rather an interaction between the abilities of the psychologist and the demands of a given setting. A psychologist may be competent in one setting and incompetent in others. A prerequisite to the development of competence in any setting is a thorough knowledge of the system in which the psychologist is operating.

Perhaps the criminal justice system more than other organizations presents an initial challenge to the competence of the psychologist who would work in it. That challenge takes the form of knowing what the system is and how it operates. While all psychologists have been in schools and many have some acquaintance with the mental health system, their prior interaction with criminal justice often does not go beyond receiving a traffic ticket. Legal education generally is not part of the education of a psychologist, and confusion on the part of mental health professionals in court concerning basic concepts of criminal law appears to be common (McGarry et al., 1973). Given that the decisions made in the criminal justice system on the basis of psychological reports and testimony are so often fateful for the individuals involved, ignorance of relevant legal concepts and the organizational context in which they operate is particularly distressing. Shah (1975) has put it forcefully:

[Psychologists and others] who work in forensic or legal settings, or those who choose to function in situations requiring involvement with the legal system, have a clear and definite responsibility to become properly informed about the relevant legal issues, questions, and criteria pertaining to their roles and functions. It is quite presumptuous, to put it mildly, for mental health and medical professionals to render opinions and recommendations on issues of pretrail competency, criminal responsibility, involuntary civil commitment, sexual psychopathy, and the like, when the relevant legal issues and criteria are not properly understood. Acquiring a sound and accurate understanding of the relevant issues must be viewed as a *professional and ethical requirement*. (p. ix, emphasis in original)

Recommendation 5: *Since it is not within the professional competence of psychologists to offer conclusions on matters of law, psychologists should resist pressure to offer such conclusions.*

Those who attempt to educate themselves in criminal justice will soon discover, among other things, that a recurrent criticism of psychologists and other mental health professionals in the courtroom is that they render conclusions that are more properly within the province of the judge or the jury. Psychological testimony, the criticism goes, is often an imposition of the psychologist's personal value preferences into moral or policy issues more appropriately left to other decision makers in a democratic society (Morse, 1978).

A psychologist who, for example, offered the opinion that a given person had a certain probability of committing certain criminal acts in a specified time period, would be making a *professional or scientific statement* (although it would likely be grossly inaccurate—see below). However, a psychologist who simply offered that an individual was "too dangerous to be released" would be making a legal or social value statement. The psychologist would be imposing his or her values as to the degree of risk society should bear in releasing the individual. Other examples could be found in the areas of the insanity defense and incompetence to stand trial. We would note that often it is not that the psychologist volunteers such conclusive statements, but that the courts, in an attempt to evade their responsibility to deal with difficult issues, pressure psychologists to answer legal questions for them.

Recommendation 6: *Psychologists should be clear about what they are trying to accomplish*

in the criminal justice system and the state of the empirical evidence in support of their ability to accomplish it.

The history of research in psychotherapy has shown that it is fruitless to attempt to assess the global competence or effectiveness of psychologists in treating psychological disorder. The question needs to be much more task-specific: *How* competent are *which* psychologists at treating *which* people for *what* problems? Likewise, one cannot address the issue of the competence of psychologists in the criminal justice system without specifying the range of tasks on which competence is to be measured.

A close reading of recent literature on the effectiveness of psychological services in criminal justice settings reveals that (a) for some tasks the research is moderately encouraging (e.g., some forms of police training, restoration of defendants for competency to stand trial), (b) for other tasks the research is discouraging (e.g., the prediction and treatment of violent criminal behavior—see below), and (c) for the great majority of tasks there are no data at all.

If one accepts this assessment of the state of the art of empirical research on the competence of psychologists in the criminal justice system, one is not led to throw in the professional towel, since practice has preceded progress in virtually all areas of psychology (and medicine as well). But one *is* led to be exceedingly modest in how psychological services are "promoted" in criminal justice. "Caveat emptor" has long ago given way to "truth in advertising" in other areas, and the need for frankness in representing the effectiveness of psychological services in criminal justice appears to be acute.

Note that we are not recommending that "unproven" or novel programs be abandoned. To do so would be to put the criminal justice psychologist in a classic Catch-22 situation: A program cannot be documented until it is initiated and cannot be initiated until it is documented. We are recommending frankness and an avoidance of "oversell." If a service has not been adequately researched in the past, it should not be represented as "effective." Rather, the psychologist should inform the police chief, judge, warden, or offender to the effect that "Here is what I would like to do and what I hope it would accomplish. There are theoretical reasons why I think it could be effective, but there has been no good research on the topic, so I cannot be sure. Shall we give it a try and evaluate the results?"

Recommendation 7: *There is an ethical obligation on psychologists who perform services in the criminal justice system, as elsewhere, to encourage and cooperate in the evaluation of those services.*

Frankness about the limitations of knowledge concerning psychological services in the criminal justice system must be augmented by a commitment to develop that knowledge wherever possible. We do not see empirical research in criminal justice as a luxury to be indulged in after the psychologist's "service" activities are completed. Rather, we see the empirical evaluation of psychological services in the criminal justice system as an *ethical necessity* for the profession. We do not underestimate the formidable methodological difficulties and bureaucratic hurdles confronting the would-be evaluator. We also realize that psychologists are most often hired by criminal justice agencies to provide services, not to perform research. Yet it is worth the effort to climb the ladder of methodological sophistication even if one does not reach the top rung. Much can be learned from nonrandomized designs, and there have been some successful efforts at controlled evaluations of psychological services in criminal justice settings (Kassebaum, Ward, & Wilner, 1971; cf. Quay, 1977). Research provides us with the only way of validating the competence of the psychologist in criminal justice through alerting us to those areas in which psychological services are effective. It provides the empirical basis for making

informed ethical decisions on the roles psychologists should assume.

Recommendation 8: *Psychological research in prisons should conform to the ethical standards proposed by the National Commission for the Protection of Human Subjects.*

Psychologists in the criminal justice system may sometimes feel that, regarding research, they are damned if they do and damned if they don't: condemned as "having something to hide" if they fail to pursue vigorously the evaluation of their services and vilified as turning prisoners into "guinea pigs" as soon as they ask people to fill out a form. It is our belief not only that the pursuit of empirical knowledge regarding psychological services in criminal justice is an ethical necessity for the profession of psychology but that it is ethically possible to obtain such knowledge.

The ethics of research in criminal justice settings is an area that has attracted a great deal of scholarly attention (Bloomberg & Wilkins, 1977). Fortunately, we can benefit from the intensive review and recommendations regarding prison research—and it is in prisons that most criminal justice research by psychologists takes place—recently published by the National Commission for the Protection of Human Subjects of Biomedical and Behavioral Research (1977).

The National Commission identified three broad categories of research in prisons. The first category is one in which research is conducted in the hope of improving institutional or program effectiveness. This would include research on psychological treatments that have "the intent or reasonable probability of improving the health or well being of the individual prisoner" (p. 3080). The second category is one in which the research is inherently related to confined persons but does not have the purpose of benefiting the prisoners, such as research on the psychological makeup of prisoners or "studies of the possible causes, effects and processes of incarceration and studies of prisons as instituional structures or of prisoners as incarcerated persons" (p. 3080). The final category consists of research that uses prisoners as subjects because they are available but does not particularly relate to their status as prisoners–for example research that uses prisoners as subjects for psychopharmaceutical testing.

The National Commission recommended that research whose purpose is to benefit prisoners be allowed only if it is

> reviewed by at least one human subjects review committee or institutional review board comprised of men and women of diverse racial and cultural backgrounds that includes among its members prisoners or prisoner advocates and such other persons as community representatives, clergy, behavioral scientists and medical personnel not associated with the research or the penal institution. (p. 3081)

The review committee should consider the risks involved in the research, the provision for obtaining genuinely informed consent, safeguards for confidentiality, and other concerns. Parole boards should not take into account prisoners' participation in research.

Research in the second category—related to prisoners but nonbeneficial in intent—is to be conducted only if the above review board approves it and, in addition, only if the studies are such that "they present minimal or no risk and no more than mere inconvenience to the subjects" (p. 3080).

Research in the third category—research on prisoners because they are "there"—is to be conducted only if the above review board approves it and if three additional requirements are satisfied: (a) The research must fill an "important social and scientific need," (b) it must "satisfy conditions of equity," and (c) it must be characterized by "a high degree of voluntariness" on the part of the prisoner. The conditions necessary to infer this voluntariness include uncensored communication to persons outside the prison, a grievance committee com-

posed of elected prisoners, and 17 detailed standards of living in prison, including adequate food, recreation, and living space, a prison staff adequate to provide for inmates' safety, work opportunities that pay the same as the research, and "adequate mental health services and professional staff" (p. 3080).

In approving research of this type, the National Commission noted studies such as that of the University of Michigan's Survey Research Center (Tannenbaum & Cooke, 1976), which found that 80% of the prisoner-subjects interviewed expressed strong support for giving prisoners the option to participate in research. As Brodsky (Chapter 4) notes, "If these same individuals were free research subjects, it is possible that their evaluations would be more negative." Likewise, one can question the sufficiency of the living standards that the National Commission proposed to assure voluntary participation. For example, some of the task force hold that conjugal visits should be considered a minimal standard of prison life.[3]

In general, the task force believes that the recommendations of the National Commission represent a significant advance in the protection of prisoners and in the conduct of ethical research by psychologists and others in prisons. We urge psychologists to read and conform to these recommendations.

Ethical Issues Psychologists Create for the Criminal Justice System

Recommendation 9: *Psychologists should be exceedingly cautious in offering predictions of criminal behavior for use in imprisoning or releasing individual offenders. If a psychologist decides that it is appropriate in a given case to*

---

[3] It should be noted that the Proposed Regulations on Research Involving Prisoners, which is the government's response to the National Commission, would prohibit Department of Health, Education and Welfare funding of any research in this third category (*Federal Register*, January 5, 1978, p. 1053).

provide a prediction of criminal behavior, he or she should clearly specify (a) the acts being predicted, (b) the estimated probability that these acts will occur during a given time period, and (c) the factors on which the predictive judgment is based.

The task force considered in detail only one general issue created for the criminal justice system by the presence of psychologists and the assumptions that guide their current role assignments. That issue concerns the nature of imprisonment and the judicial procedures for determining its severity. While, ideally, we would like to have dealt in similar detail with other system-level issues related to psychology, such as the function of the police or the role of psychological factors in the determination of guilt, considerations of time and resources precluded our doing so. Our choice was guided by the fact that the majority (70%) of psychologists working in the criminal justice system are working in correctional institutions and that significant developments in how prisons are to be conceptualized are now taking place across the nation.

On the one hand, there are those who believe that the rehabilitation of offenders through psychological and vocational treatment is a principal justification for imprisonment (Clark, 1970). Advocates of this model see psychologists and other mental health professionals as having a significant role in humanizing prisons and moderating excesses of retributive punishment. They also believe that the diagnostic and therapeutic skills of psychologists can serve important utilitarian functions by protecting society from the release of dangerous persons and by helping offenders overcome antisocial propensities. Indeterminate sentences, to be terminated in part on the basis of psychological reports, are a major component of this model.

On the other hand are those who see the presence of psychologists in decision-making roles in prisons as preventing more basic reform. Psychologists in prisons, according to

this view, serve the latent function of legitimizing an "offender-blame" (Ryan, 1971) or individual pathology model of crime that diverts attention from social system factors influencing criminal behavior. Also, by virtue of their scientific and objective image, psychologists unwittingly have usurped or have allowed themselves to be co-opted into making social value decisions, such as how "safe" an offender should be before he or she is released, which more properly should be left to the political and judicial processes (see Recommendation 5 above). Judge David Bazelon (1973) expressed this position to a conference of correctional psychologists:

> Instead of facing up to the true dimensions of the problem and society's social and economic structure, we prefer to blame the problem on a criminal class—a group of sick persons who must be treated by doctors and cured. Why should we even consider fundamental social changes or massive income redistribution if the entire problem can be solved by having scientists teach the criminal class—like a group of laboratory rats—to march successfully through the maze of our society? In short, before you respond with enthusiasm to our plea for help, you must ask yourselves whether your help is really needed, or whether you are merely engaged as magicians to perform an intriguing side-show so that the spectators will not notice the crisis in the center ring. In considering our motives for offering you a role, I think you would do well to consider how much less expensive it is to hire a thousand psychologists than to make even a miniscule change in the social and economic structure. (p. 152)

The task force believes that either of these two models, if taken to the extreme, is simplistic. A single-minded focus on changing the behavior of individual offenders can indeed blind us to larger ethical questions of social justice. But one need not perfect the world, or even the criminal justice system, to provide services to individual offenders.

The model of imprisonment that the majority of the task force believes is most conducive to the ethical use of psychologists is the "just-deserts" model (Fogel, 1975, Morris, 1974; Twentieth Century Fund, 1976; von Hirsch, 1976; von Hirsch & Hanrahan, 1979). In brief, this perspective holds that the amount of punishment given to an offender, usually operationalized by the length of a prison sentence, must be limited· to that which the community believes the offender "justly deserves." It should not be extended beyond that limit by utilitarian considerations such as whether or not an offender needs psychological "rehabilitation" or is predicted to be "dangerous." The principle establishing the upper limit for incarceration is thus an explicitly normative and moral judgment of relative harm and culpability for past behavior, rather than an assessment of relative social risk or the potential for changing behavior in the future. As Norval Morris (1974) has succinctly put it, "Power over a criminal's life should not be taken in excess of that which would be taken were his reform not considered as one of our purposes."

Whether due to outcries of prisoners and prisoner advocates (e.g., American Friends Service Committee, 1971; Mitford, 1973) that "rehabilitation" in prisons often resembles an Orwellian nightmare, or to the research on the lack of effectiveness of prison treatment (e.g., Greenberg, 1977; Martinson, 1974) and the lack of validity of predictions of dangerous criminal behavior (Monahan, 1978), there has been a substantial swing from the "rehabilitative ideal" to "just deserts" in the past few years. Many states and the proposed Federal Criminal Code Reform Act of 1979 are adopting versions of determinate sentencing statutes that eliminate or restrict parole boards and the psychological predictions that feed into them and substitute "presumptive" sentences, in which, for example, every second-offense rapist judged to be similarly culpable receives a similar sentence, regardless of his assumed potential for rehabilitation.

While one can question the extent to which

the rehabilitative ideal has been seriously implemented (there are currently fewer than 100 psychologists in the entire Federal Bureau of Prisons, with approximately 30,000 inmates) and the widely accepted conclusion that "nothing works" in prison treatment (cf. Halleck & Witte, 1977; Palmer, 1975; Quay, 1977), we believe that it would be unwise for psychologists to oppose the redefinition of their roles implied by the just-deserts model. The just-deserts model is not without its conceptual difficulties (e.g., How does one arrive at a "just" sentence for a given crime?—Cederblom & Blizek, 1977) or its own ethical quandaries, for "as long as a substantial segment of the population is denied adequate opportunities for a livelihood, any scheme for punishing must be morally flawed" (von Hirsch, 1976, p. 149). And it is surely not lacking the potential for demagogic abuse by those who literally wish to "throw away the key" on offenders. Nonetheless, the just-deserts model appears to us to be "less unacceptable than any other which can be considered at this time" (Wilkins, 1976, p. 178). It is neither antiscientific nor antipsychological. While it will not ameliorate the horrendous human degradation that is part of many prisons—and *nothing* an offender has done could "deserve" the physical and sexual violence rampant in American "correctional" institutions—it has the important virtue of placing an upper limit on the power of the state to expose persons to such conditions. If it does preclude psychologists from participating in some of their traditional roles in prisons (i.e., release decisions), it more than compensates, in our view, by increasing the fairness of the criminal justice system as a whole and by removing many of the stumbling blocks to the ethical provision of truly voluntary psychological services.[4]

---

[4] The just-deserts model has other implications for the practice of psychotherapy in prisons. If, for example, sentences were set before incarceration began and could not be extended by therapeutic considerations, it would be incumbent upon the psychologist to attend more carefully to constructing a time-limited program of treatment.

WHO IS THE CLIENT?

We reject the argument that "somebody has to make predictions" in determining sentence length and that these predictions necessarily will be made at an even lower level of validity—or a higher level of bias—if psychologists "abdicate" their roles as predictors of future crime (see Chapter 5). While that is a risk with which psychologists should be concerned, it is also possible that nobody will make such predictions or, at the very least, that predictions for the purpose of incarceration will be made on the basis of actuarial variables that are both open to judicial and public review as well as specifically keyed to the offender's criminal history (Gottfredson, Wilkins, & Hoffman, 1978). The criminal justice system, thus deprived of the opportunity to launder difficult ethical and policy questions as matters of scientific acumen, may begin to confront more honestly the value premises on which it goes about basing prison sentences. As Watzlawick, Weakland, and Fisch (1974) have stated,

> Whether the setting is a maximum-security prison or merely Juvenile Hall, the paradox is the same: the degree to which the offender has supposedly been reformed by these institutions is judged on the basis of his saying and doing the right things because he has been reformed, and not because he has merely learned to speak the right language and to go through the right motions. Reform when seen as something different from compliance, inevitably becomes self-reflective—it is then supposed to be both its own cause and its own effect. This game is won by the "good actors": the only losers are those inmates who refuse to be reformed because they are too honest or angry to play the game; or those who allow it to be apparent that they are playing the game only because they want to get out, and are therefore not acting spontaneously. Humaneness thus creates its own hypocrisies, which lead to the melancholy conclusion that in this specific sense it seems preferable to establish a price to be paid for an offense, i.e., a punishment, but to leave the offender's mind alone and therby avoid the troublesome consequences of mind-control paradoxes. (p. 69)

It is important to note that we take this position more for ethical than empirical reasons. It does appear from reading the research that the validity of psychological predictions of violent behavior, at least in the sentencing and release situations we are considering, is extremely poor, so poor that one could oppose their use on the strictly empirical grounds that psychologists are not professionally competent to make such judgments. An analogous conclusion was reached by a task force of the American Psychiatric Association (1974): "Neither psychiatrists nor anyone else have reliably demonstrated an ability to predict future violence or 'dangerousness.' Neither has any special psychiatric 'expertise' in this area been established" (p. 20).

Our position goes further. We hold that even in the unlikely event that substantial improvements in the prediction of criminal behavior were documented, there would still be reason to question the ethical appropriateness of extending an offender's confinement beyond the limits of what he or she morally "deserves" in order to achieve a utilitarian gain in public safety.

It is clear, however, that there are no facile answers to this most difficult question of public policy and professional ethics, especially when one takes into account "justice" to the potential victims of violent crime, who, like their offenders and unlike the legislators, judges, and psychologists making decisions in the criminal justice system, are often poor and nonwhite (Shah, 1978). Likewise, the complexity of accomplishing change in an organization as large and diffuse as the criminal justice system militated against the task force's taking a more absolute stand on the question of psychological predictions of criminal behavior. In those situations where the realistic alternative to distinguishing among offenders on predictive grounds is a draconian sentence uniformly given to all offenders, it is not clear to us that offering such predictions is, on balance, always ethically inappropriate. Nor is there agreement on whether predictive considerations should play a role in decisions regarding the release of certain classes of offenders (e.g., offenders with psychological disorders) from prison to community treatment to serve the length of their sentences.

While there is broad agreement within the task force, therefore, that psychological predictions should not be used to extend an offender's confinement beyond the degree "justly deserved," there is disagreement as to whether periods of confinement should be liable to reduction on the basis of a psychologist's assessment. At a minimum, we urge psychologists to exercise extreme caution in making predictive judgments, particularly given the history of abuse of such judgments by the criminal justice system in the past, and to do so only after considering the broad range of ethical issues alluded to above.

Recommendation 10: *Psychologists should be strongly encouraged to offer treatment services to offenders who request them.*

What, then, is our position on the ethical context in which prison treatment should occur? Much has already been implied. We clearly see no incompatibility between abandoning rehabilitation as the *purpose* of imprisonment and maintaining vigorous rehabilitation programs in prison. In the context of justly punishing people for what they have done in the past, we would provide them with ample psychological resources to aid in changing their behavior for the future and for coping with their present psychological pains.

As Morris and Hawkins (1977) have recently put it,

> The cage is not a sensible place in which to cure the criminal, even when the medical analogy makes sense, which it rarely does. But this does *not* mean that such treatment programs as we now have in prisons should be abandoned; quite the contrary, they urgently need expansion. No one of any sensitivity can visit any of our mega-prisons without recogniz-

ing that they contain as in all countries, populations that are disproportionately illiterate, unemployed, vocationally untrained, undereducated, psychologically disturbed, and socially isolated. It is both in the prisoners' and in the community's best interest to help them to remedy these deficiencies. (p. 67)

Various organizational strategies—for example, contracting with private therapists for prison treatment or having independent lines of authority for prison psychologists—may facilitate the provision of services in a manner consonant with our previous recommendations. We note that Principal 6d of the 1979 *Ethical Standards of Psychologists* states that "Psychologists willingly contribute a portion of their services to work for which they receive little or no financial return" (p. 5). Prisons would appear an ideal place for psychologists to perform their "pro bono" activity.

Implementing Task Force Recommendations

The recommendations of the task force mentioned so far have dealt with substantive issues regarding the role of psychology in the criminal justice system. We conclude by suggesting several concrete steps the APA might take toward implementing the recommendations we have put forward and toward continuing professional debate on the issues we have addressed.

Recommendation 11: *The American Psychological Association should strongly encourage graduate and continuing education in the applied ethics of psychological intervention and research.*

While there has been a substantial increase in recent years in the literature on the ethical aspects of psychological intervention and research (Bermant, Kelman, & Warwick, 1978; Tapp, Kelman, Triandis, Wrightsman, & Coelho, 1974), this writing has yet to become part of the "mainstream" of psychological education and generally is treated as something the practitioner or researcher will "pick up" as he or she encounters ethical dilemmas. Yet moral crises are better prepared for than reacted to. Troublesome moral issues may be commonplace in criminal justice work, but they also are increasingly present in many forms of psychological research involving human subjects, in all of involuntary hospitalization, and in much of voluntary outpatient treatment, especially in dealing with children, violent persons, the poor, or minorities. The initial problem is not so much *how* these ethical issues are ultimately resolved, but rather that psychologists be prepared to reason them through in a careful manner. This means trying to identify the relevant considerations that may be involved, examining with care the empirical and normative arguments that apply to these considerations and their application to particular cases, and then attempting to assess what—all things considered—is the morally right thing to do.

In the wake of the poverty of moral reasoning ability demonstrated by many attorneys in the Watergate scandal, the American Bar Association in 1974 voted to make a course in professional ethics required in every law school. Rather than waiting for a moral Watergate to occur in psychology, we should see that professional education in applied ethics becomes part of the curriculum in every graduate program. This might go far to sensitize neophyte psychologists to ethical issues generally, and especially to those issues involved in organizational work, and to carry on the debates begun in this task force and in other groups concerned with ethical problems (e.g., the APA Task Force on Behavior Modification).

There are several ways that APA might take the lead in fostering an awareness of ethical issues. In those areas of psychology in which APA "approves" a graduate program, the Association might make such approval contingent upon the offering or requirement of a course in applied psychological ethics. State licensing boards could be encouraged to reflect ethical reasoning in their examinations, and continuing education programs could likewise place an emphasis upon ethical issues. APA could develop model curricula, background materials, and casebooks for various types of courses in applied ethics, all of which could reflect in part the complexities engendered by work in organizational settings such a criminal justice. The involvement of philosophers and others with interests in applied ethics, as well as practitioners and researchers who have confronted the issues firsthand, should be encouraged.

Recommendation 12: *The American Psychological Association should take steps to increase awareness among psychologists and those with whom they work of mechanisms to investigate and act upon complaints of violations of its Ethical Standards. Formal advisory opinions should continue to be offered to psychologists requesting an interpretation of the Ethical Standards in specific fact situations.*

To carry out the recommendations of this and similar groups, it appears essential for APA to investigate and take action upon (a) complaints of individuals or organizations that psychologists are violating the Ethical Standards, and (b) complaints by psychologists of unethical behavior on the part of their employers. Before the Association can make such investigations and take such action, however, it must be made aware of those cases that raise ethical difficulty. In the years 1975 through 1977, the Committee on Scientific and Professional Ethics and Conduct—the APA group that deals with complaints of unethical behavior filed against psychologists—handled an average of 80 cases per year. Some of these cases were more violations of professional etiquette (e.g., violations of advertising restrictions) than of professional ethics. Only one case referred to the Committee in this entire 3-year period concerned a psychologist working in the criminal justice system. Likewise, the Committee on Academic Freedom and Conditions of Employment—the APA group that deals with complaints of unethical behavior filed by psychologists against their employers—has handled an average of approximately 30 cases per year for the past 3 years. Only seven cases during this period have been filed by a psychologist against a criminal justice agency. This is in spite of the fact that 82% of the psychologists employed by the criminal justice system who were surveyed by the task force reported personally encountering ethical problems in their work (see Chapter 6). It apperars that much more must be done to make psychologists and those they work with aware of the existence of mechanisms to redress ethical grievances.

Perhaps more important than after-the-fact enforcement of sanctions against those who violate the Ethical Standards, the APA should strengthen its proactive capacity to offer advice and consultaion to psychologists who are at ethical choice points. The Association already offers advisory opinions on ethical issues when asked to do so, but its ability to respond quickly to a psychologist's request for an interpretation of the Ethical Standards in a specific fact situation is hampered by a lack of staff resources and the absence of networks of expert consultants in specialized areas (e.g., criminal justice, education) who could offer prompt "peer review" of the ethical implications of a proposed course of action.

As a sign of its commitment to its own Ethical Standards and to taking seriously the work of groups such as this task force, APA might begin the upgrading of its educational, enforcement, and advisory responsibilities in the area of applied ethics with all deliberate speed.

Philip A. Mann

2
Ethical Issues for Psychologists
in Police Agencies

Heightened awareness of societal problems during the 1960s and early 1970s brought into bold relief the role of social institutions in determining the general quality of life. One such institution, the police, was particularly highlighted as public attention focused on the increasing crime, civil unrest, and racial problems engendered in the wake of renewed concern with equality, justice, and civil liberties. A rapid and dramatic shift occurred in the degree of scrutiny given to the role and function of the police in society. This increased interest, however, was preceded by years of relative indifference toward the police function by the average citizen.

Psychologists were not noticeably different from the general public in this regard. Aside from a few scattered personality studies and the work of a small number of psychologists involved in personnel selection, most psychologists demonstrated at the least a disinterest in, and at the most an antipathy toward, the study of the police. This attitude was generally found among most social scientists (Shellow, Note 1). Psychologists were also not different from the general public in viewing police officers as macho, authoritarian personalities with limited intelligence, despite the fact that this stereotype is not supported by psychological test results. (The history and current status of police personality studies have been reviewed by Niederhoffer, 1967, and by Lefkowitz, 1975.)

Although the police comprise a major be-havior-regulating structure in society (Rhodes, 1972), this fact was little appreciated by psychologists until the 1960s when two different developments helped bring it to their attention. One was the increased public concern with racial relations and civil unrest, which contributed to a view of the police as a forceful, sometimes unjust, embodiment of the power of the dominant majority. In this view, the police were perceived as in need of greater sensitivity to the wishes, feelings, and rights of minority groups. The second development was the growth of the community mental health movement, which fostered a view of the police as a major help-giving resource in the community, especially in dealing with those having mental and emotional problems (Cumming, Cumming, & Edell, 1965; Liberman, 1969). In this view, police officers were seen as in need of improved knowledge and skills for recognizing and managing such problems.

These two sources of emphasis on the importance of the police function involve different assumptions concerning the police role and emphasize contrasting views of police behavior. They also spring from different ideologies and hold different goals for interventions with police officers. Both share a concern with improving police behavior, however, especially the quality of police-citizen interaction. This common concern has been addressed most often through efforts to improve police training, but an exclusive focus on training technologies tends to obscure the important differences in motivation underlying these two approaches to work with the police. Failure to recognize and maintain these distinctions has sometimes led to confusion in the minds of police trainers and trainees, as well as among the observant public.

There is little doubt that both of these thrusts toward change in police behavior arose from the spirit of reform dominant during the 1960s. This reform spirit was based strongly on the assumption that behavioral science technology could effect changes in individuals through specialized training, the same sort of assumption that characterized the initial strategy of the War on Poverty (Rein, 1969). In the 1970s however, reaction to widespread civil disturbances and a change in political administration and philosophy altered the assumptions and strategies behind this spirit of reform. For whatever reasons, change efforts in social institutions shifted from reform strategies to more bureaucratic and organizational solutions. In the welfare field, for example, emphasis shifted to income redistribution, in theory if not in fact, and to the development of affirmative action plans to enhance equality of employment opportunity. In the police field, one of the dominant themes in recent years has been the development of team policing (Block & Specht, 1973), and the most salient concern of many police administrators today is the development of selection procedures that are effective in selecting competent personnel while not discriminating against minority groups and women. The former is an organizational concern, while the latter comes directly from affirmative action programs for insuring equality of opportunity. These changes reflect a shift in emphasis from individual change strategies to techno-structural solutions (Hornstein, Bunker, Burke, Gindes, & Lewicki, 1971).

Another focus of concern in the police field is disagreement over the definition of the police officer's job. Many among the ranks of the police, as well as the public, see law enforce-

ment activity, that is, "crime fighting," as the primary function of the police. While few would argue that law enforcement is not, in fact, an important police function, the data of most police departments reflect the reality that police work consists approximately of 20% law enforcement and 80% "order maintenance" including a variety of human services (Bard & Shellow, 1976a). In view of this data, it is unfortunate that some see efforts to improve police training and sanctions in the area of human services as an unnecessary and undesirable distraction from a major focus on crime control. Nevertheless, as crime itself has become an increasingly serious problem, relatively more public emphasis has been placed on law enforcement activity, training, and hardware and relatively less on providing services. Each of these developments is the result of a political process changing in response to perceived social needs.

Other current concerns in the field of police work, though somewhat in the background, include community control and public accountability, reform of corruption, professionalization and improved economic standing for police officers, enhancement of the ability of individual police officers to cope with job and family stresses associated with their work, and, most recently, the development of programs for the prevention of rape and the humane treatment of rape victims.

Thus, society has moved in the space of a few years from relative disregard of its police system to an increasing awareness of its multiple facets and a dramatic upswing in expectations for this social institution. Many of these expectations are potentially conflicting, and each is backed by substantial interest groups.

While psychologists' involvement with police departments is still relatively small, psychologists are increasingly filling a growing variety of roles that address the concerns mentioned earlier. Psychologists working with the law enforcement system operate from a number of different organizational bases and bring to the police setting a diversified array of technical expertise. Since most of the techniques employed by psychologists in working with the police antedate the recent increase in the number of psychologists so employed, it is safe to say that new technology is not the major factor drawing psychologists to such work. Rather, it can be assumed that psychologists working with the police do so from a variety of motives and incentives that derive from a number of sources. During the 1960s, increased employment of psychologists in police agencies resulted, at least in part, from psychologists' desires to be engaged in "relevant" activities and from a sense of crisis in society. Today, psychologists' work with the police is more of a response to the recognition on the part of law enforcement administrators of a need for increased expertise in meeting the problems confronting police organizations and communities.

The multiply determined concerns with the police function outlined above underscore the importance of first examining the various bases for the involvement of psychologists in police departments, as well as the variety of roles and functions these psychologists perform, if we are to understand fully the issues that arise in such work. We can then examine questions of ethics, public policies, and future roles for psychologists in the law enforcement system.

Current Roles and Functions of Psychologists Working in Police Settings

Twain, McGee, and Bennett (1973) identified five functional areas of psychologists' activities in the criminal justice system: assessment, treatment, training, consultation, and research. These functional areas were derived with the entire criminal justice system in mind, not just police departments. Psychologists working with police departments have functioned in most of these areas, although not necessarily in ways

characteristic of those areas in other parts of the criminal justice system. However, if we substitute for assessment the selection of police personnel through psychological tests, and if we define treatment to mean the provision of direct psychological services to police officers, then these categories do encompass the activities of psychologists in the law enforcement system.

Personnel Selection

Psychologists working in police personnel selection may be involved either directly in the assessment of police applicants or indirectly in the development of selection procedures. They may be employed by civil service commissions and police departments, or these organizations may make use of them primarily in a research capacity, often through contractual arrangements.

Although the use of psychological technology in the personnel field has a long history, its use in selecting police personnel has been surprisingly limited. While Narrol and Levitt (1963) reported that 55 large cities they studied used some psychological tests in personnel selection, Murphy (1972) found that only 80 of 203 police agencies responding to a questionnaire indicated that they used psychological testing. And although the Task Force on the Police created by the President's Commission on Law Enforcement and Administration of Justice (1967) recommended psychological testing of police applicants as a means of improving the quality of police personnel, this recommendation has not been widely implemented to date. Moreover, equal employment opportunity guidelines and court decisions make it quite clear that tests and other selection procedures must have demonstrated validity in predicting job performance and must not discriminate against persons because of their minority group status or sex.

While the requirement for sound research findings is quite clear, knowledge in this area is still largely undeveloped. Rhead, Abrams,

Trossman, and Margolis (1968) reported on a psychological assessment program of police candidates for the Chicago civil service commission. These investigators used a battery of psychological tests and interviews to make clinical assessments of police applicants. Blum's (1964) finding that three MMPI scales were correlated with subsequent serious misconduct by police officers is one of the best known attempts to relate psychological test scores to subsequent performance criteria. However, this finding was not replicated in later studies by Azen, Snibbe, Montgomery, Fabricatore, and Earle (1974) or by McDonough and Monahan (1975).

The latter two studies are representative of a small number of recent studies that have begun to use sophisticated research methodologies to establish the validity of selection procedures. Azen and his co-workers (Azen, Snibbe, & Montgomery, 1973) conducted a 20-year follow-up study using a variety of physical, social, and psychological predictors of a number of different criteria of success.

Another important study was that of Baehr, Furcon, and Froemel (1969) with Chicago policemen. Using a battery of tests of their own devising, these researchers developed separate predictive methods based on the differences they found between black and white police officers. They hoped to stimulate the development of nationally standardized selection procedures as well as to overcome racial discrimination in test results. However, Snibbe, Fabricatore, Azen, and Snibbe (1976) did not find these same racial differences when they administered the same tests to black, white, and Mexican-American members of the Los Angeles County Sheriff's Department, a result that casts doubt on the advisability of uniform selection procedures.

The use of psychological tests in selection procedures is a new and relatively undeveloped area in the law enforcement system. Researchers in this field are faced with a number of significant obstacles, not all of which may be

possible to overcome. One persistent problem is the choice of selection criteria. While most recent studies have employed several criterion variables, it appears that the same criteria do not apply in different communities or in different law enforcement agencies. In this context it should also be noted that while emotional stability and other personality characteristics are often thought of as critical for police candidates, the question of aptitudes and interests suited to the tasks required of the police officers must also be considered. Sterling and Watson (1970), for example, found that while many police recruits had aptitudes and interests well suited to crime fighting, they were actually poorly fitted for the clerical and service tasks that comprise the majority of police work. Thus, task analysis is an important source of job criteria that has not appeared in many studies to date. Even the few studies mentioned here indicate the need for replication and cross-validation, since it is not unusual for findings in one sample to be conspicuously absent in another. A related problem is the question of long-term follow-up. In addition to the usual problems encountered in longitudinal research, such as the staying power of the researchers and social changes that may bring about changes in the criteria desired, researchers in this area must take into account the personal and social changes that police officers undergo in the course of their careers. Only long-term studies can answer questions concerning the prediction of successful performance in the light of these changes.

A number of practical problems limit the adequate design of research studies on the selection process. If a wide range of applicants could be employed and their performances monitored for a period of time, the increased variability of their performances would increase the chances of obtaining satisfactorily high validity coefficients between test results and performance criteria. Since such a procedure is impractical and undesirable from a number of other points of view, the consequence is that

21

most studies must rely on the more homogeneous group of applicants who are actually employed as police officers. The greater homogeneity of this group thus restricts the range of performance variability and reduces the chances of obtaining powerful predictors of successful police officers. If data for predictors and criterion measures are collected simultaneously from officers already in service, the restriction of range is even greater, particularly if some of the predictors used were also employed in the original selection of these personnel.

Accordingly, a minimally acceptable approach is to follow a group of new employees from applicant status through criterion status and to repeat this procedure on several samples. Admittedly, this procedure tends to perpetuate present standards, but that is more of a policy problem than a technical problem.

Finally, small communities have neither the resources nor sufficient pools of applicants to allow the development of valid selection procedures through adequate validity studies. Many such small communities exist, and unless one is willing to make the assumption that the selection process is not important in these communities, this fact also poses significant problems for the researcher. In summary, both technical and practical problems in the personnel selection area present sizable challenges to psychologists and police departments.

Direct Psychological Services to Police Officers

The physical dangers of police work are well known. Somewhat less recognized are the many psychological stresses of the job. The stresses of the socialization process that begins when a person enters police work have been the subject of several studies (Niederhoffer, 1967; Reiser, 1976; Westley, 1970). Mann (1971, 1973) has noted the uncertainty involved in the numerous decisions police officers are required to make in situations not covered by either law or policy. The shift-work nature of police tours of duty, especially rotating shifts, creates adaptive stresses (Reiser, 1976) and tends to limit the social relationships of police officers to those with whom they work (Mann, 1973). All of these factors contribute to the high degree of marital strain experienced by those in the police force (Reiser, 1972).

In 1968, the Los Angeles Police Department employed Martin Reiser as a full-time, in-house psychologist. Without precedent and with the opportunity to create his own job description, Reiser assumed the function of providing crisis intervention counseling to police officers and their families. Reiser's position put him in a unique situation with respect to two important factors. First, as an employee of the department, he was well ahead of the game in overcoming a barrier that any psychologist working with police departments must surmount—being an outsider in a tightly knit organization (Shellow, Note 1). Second, he was in an excellent position to maximize familiarity with the stresses of police work and to share his perception of such problems with police personnel.

In subsequent years, this precedent has been followed by several other police departments (Hillgren & Jacobs, 1976). The literature suggests that direct counseling or psychotherapeutic services is provided only by those psychologists employed full time within police departments and not by those employed as outside consultants. Moreover, the provision of such services is seldom the only function of such psychologists but is one of several duties, including most of the functions discussed here.

Provision of direct psychological services to persons with whom the psychologist interacts in other roles within the police organization creates special problems that have been recognized by those involved in such work (Hillgren & Jacobs, 1976; Reiser, 1972). These problems are discussed further in the section on ethical issues.

The police-agency-based psychologist enjoys certain intraorganizational freedoms not always shared by the external consultant. However, there are also some constraints involved. Lambert (Note 2) examined the different forces operating on consultants who were full-time employees of school districts (school-based) and those who were employees of outside organizations (community-based.) The differences she found are analogous to those that apply to the internal and external bases of operation of psychologists working with the law enforcement system.

The internally based psychologist is more likely to be perceived as identified with the goals of the police organization; in fact, such an image seems to be essential to job security. Accordingly, administrators may more readily seek the services of the in-house psychologist for work that is seen as part of the ongoing business of the department. When the external consultant's help is sought, the emphasis on change, and consequently on resistance to change, is likely to be more explicit and deliberate. Since police agencies are public organizations, employment of an external consultant will likely call attention to the change project and the need for it, placing administrators and organizations in a position of vulnerability to criticism they might prefer to avoid. On the other hand, the internal psychologist is not free to refuse to accept an assignment or a request, while the external psychologist is.

Definition of the psychologist's role is a critical item of business for both the internal psychologist and the external consultant. It would seem to be a continual task for the internally based psychologist, however, in order to avoid confusion among the several roles he or she may be expected to fill. The external consultant is more likely, although not always, to fill a single, more readily definable role. The sources of resistance confronting the psychologist's efforts to bring about change are more likely to be organizational and structural for the external consultant and will more often be based on personal likes and dislikes for the internal consultant. While both types of

consultants must deal with the question of confidentiality, it seems to be more troublesome for the internally based psychologist because of the potential for role confusion.

External consultants make frequent use of contractual agreements in which the goals of consultation are made explicit and concrete. This process can serve as a reference point for continuing review and modification of the consultation process (Mann, 1973). These aspects of the consultant's work may be more readily overlooked in defining the work of the in-house psychologist, so that objectives are less clear. Similarly, external consultation has a clearly definable beginning and ending point, if so desired, which makes evaluation of the consultant's work somewhat easier but also makes the question of specific outcomes more salient. Since the internally employed psychologist is part of the organizational structure being evaluated, the evaluation process can become more obscured and also more difficult. That is, allocation of the respective responsibilities for change between the psychologist and the organization is made problematic. In addition, the internal consultant has less freedom to criticize than the external consultant, although the acceptance of the criticism in either case will depend on the quality of the relationship the psychologist has with the police organization.

Finally, the external consultant, in contrast to the in-house psychologist, seems to have somewhat more freedom to employ psychological techniques in either consulting or training roles without their being confused with psychotherapeutic techniques, a distinction maintained only with some difficulty even by the external consultant. The importance of this problem is discussed further in the section on consultation.

Training

The Task Force on the Police created by the President's Commission on Law Enforcement and Administration of Justice (1967) found that the amount of training provided for police officers lagged far behind the need for such training:

> While considerable progress has been made in recent years in the development of training programs for police officers, the total training effort in this country, when related to the complexity of the law enforcement task, is grossly inadequate. (p. 36)

For the purposes of the present discussion, training needs to be differentiated from other activities. In an effort to upgrade the quality of police personnel, programs have been implemented that provide financial aid to police officers to continue their education, and grants have been made to universities and colleges to provide curricula in criminal justice fields (President's Commission on Law Enforcement and Administration of Justice, 1967). However, these efforts should not be confused with, or considered substitutes for, police training programs. Training is concerned with the acquisition of knowledge and skills required to perform the duties expected of police officers in particular jurisdictions. Thus, training deals not just with knowledge and techniques but also with their relationship to local policies, laws, and public expectations. Additionally, for purposes of this discussion, we will distinguish between training and consultation, in the sense that the latter involves the use of an expert in some particular field to help the police agency solve a specific problem. While consultation may involve some forms of training at times, this is not always the case, as is discussed in the next section.

The Task Force on the Police also outlined goals for the training of a police officer: (a) to "elicit a commitment . . . to the importance of fairness as well as effectiveness in the exercise of authority," (b) to "provide guidance to assist him in the exercise of his discretion," (c) to provide "a basis for understanding the various forms of deviant behavior with which he must

deal," and (d) to acquaint "him with the various alternatives and resources that are available to him, in addition to the criminal justice process, for dealing with the infinite variety of situations which he is likely to confront" (President's Commission on Law Enforcement and Administration of Justice 1967, p. 37).

Psychologists have been involved in training activities that address each of these goals. These training activities include a variety of approaches to human relations training, recognition and management of abnormal behavior, crowd control and the handling of sensitive situations, and the treatment of rape victims. In addition, psychologists participate in teaching courses or sections of courses on psychology (Green, 1976; Mann, 1970).

Human Relations Training

Among other recommendations on police-community relations, the Task Force on the Police recommended that police officers receive from 60 to 120 hours of human relations training but noted that surveys indicated that few departments provided more than from 10 to 20 hours of such training for recruits and very little for officers in service. The task force further recommended that police departments expand their personnel in this area:

> Civilian experts in such fields as psychology, sociology, and urban problems should be recruited as full-time employees of units in large departments. Both large and small departments can also utilize experts from universities and other sources as consultants for planning and carrying out training programs and for other important tasks. (President's Commission on Law Enforcement and Administration of Justice, 1967, p. 155)

Human relations training covers a wide range of topics and techniques. Aside from the core subject-matter areas of psychology, sociology, and social history, perhaps the best known approach is what is referred to generally as sensitivity training. In fact, this type of training may involve several varieties of activities including (a) small-group discussions (Lipsitt & Steinbruner, 1969), (b) T-groups modeled after the approach of the National Training Laboratories, which employ a particular methodology (Sata, 1975), (c) an exchange-of-images approach, such as that employed in the Houston Program (Sikes & Cleveland, 1968), and (d) a number of other approaches that may emphasize confrontation of racial stereotypes or attitudes. In these activities, the psychologist functions as group leader or facilitator. He or she may be relatively active or passive and may or may not introduce structure into the group process in the form of task assignments or role-playing situations. Civilian community members may or may not be involved in the group process. The important point to be noted is that these activities represent a variety of approaches despite their being lumped together under the term *sensitivity training*.

These activities have in common the use of a group process, an active approach to learning as distinct from the lecture method, and an emphasis on feelings as well as ideas. In general, such sensitivity training is based on sound principles of learning, yet much of this type of training has generated strong reactions, some of them irrational, some of them substantive.

In this context, it must be pointed out that many of these sensitivity training programs were organized hastily in an atmosphere of tension and crisis. While crisis theory (Rapoport, 1962) predicts that change is easier during periods of crisis, it does not guarantee the success of any method whatsoever, and tensions can arouse resistance impervious to all efforts at change. Indeed, some psychologists have commented about the defensive climate in which they attempted to conduct sensitivity training or similar activities (Reddy & Lansky, 1975; Sikes & Cleveland, 1968).

Thus, it is not surprising that evaluative studies of these programs have produced mixed results. A typical approach to evaluation has been to employ pre- and posttraining attitude scales, and attitudes measured in this way have been shown to improve, to stay the same, and to worsen. More disturbing is the finding of both Sacon (Note 3) and Teahan (1975) that despite initial improvement in attitudes, there is a net worsening of attitudes over a longer period of time. Whether these effects are due to sensitivity training or to the effects of socialization experiences within the police organization cannot be determined from these data.

However, the use of verbal attitude measures may not be an appropriate approach to evaluation with police officers Shellow (1975) and Gustin (1975) have commented on the limited utility of such measurements, the latter suggesting that it is merely another instance of the well-known phenomenon of verbal expressions and behavior not being highly correlated among the police. Moreover, Mann (1973) found that police behavior was changed without measureable changes occurring in their attitudes. Pfister (1975) presents some well-designed evaluative studies of the effects of a T-group experience. His study used behavioral data and questionnaire responses from citizens having nonadverse contacts with both police officers who had been through the training and a control group of officers who had not had the training. The results were positive in favor of the trained officers. Pfister's work is one of the few reports to employ both behavioral data and control groups in the research design.

The observation in the report of the Task Force on the Police that human relations training tends to improve the attitudes of only mildly prejudiced officers and to generate antagonism toward the training method, an observation made before most of these programs were conducted, may have been an accurate forecast. However, few would contend that sensitivity training should be expected to solve all of the problems in this area without accompanying changes in departmental policies, supervision, and reward structures. Moreover, the important task of mutual learning between citizens and police deserves a fairer trial under more favorable conditions. As Mann and Iscoe (1971) have noted, the best way to deal with a crisis is to establish working relationships before it arises. Under such circumstances, both police and citizens are more free to engage in mutual learning.

Recognition and Management of Abnormal Behavior

The police have long been an unrecognized resource for intervening in disturbed behavior in the community. Hollingshead and Redlich (1958) found that over half of those from the lowest socioeconomic class who find their way to psychiatric treatment do so via the police and courts. Liberman (1969) found that most people who had used the police for help with a mental health problem in their family considered the police a natural source for such help and would call on them again even after having had contact with the mental health system.

Early efforts on the part of mental health professionals, including psychologists, to teach police about abnormal behavior were backed by the National Association for Mental Health, which was concerned about the treatment of the mentally ill who were apprehended and placed in jails. This organization sponsored an informative booklet written especially for police officers (Matthews & Rowland, 1974), which has now gone through several editions.

In the late 1960s, Morton Bard and his coworkers (Bard, 1970; Bard & Berkowitz, 1967) began training special units of police in New York City as specialists in crisis intervention in family disturbances. Using a combination of role playing, group discussions, and individual consultation, Bard and his colleagues sought to increase the personal and social effectiveness of police officers in handling situations that pose a high risk of injury to both officers and participants. While the original project aim of creating family-crisis specialists was not adopted by the police department, such training is now included for all officers entering the de-

partment, and Bard's demonstration of training in this area of police activity has stimulated similar efforts in other cities.

Driscoll, Meyer, and Schanie (1973) conducted a training program for police in Louisville, Kentucky, that was structured after Bard's model; Mann (1973) and his colleagues provided training and consultation in family crisis intervention as part of a broader consultation program with police in Austin, Texas; and Bard, Zacker, and Rutter (Note 4) reported on a subsequent family crisis-intervention training program for New York Housing Authority police officers.

Evaluations of these training programs are generally favorable, although interpretation of the data are not without problems. In Bard's original New York City project (Bard, 1970), data on the frequency of (a) assaults within families and against officers, (b) murders, and (c) repeat calls showed inconsistent results in the experimental and control precincts. In the New York Housing Authority project (Bard et al., Note 4), data indicated that the trained police showed generally better performance in crime management than did police in control projects; also, residents' attitudes reflected an increased sense of being protected, although not a better opinion of police officers.

In the Louisville project (Driscoll et al., 1973), the effects of the training were assessed with questionnaire responses obtained by telephone from persons who had been involved in family disputes handled by either trained or untrained police. The results showed a more favorable response toward the police trained in the program. The police who were trained also reported that they felt more effective in handling family disturbances than they did before the training.

The finding in the New York City programs that a high percentage of disputes were handled by mediation techniques (Bard, et al., Note 4) is of significance in itself. It represents a shift from a modal pattern of nonintervention, referral to legal resources, or occasional force

(Bailey, Note 5). In the Austin project, (Mann, 1973), in addition to a shift from legal interventions (that is, referral to courts or refusal to intervene on grounds of lack of a legal basis) to personal/social interventions and referrals, Mann found a significant increase in the number of persons who followed through on referral advice by contacting a community mental health center. These changes represented an implicit show of faith in the training on the part of the officers involved.

The Austin project also included training for police recruits in the recognition and management of different types of abnormal behavior. Psychologists participated with police recruits in role-playing situations in which a variety of disturbed behavior was portrayed, and the recruits were asked to role play what they considered to be appropriate handling of the situation. Following the role play, a group discussion was held concerning the type of behavior portrayed and its psychological basis, a critique of the recruit's performance was conducted with suggestions for alternative approaches when indicated, and legal and policy implications were examined and clarified.

Crowd Control and Sensitive Situations

One of the earliest reported examples of psychologists' roles with police is Shellow and Roemer's (1966) account of the application of social psychological principles to the successful police management of a potentially dangerous mob situation. Shellow and Roemer analyzed a particular anticipated incident, selected social psychological principles applicable to it, and assisted police in preparing a plan of police behavior that resulted in the avoidance of disruptive behavior. Shellow has used a similar approach in helping police departments in other cities cope successfully with demonstrations and other potentially destructive crowd situations (Shellow, 1976, Note 1). A somewhat similar approach was taken by Mann and Iscoe (1971) in helping a police department cope with a

massive antiwar demonstration that had a peaceful conclusion.

Such activities, while successful, have been limited to dealing with specific anticipated events. How much carry-over value such training has is not known. Mann has recently conducted regular recruit and inservice training in crowd control and incident management for police officers in a medium-sized city. In addition to general social psychological principles governing mass behavior, the training focuses on the police officer's decision making under stressful situations. The approach is similar to that described by Argyris (1976) in which officers are presented with hypothetical situations based on actual events, asked to react to them, and then asked to examine the assumptions that led to the action. This approach allows for examination of the laws and policies applying to such situations but assumes that the police officer's immediate decision making is more critical, since most such situations are too unpredictable to allow reliance on specific guidelines entirely (Mann, 1971). However, so far, the effects of this training program have been neither evaluated or seriously tested.

Rape Prevention and Victim Treatment

Public Law 94-63, amending the Community Mental Health Centers Act, requires that community mental health centers develop programs for the prevention of rape and the sympathetic treatment of rape victims. Stemming from growing awareness of the problems of rape and its victims and increasing political pressure to attack these problems, these programs will undoubtedly involve psychologists, among others, in training police personnel to assist victims, in providing referral services, and in planning preventive efforts. Already a number of rape crisis centers have been established around the country (Eron, 1973; Fox & Scherl, 1972), and many police departments are establishing special units to handle these cases (Brown, 1970).

Ellinson (1976) describes training seminars

held for officers of the New York City Police Department who deal with sex crimes. A Rape Investigation and Analysis Section, an all-female unit, was formed in 1972. Several additional units with officers of both sexes have been formed subsequently. The three-day seminars cover the legal, criminal, and psychological aspects of rape. Crisis intervention techniques are emphasized, along with effective investigation techniques that also incorporate sensitivity to the victim's circumstances.

Activities for the prevention of rape are largely undeveloped. Aside from community workshops for increasing community awareness of the problem and discussing possible defensive actions and the provision of self-defense courses for women, there are no well-developed programs for rape prevention. Professional and legal opinion is still somewhat divided on which victim reactions are appropriate and effective, and knowledge in this problem area remains clouded by ambivalent and unsympathetic public attitudes. There is much room for progress.

Consultation

In law enforcement agencies, psychologists have served as mental health consultants, organizational consultants, and consultants on special problems. Each of these types of consultation has a different method and purpose.

Mental health consultation has a generic connotation, but the specific form developed by Gerald Caplan (1970) is probably more widely practiced. Caplan defines four types of consultation: client-centered case consultation, consultee-centered case consultation, program-centered administrative consultation, and consultee-centered administrative consultation. Mental health consultation is a voluntary relationship between a consultant who has expert knowledge in the mental health field and a consultee who seeks the consultant's help with some problem arising out of the consultee's work role, involving a mental health problem of the consultee's client or clients.

Within Caplan's model, it is important to note that consultee-centered consultation deals with four types of problems that consultees manifest in attempting to help their clients: a lack of knowledge, a lack of skill, a lack of confidence, or a lack of objectivity. While each of these problems is dealt with through a review of case material, consultation on problems of consultee confidence or objectivity involves techniques that could be confused with psychotherapy. The distinction lies in the fact that the consultant limits his or her help to problems associated with the consultee's work role, that is, the difficulties presented by a particular class of clients. Additionally, the consultant works by discussing information relevant to the consultee's client and does not discuss the consultee's personal life. In contrast, psychotherapy is not so limited in scope, often seeks wide-ranging personality change, and focuses on the patient's personal life.

Despite these distinctions, however, the stereotype of the psychologist as psychotherapist is still so prevalent that most consultants find it necessary to carefully define their roles to avoid this confusion. When a potential consultee does present a request for personal treatment, or seems to be seeking it actively, most consultants follow the practice of referring that consultee to another professional (Caplan, 1970). The importance of this problem was referred to earlier in the section on direct psychological services to police.

Mental health consultation may be used as part of a training function, as noted in the projects conducted by Bard and by Mann. In those projects, consultation was used in addition to training activities that involved larger group sessions. Caplan recommends that when problems of lack of knowledge and lack of skills are fairly common within an organization or agency, then training, rather than consultation, is the preferred solution. Mann (1973) has suggested that as problems of lack of knowledge and lack of skills are overcome through training activities, consultation on problems of lack of confidence and lack of objectivity may become more relevant and more effective. Conversely, it does little good to attempt to improve confidence or objectivity if consultees are lacking in the knowledge and skills required to help persons with mental health problems.

Organizational consultation involves the application of social psychological principles to organizational problems. One of the largest areas of this sort of activity in recent years has been the work of psychologists in helping to develop police teams (Bard & Shellow, 1976b). Toch and his associates (Toch, Grant, & Galvin, 1975) used an organizational technique in the development of internal change agents to introduce innovative approaches to a number of police problems in Oakland, California. Mann (1973) and his associates studied a problem of poor morale within a police department; after observation and interviews, they made recommendations for changes in communication patterns and personnel duties that alleviated the problem.

These approaches may or may not involve the use of group process methods—similar to those employed in human relations training but differing in their purpose—to aid in the improvement of internal organizational functioning. In each case, the goal of consultation is to assist the organization to become self-sufficient in managing its organizational problems.

As is the case with organizational consultation in other bureaucratic structures (Bennis, 1966), changes in organizational structure or function often create serious problems of resistance simply because of the systemic nature of existing structures and functions. The fate of team policing seems to illustrate this phenomenon particularly well. Bard and Shellow (1976b) describe a problem that has occurred frequently in these efforts—namely, competition between the team and nonteam elements of the department. Team policing involves a much more horizontal organizational structure than the vertical, quasi-military form of most police agencies, and this change in pattern is not easily absorbed by the existing structure. Thus, despite many apparently desirable qualities and evidence of its effectiveness, team policing has often been short-lived. On the other hand, the data presented by Toch and his associates suggest a widespread lack of shared expectations within a police department on critical incidents, a problem that is probably typical of many law enforcement agencies. Mann (1971, 1976) has observed that after critical and dangerous police incidents, rather intense social comparison processes occur in which police officers search out some common norm against which to compare their own reactions. Apparently the typical organizational structure of most police departments does not provide for the regularization of this process or for improved communications within the organization.

Reiser (1971) describes a number of special problems on which the psychologist may be asked to provide consultation. These include such diverse problems as driver training programs for police officers, analysis of officer-community interactions, developing psychological profiles in bizarre murder cases, testifying as an expert witness on pornography, as well as some of the activities mentioned elsewhere in this paper. Some of these activities go beyond the usual notions of the consultant's role as defined here and quite clearly would depend upon the special competence of a particular consultant for their appropriateness. In fact, Reiser's description of the variety of consultant activities of the psychologist employed full time by the police department contrasts with the more limited role assumed by most consultants. This contrast is no doubt a function of the differences in employment conditions, since the external consultant is more likely to be engaged for a more specialized purpose, while the in-house psychologist is available for more varied tasks. The in-house consultant is probably able to compensate for the greater diffuseness of his or her impact by the greater familiarity with and accessibility to the department that goes with the position, while the external consultant must first overcome the barriers encountered as an outsider before the more concentrated impact of his or her limited role can be achieved.

Research

In the preceding discussion a deliberate effort has been made, whenever possible, to describe the findings of research and evaluative studies connected with each of the projects mentioned. The point of doing so was to call attention to the importance of the evaluation function for psychologists working with law enforcement agencies. Evaluations of training and consultation programs and research on the selection process comprise the largest areas of research in which psychologists working with police organizations have been involved. Other forms of research, much of it newly emerging, include research on the effects of police activities and on community planning in relation to public safety.

In the previous discussion of research on the selection process, it was noted that the choice of criteria presents a problem of central importance. This is also true in most other areas of research activity involving police organizations, for example, in the question of whether attitudinal or behavioral measures are preferable or more meaningful in assessing the effects of training and consultation activities. The selection of one or the other should not depend solely on theoretical assumptions such as whether or not attitudinal changes lead to behavioral changes but should also depend in part upon the expectations of the audience to whom the research findings will be directed. As is the case in doing research with any client organization, the participation of the police department, and at least in some instances the community,

in selecting criteria is an important ingredient of a meaningful research study.

Another factor influencing the quality of evaluative studies is that their design is too often an afterthought. Applied psychologists are often much more oriented to methods of intervention than to outcomes and evaluations. In the mental health field, for instance, there have been few expectations of or standards for demonstrating the effectiveness of treatments until recently. If a patient was considered ill, it was felt more important to see that the patient received treatment than to ask how effective that treatment was. Accordingly, few resources were allocated to evaluation. Psychologists coming to the law enforcement field with clinical backgrounds may hold similar assumptions, but it is clear that expectations for outcome evaluation are more demanding in work with public institutions than has been true for psychologist's work in other fields.

On the other hand, until recently, evaluation of work done by public institutions has not been significantly more in evidence than evaluation of work in the mental health field. One of the first studies to question seriously an important assumption concerning the effects of police activity was the Kansas City Preventive Patrol Experiment (Kelling, Pate, Dieckman, & Brown, 1974). It has long been an accepted, but untested, belief that patrol activities deter crime. The Kansas City Police Department, with the help of the Police Foundation, set out to test this assumption. Using by far the most sophisticated research design employed in any study of its type, the researchers assigned 15 precincts to one of three conditions: reactive patrol, in which cars responded only to calls; control, in which normal patrol activity was maintained; or proactive patrol, in which an increased number of cars conducted more vigorous patrol activities than usual. Precincts in these three conditions, which were maintained for a one-year period, were compared on 13 different measures, including victimization and reported crime, rate of crime reporting, arrests, response time, and citizen and businessperson's attitudes toward police and toward their own safety. No significant differences among the precincts in the three patrol conditions were found.

In addition, this study found that 75% of the Kansas City police officers believed that patrol activity was the most important activity of the police department and that 60% of the officers' time was noncommitted, that is, not involved in answering calls for service. On the basis of these results, Kelling et al. concluded that this 60% of officers' time could be put to better use in more effective preventive activities than patrol duty.

Addressing the problem of prevention from another perspective, Monahan and Catalano (1976) describe how some states' requirements for environmental impact statements on new construction and development provide police agencies an opportunity to review such plans and to comment upon how they may affect demands for police service. In addition, using the findings of environmental psychological research, police departments can make recommendations for planning developments so as to increase public safety. Along this line, Monahan (1976) presents several suggestions for how research may be employed to design environments and to intervene in specific situations so as to reduce violent crimes. This approach to prevention is a new area of activity but hopefully one that will be further developed. Many are inclined to regard such a planning and environmental design approach to crime prevention as having a relatively low yield yet when one considers the low percentage of crimes cleared by arrest, a modest difference in the occurrence of crime could have a significant impact. For example, Monahan and Catalano (1976) cite a study by Wright, Heilrveil, Pelletier, and Dickinson (Note 6) which found that a program to improve street lighting produced a 52% decrease in robberies and a 41% decrease in assaults, figures that exceed the usual arrest clearance rates for those

crimes. Again, this is an area of research with much room for increased activity.

The activities of psychologists working with law enforcement agencies that have been reviewed in the preceding sections are only a sampling of those generated by the proliferation of such activities in recent years. The ones reviewed here are mainly those that have been reported in publications, and not all of the different projects described in print have been mentioned here. Nevertheless, substantial growth in both the number and variety of such activities is evident.

The rapid growth of this activity confronts the psychologist with a number of complex and unique situations that call for the exercise of professional judgment. Since such work takes place in an atmosphere of conflicting and changing public values, ethical issues may arise in which the application of judgmental guidelines developed in other work areas may not be clear-cut. Examples of such ethical issues need to be considered both for the purpose of clarifying the application of ethical principles and for deriving implications for public policy.

Examples of Ethical Issues

Ethical issues arise out of conflicts among interests and values when one or more of these interests and values involve moral standards, matters of human dignity and decency, or the constraints that professionals self-consciously place on their work in order to safeguard the welfare of their clients and to meet their responsibilities to the general public. Psychologists working with law enforcement agencies must be aware of a number of audiences to which they are directly or indirectly responsible: the police organization that employs them, the diversity of groups making up the public interest, and the profession of psychology.

It is important to distinguish ethical issues from questions of legality and of strategy. It is

31

assumed that psychologists' work will be conducted according to whatever legal considerations apply in particular situations. Ethical considerations do not apply to questions of whether or not certain strategies are successful or certain techniques are effective. However, the direct and incidental effects of such strategies and techniques have ethical implications.

The *Ethical Standards of Psychologists* of the American Psychological Association were developed from the experiences of psychologists in a variety of settings and have been revised periodically on the basis of subsequent experience (*Ethical Standards of Psychologists*, 1953, 1963, 1977, 1979). The emergence of community psychology during the 1960s led Golann (1969) to examine the ethical issues that arose as psychologists began to work increasingly in community settings. He reported that a survey of members of the APA's Division of Community Psychology indicated that the existing code of ethics was deemed adequate to cover such situations but that a collection of examples of ethical concerns in such work would be desirable. Similarly, the purpose of this discussion is not to generate ethical principles but to provide examples of ethical concerns that arise in the work of psychologists with law enforcement agencies.

APA's Task Force on the Role of Psychology in the Criminal Justice System surveyed 349 APA members whose primary employment setting was related to the criminal justice system. The law enforcement system was reported to be the principal employment setting for 38 of these psychologists and the secondary employment setting for 97 of them. Responses were received from 203 of the 349 psychologists in the original sample (58%). Among these respondents, only 6 reported ethical concerns derived from work with law enforcement agencies. This sampling can be used as a beginning point and a number of issues added that arise in the activities described previously. The resulting issues may be grouped into the following categories for discussion: (a) representations of the adequacy or effectiveness of psychological programs or services, (b) representations of the competency of the psychologist, (c) confidentiality, (d) responsibility to client organizations, and (e) design of research and utilization of research findings.

Representations of Programs and Services

One respondent to the task force survey listed seeking grant money for projects with unrealistic goals and overstaffing projects funded by government money as examples of unethical practices. These comments suggest ethical concerns that may arise when there are important problems to be solved and limited funds are available to support efforts at their solution.

The issue may occur in two forms. On the one hand, a sincere desire to apply psychological concepts and methods to problems of law enforcement agencies might lead to overselling or overpromising of results. On the other hand, the psychologist may be asked by a police organization to provide services to solve a problem when he or she has reason to doubt the effectiveness of those services for solving that particular problem.

The latter form of the issue is likely to occur when client organizations, under some pressure, are seeking solutions to problems that have been incorrectly identified or incompletely analyzed. In the extreme instance, the psychologist might have reason to believe that the services are sought by the client organization for largely cosmetic reasons, with minimal commitment to solving the problem(s). This may be the case when a psychologist is asked to provide interpretations of test data in personnel selection when the validity of the tests is questionable or when a psychologist is hired to design and conduct programs of selection, training, or consultation for the purpose of changing some particular police behavior when the problem may lie with some aspect of the client organization not affected by these procedures, such as policies and their enforcement.

A rather dramatic example of such questions is provided by the Washington, D.C., Pilot District Project (Kelly, 1975; Lalley, 1976). Funded by the U.S. Office of Economic Opportunity and designed by psychologist Robert Shellow, this project generated intense disagreement among citizen groups, the police, officials of the funding. source and government, and evaluators of the project. While much of this disagreement concerned other areas, the question of adequacy of methods was among the issues raised.

It should be emphasized that reasonable people with sincere motivations may disagree over various approaches. The question is how much doubt about the effectiveness of various programs and methods is acceptable in the psychologist's decision to proceed with the activity. The fact is that the effectiveness of many psychological techniques in solving the problems of particular police agencies has not been widely demonstrated. Should the psychologist accept opportunites to engage in projects of doubtful efficacy (a) for the sake of establishing a relationship that may allow more effective work later or (b) in order to demonstrate the utility or ineffectiveness of such programs?

Representation of Competence

Another respondent to the task force survey listed providing incompetent or useless services as an example of unethical behavior. This issue is related to the previous one but extends to the competencies that psychologists claim for themselves as individuals. The APA code of ethics states that psychologists represent their competencies accurately and recognize their limitations. However, the issue extends beyond this in certain instances. In discussing ethical issues for sociologists in applied settings, Angell (1967) noted,

> In professional relations the maxim *caveat emptor* does not apply. The buyer cannot beware because he does not know enough about what he is purchasing to tell whether he is getting the kind of service he is paying for. (p. 727)

This issue is particularly critical for those psychologists who may be competent to perform the generic functions desired by the client organization but may not be familiar with the requirements of and constraints operating on the psychologist's role in a particular police agency. For example, a psychologist who is competent in clinical psychological test administration and interpretation may be asked to assist in a program of police personnel selection. In addition to involving a different level of psychometric theory and technique than many clinicians are accustomed to practicing (such as the ability to conduct validity studies, develop selection ratios, and construct criterion measures), such work requires familiarity with equal opportunity guidelines, the requirements of police work, and the role of personality factors in police performance. Lack of competence in these areas can have serious financial, legal, and social consequences.

Another example of an issue of competence arises in training and consultation programs aimed at helping police officers recognize and manage abnormal behavior. A question in which police officers have an important interest is the assessment of potential dangerousness. At one level of this issue is the doubt cast on the ability of psychologists to predict dangerousness among the mentally ill (Monahan, 1975). At another level is the difference in the circumstances and consequences of making such predictions for the police officer and for the psychologist in their respective work roles, a difference that emphasizes again the necessity for familiarization with the police officer's work situation. Since the legal basis for police intervention into disturbed behavior requires an assessment of dangerousness in most jurisdictions, the psychologist must understand both the legal definition of evidence for such judgments in that jurisdiction (usually the county or district attorney's view of such behavior) and the limits of clinical knowledge in making assessments of dangerousness in the context of police work. Without similar knowledge of the constraints and legal bases operating on the police officer's interventions into human behavior, the psychologist risks giving advice or teaching techniques that may lead the officer to take actions placing him or her in legal or organizational jeopardy or that are worthless because they cannot be implemented.

Confidentiality

Psychologists are accustomed to observing confidentiality in their work with individual and organizational clients. In certain roles, however, psychologists and their clients may not be prepared for some of the conflicts that may arise in work with law enforcement agencies. This problem has been alluded to earlier in discussing the psychologist's role in providing psychotherapy or counseling to police officers, but it may also arise when the psychologist acts as a consultant. If the psychologist is also asked to make evaluations of police officers for administrative reasons, a clear ethical conflict exists. Even if the psychologist is not asked to divulge confidential information, no guarantee can be given that such information will not enter into the psychologist's judgment. Although an analogous situation may exist with the psychologist's evaluation of other individual patients or clients, the analogy breaks down when one realizes that the police officer may not have accepted the client or consultee role with the understanding and consent that such confidential information might be used later for other purposes.

On the other hand, a psychologist may obtain information in such a confidential relationship that he or she feels poses a serious threat to the welfare of the public, the police department, or the police officer. Yet revelation of this information would violate the confidence of

the relationship. What is the psychologist's responsibility in such situations?

Similar concerns about confidentiality apply to other information obtained about the police organization in a professional relationship. This may be in the form of research data, gossip, or other "inside knowledge" to which the psychologist may have access solely because of his or her position. Even though individual identities may not be involved, the public, the psychologist's colleagues, and representatives of the media may seek such information. Many psychologists are probably not accustomed to treating a public institution the way they would treat other clients or organizations, and they may be apt to reveal privileged information through publication of research data, interviews, or professional symposia. What conditions govern the confidentiality of such information?

A final aspect of this issue involves the possibility that the psychologist, in the course of observing or becoming familiar with police activity, may witness events with legal implications. Should the psychologist agree to serve as an eyewitness to criminal behavior he or she may have observed that involves civilians? If so, the psychologist might then be asked to give testimony in inquiries involving officer indiscretions or unlawful behavior, either in court proceedings or internal investigations. Might the psychologist's observations then be given a different weight than those of the ordinary citizen or police officer testifying in such a case? What is the legal and professional status of the psychologist in such situations?

Responsibility to the Client

One respondent to the task force survey noted simply, "Always remember who the client is. My client is the police department, not the offender or the victim." This psychologist clearly perceives his role to be working for the police department. However, such clarity of role may not always be present. Psychologists may be employed *by* a civil service commission but be working *with* a police agency in order to develop performance criteria. Psychologists involved in police-community relations programs may see themselves quite correctly as working for the community. Other psychologists may be employed by community mental health centers and working with police organizations.

Without a clear perception of their responsibilities to the various groups in these employment situations, psychologists may be subject to conflicting loyalties, and personal biases or professional commitments may intrude on the work roles they adopt with regard to the police organization. For example, a mental hospital may implement an open ward policy, a policy with which the psychologist may agree for professional reasons. However, the officials of a police agency with which the psychologist consults may denounce the policy, reasoning that an increase in patient elopements will pose a threat to the community and thus more work for the police. What position is dictated by the psychologist's work role in this situation?

Similar conflicts may develop during times of civil tension and intergroup confrontations. Incidents between police and members of minority groups may generate sympathy for the latter and antagonism toward the police among the public. The psychologist's colleagues or employer may then assume that the psychologist should be trying harder to correct what they see as improper or ineffective police practices. Regardless of the correctness or incorrectness of these perceptions, the principle of confidentiality may be invoked against a psychologist who provides inside information that might clarify the situation in the public's eyes. Conversely, a psychologist's sympathetic portrayal of the police may be perceived by the public as a loss of objectivity. Or, if the psychologist is employed by an organization such as a mental health center that has an important constituency among poor and minority groups, such a step might serve to discredit the psychologist's employing institution.

On a more personal level, the psychologist may be asked to participate in activities that conflict with his or her personal ideologies with respect to the means to be pursued, the ends to be obtained, or both. The psychologist might decline to participate, but such a refusal might become public knowledge and suggest disapproval of the activity and reflect adversely on the police organization. On the other hand, continued participation may mean that the psychologist makes less than an enthusiastic contribution to the activity. What are the psychologist's obligations under such circumstances?

Finally, conflicts of loyalty or personal biases may appear in interpretations or conclusions presented in published material based on the psychologist's experiences or research. What guidelines should influence this sort of activity?

Research

Three concerns with the research process were listed by one respondent to the survey. These were the use of adequate experimental designs, the selection of criteria in evaluating programs, and the dilemma of whether to release data that may be damaging to program continuation. These concerns implicitly reflect some of those already discussed, such as representation of competence, confidentiality, and responsibility to the client. It must be recognized that well-designed research is difficult to conduct in many police settings, as it is in other public institutions. The lack of readily comparable control groups when an entire department's performance is evaluated, the effects of pretesting, maturation, and extraneous socioeconomic changes in pre- and posttest designs (Campbell & Stanley, 1966) all contribute to this difficulty.

The problem is compounded, however, when, as often happens, the psychologist is asked to evaluate a program in process or to participate in an evaluation that has already begun. In both cases, inadequate research design or pretest data may be involved. The psychologist's participation may lend a certain expert credence to the evaluation that could be misleading if the findings are not reliable or if the conclusions suggested by the data are not warranted by the research design. On the other hand, if the psychologist declines to participate, the evaluation may be conducted anyway, with less sophistication than if the psychologist were to lend whatever help was possible under the circumstances. Similar problems may arise from participation in an inadequately validated selection process.

The release of research findings, discussed earlier, may also be involved in this category of concerns. The psychologist may have access to research findings that have been suppressed because their implications are clearly unfavorable to the police organization or to a program. Should the psychologist knowingly participate in such suppression? If not, how do the requirements for confidentiality operate here?

Approaches to the Resolution of Ethical Issues

Before beginning to explore approaches to the resolution of the specific ethical issues raised in the preceding section, it must be noted that many of these issues can and should be readily resolved through adequate forethought and planning. The same advance clarification of roles, expectations, and work conditions that applies in therapeutic, training, or consulting work in other settings applies to such work in the police setting. By clarifying in detail the nature of the psychologist's contract with the law enforcement agency, an understanding of the importance of ethical concerns to the psychologist's work can be generated that may be of considerable benefit in defining other aspects of the psychologist's role as well. For strategic reasons as well as to satisfy the psychologist's desire to be accountable for his or her work, periodic reviews of the progress of the psychologist's work relationship should also be specified in the initial planning. These pre-planned reviews give both the police agency and the psychologist a regularly scheduled opportunity to correct misunderstandings and modify procedures as needed. They also underscore the need for flexibility and openness in the relationship.

A second a priori consideration is the psychologist's commitment to empirical resolution of disagreements over matters of fact. This principle implies more than may be apparent at first glance. While it emphasizes that the psychologist's work should not be evaluated on the basis of belief or opinion alone, it also imposes the burden of empirical demonstration on the psychologist, including the possibility of finding that his or her efforts are not producing the effects desired. Moreover, this principle represents one of the psychologist's primary contributions to work with law enforcement agencies. A minimal requirement of acceptable working conditions for the psychologist is the willingness of the client law enforcement agency to submit its problems and proposed solutions to empirical examination. This commitment to empirical investigation is what distinguishes the work of the psychologist from the ideological do-goodism of various persons in the public arena in which the law enforcement agency operates (Reiff, 1971; Sarason, 1976). Of course, with the increasing emphasis on evaluation and accountability, whether by grant-giving sources or taxing bodies, this commitment is coming to be more widely expected of law enforcement organizations also.

These two ideas—early role clarification and a commitment to empirical investigation—form both the background and an initial basis for the discussions of specific ethical issues in the sections that follow.

Representations of Programs and Services

In representing psychological programs and services, the requirement for empirical verification of the effects of psychological services applies directly. Increasingly, informed funding sources are looking not only at the conceptual merit of proposed programs but at the adequacy of the design of evaluative studies that go with them. As a matter of ethical responsibility, the psychologist should expect such requirements and apply them to his or her own work whether required to by funding sources or not. At the same time, the psychologist must remember that the client organization has its own standards for evaluation that must be honored. Advance agreement on the dimensions of this aspect of the psychologist's work will answer many of the concerns raised by issues of this type.

Should the client organization be uninformed of other requirements bearing on evaluation of the work, such as standards for test validity to insure against discrimination on the basis of race, sex, and ethnicity, it is the psychologist's responsibility to supply such information and tailor research efforts accordingly.

Psychologists must be aware that in working with public organizations such as the police, they must take responsibility for the effects of their work not just on the police organization but on the public and on their profession as well. Principles 1e (Responsibility), 3b (Moral and Legal Standards), and 6e (Welfare of the Consumer) of the *Ethical Standards of Psychologists* (1979) apply, respectively, to the psychologist's acceptance of accountability for his or her efforts, the necessity for conformance of those efforts with legal requirements, and the psychologist's obligation to terminate a relationship when it is clear that the client is no longer deriving benefit from it. Psychologists must also be aware that failure to observe these standards reflects adversely not only upon themselves but upon their professional colleagues.

Representation of Competence

The psychologist is responsible for recognizing both the bases and the limitations of his or her competence. Principle 2 of the *Ethical Standards for Psychologists* deals with the bases of education and experience on which the psychologist claims competence. The psychologist claims competence only on the basis of legitimate degrees and relevant experience, recognizes the appropriateness of making such information openly available, and acknowledges the limitations of both his or her own competence and the techniques he or she employs.

Recognition of the limits of competence and techniques does not apply only to the insufficiently trained or the inexperienced. The psychologist must take pains to point out the limitations of psychological knowledge and to make appropriate qualifications on psychological generalizations, as, for example, in assisting police officers to make assessments of dangerousness. When the psychologist's competence for a particular task is limited, the psychologist should help the police organization seek the help of another professional whose competence is equal to the task. When the psychologist's experience is limited, as in familiarity with police operational procedures and requirements, the psychologist assumes the responsibility of gaining the appropriate experience or training as part of the obligations of providing relevant services. In keeping with Angell's observation that *caveat emptor* does not apply to professional services of this type, the psychologist does not leave questions of competence to be determined solely by the client organization.

Confidentiality

The requirement for confidentiality in the psychologist's work with individuals within the police organization should be among the priority items for clarification when the psychologist is defining his or her role prior to undertaking work in the police setting. That is, the psychologist must point out to police administrators the potential conflict that would arise from asking the psychologist to make evaluations of police officers with whom he or she works. Further, at this time the psychologist must communicate the principle of confidentiality to potential clients or consultees within the organization. Both Reiser (1972) and Hillgren and Jacobs (1976) have commented on the importance of this clarification. Any qualifications on the limits of confidentiality, such as the need to reveal information when a situation of which the psychologist has knowledge threatens imminent serious injury or death to the client or others, should be spelled out at this time also. In the latter instance, every effort should be made to alleviate the threat through discussion with the individual(s) involved, when this is possible, before confidential information is revealed.

The principle of confidentiality applies to organizations as well as individuals, and the police organization is no different from any other client organization in this respect. This confidentiality applies to inside knowledge gained through experience as well as to research findings, but there is an important difference from applying confidentiality to individuals. Frequently the psychologist wishes to publish data related to work with the police as part of his or her responsibility to contribute to the body of knowledge of the profession; and in some instances, outside funding sources will require such reports. Again, this is a matter to be clarified prior to initiating work—agreement must be reached on the procedures for publishing or otherwise divulging such information. Frequently, police organizations require the right to review and approve any data or information to be published. The psychologist must weigh the professional need to publish, which may be of benefit mainly to the psychologist, against the interests and prerogatives of the client organization.

If asked to serve as a witness, the psychologist should again reach an understanding with the client organization as to his or her expected role in such instances. Where the clear interest of justice is involved, the psychologist may be expected to serve as a witness just as any other citizen might be, but the psychologist must make it clear whether he or she is filling the role of professional/expert or functioning as a citizen because of the difference in legal weight given to testimony in these respective roles. It must also be understood that if the psychologist is to be called upon to testify as a witness, this function must be applied equally regardless of the issue or parties involved. Again, the psychologist must determine whether the information he or she might be asked to reveal is covered by the principle of confidentiality, that is, whether it became available in the context of a professional relationship with the persons involved.

Responsibility to the Client

Again, advance clarification of the psychologist's role will alleviate many conflicts concerning responsibility to the police organization as a client. In addition to those concerns discussed already, psychologists must also be careful to clarify their work roles with other parties or organizations that may be their major employers or constituencies, whether these be universities, community mental health centers, or other members of the community. Psychologists employed primarily in a university setting may have few limitations placed on them in this respect because they operate under a tradition of academic freedom that gives them considerable autonomy to function in other settings provided they otherwise meet their obligations to the employing academic institution. However, psychologists functioning out of other employing institutions may not be able to assume such freedom. In either case it is well to clarify these matters in advance so that conflicts in loyalties can be prevented or at least more easily resolved.

The psychologist is obligated to bring to the attention of the police organization any ideological conflict that may influence his or her performance of tasks that the client organization might request. This does not mean that the psychologist is obligated not to participate in such tasks. If the client organization, being informed of the psychologist's ideological position, wishes the psychologist to continue with the work, he or she may do so ethically at his or her own discretion. The primary obligation of the psychologist is to inform the client. This issue is discussed clearly by Angell (1967) in regard to sociologists.

Whether to reveal research data and other inside knowledge has been discussed at some length already. In this regard, Angell makes another worthwile point applicable to psychologists as well as sociologists: One should distinguish between data collected primarily for the purpose of making a contribution to scientific knowledge and data collected for some practical purpose incident to the client organization's functioning. In the latter case, the psychologist is under no ethical obligation to seek to publish the information out of responsibility to the profession of psychology. In the former instance, however, and where such information is relevant to evaluative studies required by funding sources, the psychologist is ethically bound to seek its publication. Again, these matters should be the subject of agreements reached prior to the psychologist's undertaking a working relationship with the police organization.

Finally, it should be emphasized that the psychologist must conduct work with the police organization with the same respect for members of another profession and for the operational patterns of another institution that would be accorded other professional groups. Principle 7 of the *Ethical Standards of Psychologists* refers to relationships with other professions and institutions, and it applies here. It is as much a matter of competence as of ethics that the psychologist maintain objectivity and develop an appreciation of the need for police personnel to function differently than psychologists and for police organizations to follow different practices than those adhered to by other organizations with which the psychologist may be associated. There is no reason to assume that this type of mutual respect is not as important in work with police organizations as it is in work with any other client.

Research

The adequate and appropriate design of research studies is, of course, an integral part of the competence of the psychologist. The difficulty and complexity of research in the police setting has already been noted. It is assumed that the psychologist conducting research in this setting will take pains to conceptualize the problem and develop a competent research strategy, but the necessities of practical circumstances often make research designs that allow for well-controlled variables and straightforward interpretation of results difficult or impossible. When the psychologist involved does not possess skills in designing and interpreting research under these conditions, consultation with an expert in research design is advisable.

More often than not, the realities of research in applied settings pose problems that cannot be overcome entirely. Accordingly, the proper qualifications that must be placed on the interpretation of results, including the limitations on the applicability of the findings and plausible alternative hypotheses, become as important a part of the information to be communicated about the research as the data on which the conclusions are based. These concerns are covered by Principle 1a of the *Ethical Standards of Psychologists*.

In discussing the problems involved in selecting criteria for research studies, the importance of participation on the part of the client organization and other relevant constituencies was mentioned. It was also pointed out that behavioral data offer advantages over other types of data, such as attitude scales, when such measures are appropriate to the research questions. In many instances, the law enforcement agency will have available an adequate source of behavioral data that other public institutions may not possess. Thus, the psychologist called in to assist with an evaluative study already under way, or to evaluate a project in which adequate pretest data were not collected, may not be at quite the disadvantage that might exist in other settings. The psychologist does have a commitment to competent conduct of evaluative research and must not allow the express or implied impression that he or she will permit improper conclusions based on research in which he or she participated to go uncorrected. However, the psychologist's main ethical responsibility in these circumstances is best discharged by encouraging thorough presentation of any qualifications and limitations that apply to research data and by discouraging the publication or other release of misleading research findings.

Finally, the psychologist should bear in mind that while practices and policies may follow from research results, such data may not be the only determinant of action by a client organization. When the psychologist feels that data are ignored in the formulation of practices and policies, he or she may understandably wish not to continue a professional relationship with that organization. However, the ethical requirements concerning confidentiality of information, as discussed above, still hold, and release of any such data should be considered subject to whatever agreements have been reached previously concerning publication or other dissemination. The psychologist may advocate the empirical point of view within the police organization and remain well within the limits of ethical standards, but other ethical requirements make it clear that the responsibility for initiating action remains with the client organization, as it does with any client. Moreover, the psychologist's observation of confidentiality must also remain the same as for any other client.

This review of examples of ethical issues in work with law enforcement agencies is a representative, but not exhaustive, sampling of

the concerns in this area. Some of these issues have implications for public policies, a subject addressed in the next section.

Questions of Public Policy

Thus far, past and present contributions of psychologists to the work of law enforcement organizations have been discussed. Most of these studies have been conducted only in recent years, and there is much more to be learned about law enforcement work. The potential for further contributions by psychologists appears to be largely undeveloped. Whether or not this further potential will be realized depends more on the formulation of public policies requiring the utilization of psychological knowledge than on the efforts of psychologists to offer further services. The concept of team policing, for example, while grounded in sound psychological theory, has often been discarded despite its proven usefulness. The technical knowledge to develop valid selection procedures that do not illegally discriminate has been present for some time, but not until government regulations and court decisions forced the use of such selection procedures was attention paid to this knowledge.

Policy development is not always under the sole control of the police organization. Politicization of the problem of crime and use of the patronage system in selecting police personnel, abuses with a long history that persist to this day in many jurisdictions, influence police policies and practices. As society has been ambivalent in its attitudes toward the law enforcement function, so has it been ambivalent in its view of the role of social and behavioral science in its public business. Society has been inclined to look at costs first and effectiveness later.

Psychologists should be among the first to recognize that the police function is viewed through the lens of human ambivalence toward authority, a fact that places limits on the possibility of clear and logical assessments of the police role. Yet, psychologists should also be quick to point out that they can and should strive to remove those limits by an objectification of the phenomena under study. As Bittner (1970) observed,

> It would appear more probable that in the heat of polemics some facts and some judgments shifted out of line, that many polemic opponents argue from positions that are submerged in tacit and conflicting presuppositions, and the task of analysis and pending reform could only be advanced beyond its present impasse by first setting forth as unambiguously as possible the terms on which the police must be judged in general and in all the particulars of their practices. (p. 2)

The establishment of goals and objectives for the police and of standards for police performance and personnel selection would reduce the influence of the political and polemical process that ultimately contributes to an erosion of public confidence in police work and to the alienation of police officers. To the extent that psychologists become identified with police agencies, they are subject to the same forces. Mann (1973, p. 152) has noted that the process of setting goals and standards for police organizations is properly a community process in which both police and citizens should take part. While avoidance of this process may give police departments an illusion of freedom from societal sanction, the absence of goals and standards jointly shaped by the police and society is eventually paid for by the low public confidence and police alienation noted above.

A first step toward such mutual goal definition is education of the community about the functions of police organizations, a responsibility both police agencies and psychologists may share. Without such education, the many service functions police officers perform will continue to be either unrewarded or noticed only sporadically, a condition that can result in less than effective performance. Without clear goals, the effectiveness of police work in general

and of programs to improve police performance in particular cannot be evaluated unambiguously.

A whole series of consequences follow from a lack of goals and standards. Upgrading the quality of police service, development of professionalism among police officers, and improvements in public safety all require clear goals and standards. Without them, political expedients and funding sources become the determinants of police practices to a greater extent than desirable. On the other hand, some are concerned that professionalization of the police will create an autonomous police function unresponsive to public needs. The issue of developing goals and standards for the police must be squarely faced; otherwise, token and superficial efforts at improvement will tend to persist. Each policy development undertaken will inevitably involve costs as well as benefits, but it is a disservice to both the police and the public to pretend this is not so.

Progress in the area of policy formulation is essential to the development of new capabilities among police officers that changing social conditions require. In turn, as these requirements emerge, new roles for psychologists in the law enforcement system are needed. Some of these future roles are considered in the next section.

Future Roles of Psychologists in the Law Enforcement System

Recent development of certain public policies has defined new roles for psychologists working with law enforcement agencies and has increased the salience of some already existing roles. The requirement for demonstrably valid selection procedures, for example, places a new emphasis on the role of psychologists in developing meaningful performance criteria and tests to select police candidates who can meet these criteria. Public Law 94-63, which amends the Community Mental Health Centers Act, places new responsibilities on community mental health centers to develop programs for the prevention of rape and the humane treatment of rape victims. Psychologists involved in developing such programs will need to achieve close working relationships with police officers in training and consultation programs, as well as to plan with police agencies to disseminate knowledge about prevention efforts that is not presently available to any appreciable degree.

These relatively new roles and functions are examples of the results of social processes set in motion as a response to social problems. Yet surprisingly few new roles for psychologists have developed in response to recent increases in concern over crime as a social problem. Perhaps this is in part because psychologists and police officials realize that the police do not control the causes of crime. Nevertheless, some promising beginnings are suggested by Monahan and Catalano's (1976) proposal that police agencies take on a research and planning

function to review the public-safety impact of commercial or residential developments still in the planning stages. This is a function in which psychologists could make a significant contribution. Its implementation in most parts of the country awaits a stronger societal commitment to the community planning process, but already there are signs of increasing awareness of this need. As this process develops, psychologists will need to be alert to the issues involved and prepared to preserve human values and democratization of the planning process.

In the meantime, there remains room for significantly more involvement by psychologists (a) in providing assistance to research programs on innovations in police services, (b) in predicting and anticipating responses to changes in crime trends, and (c) in consulting on organizational problems within police agencies. These problems as well as newly emerging challenges pose a need for continuing participation by psychologists in the law enforcement setting.

Ellsworth A. Fersch, Jr.

3
Ethical Issues for Psychologists
in Court Settings

There is little doubt that all of the participants in the criminal justice system call upon their own notions of psychology in an effort to see that justice is done in the courts or at least to see that their own side wins. Even the adversary system is said to embody important psychological principles: the importance of confronting one's accusers, of being able to cross-examine witnesses, of having evidence presented orally by the individuals concerned, and of preventing hearsay testimony. And the components of the court setting—including the traditional symbols, the location of the participants, and even the judge's attire—are said to spring from psychological truths about fairness and the appearance of fairness (American Friends Service Committee, 1971; Donnelly, Goldstein, & Schwartz, 1962; Freedman, 1975; Saks & Hastie, 1978).

The role of commonsense psychology is unlimited in the courts. More recently, the role of the specific scientific and professional field of psychology has been increasing in the courts. When the findings of scientific psychology back the practices of commonsense psychology, there is of course no conflict, and hardly any note is taken of the relation between the folk wisdom and the scientific findings. It is only when the two conflict that there is much stir: Thus, in questions of eyewitness identification (Loftus, 1979) or of jury selection (Saks, 1976), for example, scientific psychology is set against commonsense psychology. While the courts rely

on eyewitness identification, scientific psychology seems to say that such identification is shaky and unreliable; and while lawyers select jury members through their own collective psychology, scientific psychology seems to say that such methods are haphazard and potentially self-defeating. It is primarily in these instances of conflict between the traditional and newer ideas of psychology that psychologists, those specifically trained in the science and profession of psychology, find their roles in court settings.

It is no wonder, then, that psychologists often find themselves in the center of controversies in the criminal justice system as a whole, and especially in court settings (Brakel & Rock, 1971; Fersch, 1979, 1980; Saks & Hastie, 1978; Stone, 1975). For psychologists are often used in the courts to challenge accepted truths, to implement new truths, and to help as well as undermine the system. They are asked to help the system by backing one defendant's testimony, by examining potential witnesses, by determining the competency of a defendant to stand trial, or by explaining such matters as perception and memory to the court. They are asked to undermine the system by challenging some of its basic assumptions—the value of eyewitness identification, the possibility of psychologists' predicting dangerousness, the fairness of jury selection and composition, the impact of procedures in the court—sometimes without offering any proven substitutes in their place. Whether they present their findings through articles or are allowed into the courtroom itself to present their views, psychologists have increasingly become involved in the criminal justice system and, of interest to us here, in the courts (Brodsky, 1973; Fersch, 1980).

As already noted, psychologists face many problems in the courts because of the tasks they are asked to perform by the system itself or by participants within the system. But there is another important set of problems they face once they become involved in the criminal justice system. That set of problems arises from within their own profession, for many ethical issues face psychologists in court settings. A close look at those ethical issues forms a major part of this chapter.

Every profession has its set of ethical standards, and the psychological profession is no exception (*Casebook on Ethical Standards*, 1967; *Ethical Standards of Psychologists*, 1953, 1963, 1977, 1979). The *Ethical Standards of Psychologists* are continually revised, and the current set was approved by the American Psychological Association's Council of Representatives on January 19–20, 1979. While the *Ethical Standards of Psychologists* are quite useful in the usual situations psychologists encounter, the special nature of the court and its power of coercion create especially complicated and troubling ethical issues for psychologists that these standards often do not go far toward resolving.

The preamble of the *Ethical Standards* both sets the goals for psychologists and suggests the difficulties that psychologists in court settings have:

Psychologists respect the dignity and worth of the individual and honor the preservation and protection of fundamental human rights. They are committed to increasing knowledge of human behavior and of people's understanding of themselves and others and to the utilization of such knowledge for the promotion of human welfare. While pursuing these endeavors, they make every effort to protect the welfare of those who seek their services or of any human being or animal that may be the object of study. They use their skills only for purposes consistent with these values and do not knowingly permit their misuse by others (*Ethical Standards of Psychologists*, 1979, p. 1)

Admittedly, these prefatory comments are broadly drawn. Yet adherence to these general standards by psychologists working in the courts is very difficult, for courts can impose sanctions that may fundamentally affect those who receive psychological services. Even these general statements make plain the dichotomy between those who seek the services of psychologists and those who are the objects of study. The latter group, interestingly, includes human beings as well as animals, for in a court setting, the person may be made an unwilling object of study.

Further, psychologists participating in an adversary system often cannot adequately protect their work from misuse. The essence of an adversary system is that one side of a case is challenged by the other side. And psychologists may in fact lend their knowledge to misuse, whether knowingly or unknowingly, simply by participating in procedures required by law: When psychologists predict dangerousness, for example, they may be misleading themselves and others and giving their own guesswork the protective coloration of scientific psychology (Dix, 1975; Fersch, 1980; Laves, 1975; Monahan, 1978; Shah, 1976, 1978; Stone, 1975; Ziskin, 1975, 1977).

Another set of problems arises because both the criminal justice and the mental health (psychological/psychiatric) systems identify social deviance and implement social control yet rest on very different assumptions about human nature (Monahan, 1975, 1976; Morse, 1976, 1978; Stone, 1975; Szasz, 1961, 1963, 1965, 1977, 1979; Tapp, 1976). The criminal justice system, of which the court is a part, (a) rests on the assumption that individuals exercising their free will are capable of choosing to do or not to do what the law commands; (b) has at its aims the punishment (and sometimes the isolation from the community) and rehabilitation of wrong-doers, deterrence of them from future wrong-doing, and deterrence of the general public from wrongdoing; and (c) is said to spring from the moral convictions of the community (Don-nelly et al., 1962; Kittrie, 1971; Powers, 1973; Wilson, 1975). On the other hand, the mental health system (a) rests more on the assumption that the actions of individuals are determined by their early lives or by a combination of their early lives and their environment; (b) has as its aim the treatment of mentally ill persons; and (c) is said to spring from concepts of mental health and social well-being (Stone, 1975).

While these two major systems, criminal jus-tice and mental health, are based on very dif-ferent theories and practice very different procedures, they are said to act in concert in the court setting. Whether this is even possible is again a question being increasingly discussed. What is clear is that the courts have come to rely more upon psychologists and other mental health personnel and that the law incorporates many references to them and gives them specific functions in the court setting. In fact, Kittrie (1971, p. 1) has termed this movement within these two systems "the divestment of criminal justice and coming of the therapeutic state."

The courts are one of the major focuses for discussion of this movement because it is often there that decisions are made on whether defendants will be dealt with through the criminal justice system or through the mental health system. It is there that their rights are protected or not protected. It is there that they have a chance to air their views or are prevented from doing so. And it is there that the traditional ideas of guilt and innocence, punishment and rehabilitation, mental health and mental illness, liberty and confinement, are tested and implemented.

It is also in the courts that the differential status of psychologists and psychiatrists is most noticeable. Statutes and court opinions limit the making of some determinations in courts to psychiatrists; psychologists in such instances are excluded by law. And psychiatric organiza-tions seek to limit further the role of psychol-ogists and other mental health professionals and to expand the exclusive roles of psychia-trists. Problems arise for psychologists, then, not only between the criminal justice and the mental health systems but within the mental health system itself.

Before I conclude this introduction, the rela-tion between the criminal justice system and scientific psychology needs to be put in a larger perspective. While we have witnessed decreas-ing use of the criminal justice model and increas-ing use of the psychological model in dealing with antisocial behavior, we are currently in a period of much dispute about what stance the law should take vis-à-vis lawbreakers. Three different positions are advanced (Fersch, 1979, 1980).

The first position, which I call the traditional one, is that the criminal justice system ought to deal with wrongdoers through accusation, trial, adjudication, and punishment. This position ac-cepts the notion that lawbreakers choose to commit their offenses, views punishment as an acceptable community response, and uses com-monsense psychology in its deliberations. It feels that scientific psychology, psychologists, and psychiatrists have little to contribute to ef-fective law and order and that matters end with the conclusion of the criminal process.

The second position, which I call the liberal reform one, is that the criminal justice system is harsh, predicated on false assumptions about human nature, blind to the true causes of crime, and less than morally acceptable. This position accepts the notion that individuals are not free to commit their offenses but do so out of deeply felt injustice occasioned by racism, poverty, and emotional deprivation; views punishment as unacceptable and individual rehabilitation and social amelioration as proper goals; and feels that scientific psychology, psychologists, and psychiatrists have much to contribute to effec-

45

tive assessment and treatment of defendants and offenders, to court proceedings, to extensive social legislation, and to crime prevention and limitation (Bazelon, 1976; Cryan, 1977; Flaschner, 1971; Joost & McGarry, 1974; Loftus, 1979).

The third position, which I call the rethinking position, attempts at the outset to return to basic questions and to reason through the problems of deviance and control and the many proposed solutions to them. Thus it asks such questions as what harm individuals' acts cause to specific individuals or to society, what methods are available to control them or that harm, what analogous situations there are and how they are handled, what important principles are at stake and what priorities there ought to be among them when they conflict, how each potential course of action functions and what its consequences are. This position seeks to balance the legal, psychological, sociological, and philosophical considerations involved in punishment and rehabilitation, denial of liberty, and forced treatment. The rethinking position attempts to look from the perspectives of the offender, the court, and society, beyond labels and customs, to see what is actually happening and to ask whether it should be happening. It accepts the criminal justice model, although it proposes changes and differentiates between situations in which psychology, psychologists, and criminal laws are useful and situations in which they are not (Fersch, 1979, 1980; Morse, 1976, 1978; Schur & Bedau, 1974).

Whatever position one adheres to, it is becoming increasingly evident that the current system neither punishes most offenders nor offers true rehabilitative services. Confused with regard to its goals and trapped between two conflicting views of human nature and of individual responsibility, the system provides neither good psychological lessons to the citizens nor safety to the community. It must do both if it is to be effective.

Current Roles and Functions of Psychologists in Court Settings

Having introduced the major problems in the relation between the criminal justice system and psychology and the various positions advanced to solve them, in this section I describe briefly the many current roles and functions of psychologists in court settings. To ease comparison of these functions with those of psychologists in other parts of the criminal justice system I have grouped them under five main headings suggested elsewhere (Brodsky, 1973) and used in Chapter 2 of this book: assessment, treatment, training, consultation, and research.

Assessment

Whether employed on a regular basis by a court or mental health center, employed for a particular case by a defendant, prosecutor, or judge, or asked for general information in a case, psychologists may function before the trial, during the trial, or after the trial. While currently some of these functions may only be performed in some jurisdictions by psychiatrists, the trend is toward letting psychologists perform them as well. One of the latent functions of psychologists in court settings may be to point up where psychologists' services can be effectively used.

Pretrial

One of the most significant interactions between the criminal justice system and mental health system occurs in the so-called competency evaluation: the determination of defendants' abilities to understand the charges against them and to cooperate with their counsel in their own defense. Anyone can raise the question of competency—the judge, the defense, the prosecution—and once it is raised, proceedings are stopped while a psychologist, psychiatrist, or other mental health professional examines the defendant for competency. These evaluations vary greatly and may take anywhere from a brief period for an interview to an extended period of incarceration of the defendant in a mental hospital. At issue is whether defendants at the time of their trials are able to proceed effectively with their cases (Bendt & Balcanoff, 1972; Laboratory of Community Psychiatry, 1973; Fersch, 1979; Leifer, 1962–1963; Lipsitt, Lelos, & McGarry, 1971; Roesch & Golding, 1977; Stone, 1975).

Another point of interaction between mental health and criminal justice is often confused with the competency evaluation, and though it happens far less frequently, it is, in the public mind, the prime example of psychologists or psychiatrists at work in court settings: determination of criminal responsibility. This determination does not involve defendants' states of mind at the time of their trials. Rather, it involves the defendants' states of mind at the time of the alleged offenses. Most often, such inquiry is made in cases where the defendant is pleading not guilty by reason of insanity or where the crime was particularly horrible. The issue is whether the defendants were mentally ill at the time of the acts and whether as a product of that mental illness they lacked criminal responsibility (Dix, 1971; Fersch, 1980; Fingarette, 1972; Goldstein, 1967; Monahan, 1973; Stone, 1975).

Psychologists in court settings also determine the dangerousness of defendants, either for the purposes of confining dangerous, mentally ill persons against their will in a hospital or of recommending to the court other appropriate measures to be taken (Dix, 1975; Monahan, 1978; Shah, 1976, 1978).

Further, psychologists aid judges in determining whether juveniles who have committed serious crimes should be dealt with as adults or as juveniles. Questions about emotional factors precipitating the alleged acts or about the potential that the juveniles show for rehabilitation often need to be answered (Bayh, 1977;

Cohen, 1977; Corbett & Fersch, 1979; Faust & Brantingham, 1974; Fox, 1970, 1977; Marino, 1977; Platt, 1977).

Psychologists are also asked to determine the potential for rehabilitation of persons before the court, often first offenders or persons accused of using drugs or alcohol or of harming family members. Here the question is whether the defendants should proceed to trial or should be diverted into some special program the court or other agency might have for such individuals. Psychologists are often asked whether a particular program would fit the individual and whether the individual has the capacity to profit from the program (Commonwealth of Massachusetts, Note 1).

Another function that psychologists and sociologists are increasingly being called upon to perform is helping in jury selection. Psychologists are retained by one of the sides in the case, usually the defendant's, and assist the lawyer in determining who to challenge from among the potential jurors (Saks, 1976; Saks & Hastie, 1978).

Finally, psychologists might be asked to assist in plea bargaining to assure (a) that defendants are able to participate in the negotiations, (b) that the plea bargain struck is consonant with the psychological functioning of the defendant, and (c) that the bargain is satisfactory in a general sense. This, however, seems to be done only rarely (Saks & Hastie, 1978).

During Trial

The most obvious role of psychologists during trial is to appear as expert witnesses. Psychologists can be witnesses for the prosecution or for the defense or witnesses called by the court. As experts, psychologists can testify about the results of psychological research on such topics as perception, sensation, confessions, eyewitness identifications, and mental states or about the results of their clinical evaluations of defendants on such topics as motivation or mental status at the time of alleged offenses or at the time of the trials. Psychologists can also rebut the testimony of psychologists or psychiatrists employed by the opposing side by damaging their credibility or calling into question their research, experience, or judgment (Buckhout, 1974, 1976; Ennis & Litwack, 1974; Levine & Tapp, 1973; Loftus, 1975, 1979; Ziskin, 1975, 1977).

Posttrial

The major assessment function of psychologists after trials is in connection with the presentence evaluations of defendants: Psychologists can contribute information concerning the psychological functioning of defendants and their potential for rehabilitation.

Assessment before, during, and after the trial can be done through interviews, with the aid of various psychological tests, or through some combination of methods. Diagnostic services are equally applicable to juveniles and adults, and in assessing defendants, especially juveniles, psychologists often assess the defendants' families as well. While most assessment concerns alleged offenders, it is obvious that in one important area, jury selection, assessment is of individuals not accused of criminal activities and is undertaken in a more indirect way than the examination of defendants.

Treatment

As with assessment, treatment can take place at different stages of the criminal process. Usually it takes place after the trial as part of the disposition, but it can also take place before the trial (Cryan, 1977; Fersch, 1974; Gorelick, 1975).

Pretrial

Before the trial a major treatment effort might be directed toward restoring defendants to competency to stand trial. This might be done through outpatient treatment with or without the use of medically prescribed drugs, or it might be undertaken in a hospital setting.

Another function increasingly assigned psychologists in court settings is provision of treatment for those individuals who have been diverted from trial and referred for treatment in lieu of trial. Often such diversion is predicated on these individuals' successful completion of treatment. Their treatment is much the same as the treatment given to defendants after trial, except that the former group may have to return to stand trial if they do not cooperate.

Posttrial

Posttrial treatment of offenders constitutes one of the largest functions of psychologists in court settings. Many offenders receive either probation or a suspended sentence for their offenses, and courts seek to require some offenders to enter treatment programs as part of their probation or as a condition of the suspension of their sentence. The treatment varies from intensive drug, alcohol, or behavior modification programs to weekly visits to a psychologist at court, to intermittent contact with some social service agency. Treatment is also offered at times to the families of juveniles and of some other offenders as well.

Training

Training is a third major function of psychologists in court settings. Often psychologists provide direct training and supervision to other mental health personnel—social workers, student psychologists, drug and alcohol counselors—working within the court setting or in agencies assisting the court. Psychologists provide training programs for probation officers on such topics as adolescence, forms of treatment, and types of mental illness. They also provide informal training around specific cases and issues, help translate professional literature for practical uses, and answer the questions of staff and clients. Sometimes they provide direct training to parents and families of offenders, suggesting behavioral methods to improve relationships and informing families of the workings of the criminal justice and related mental health systems.

Consultation

Psychologists in court settings have the opportunity and capacity to provide consultation to a number of different groups. To judges they can provide consultation on instructions to juries, judicial decisions, and the outcomes of cases; they can clarify mental health issues and help judges understand the complex relationships between the criminal justice and mental health systems; and they can contribute an amicus curiae brief when one is needed. To lawyers, both for the prosecution and the defense, they can provide consultation on mental health matters as well as on general matters of scientific and professional psychology. To probation officers they can provide consultation on referrals appropriate to the needs of offenders. And to outside agencies, such as schools, youth agencies, and drug and alcohol programs, they can provide information helpful to these agencies' programs and better understanding of the court. In all of these consultative relationships, psychologists can answer questions, suggest lines of inquiry, help interpret responses, and research important issues.

Research

Whatever assessment, treatment, training, or consultative services psychologists perform in the courts, they also have the opportunity to conduct research. While they may not have the freedom to design experiments as they might in more academic research, they can compare groups, look at outcomes, parcel out the factors that seem influential, and trace the interaction of the criminal justice and mental health systems.

Thus, with offenders, psychologists can investigate the different dispositions that are made, the relation between offenders' characteristics and dispositions, the nature of inquiries into competency and responsibility, and the effects of treatment. With regard to the adversary system itself, they can look into the processes of decision making—whether by judge or by jury, the issues concerning eyewitness identification and evidence, the selection and instruction of juries, and jury verdicts (Saks, 1977; Sales, Elwork, & Alfini, 1976; Tapp, 1976). Beyond these often-suggested topics, psychologists can of course conduct research on any facet of their roles and functions in court settings.

Another Function

One other function of psychologists in court settings ought to be mentioned, a function latent wherever psychologists appear in the criminal justice system: validation of the criminal justice system and allying of it with scientific psychology. Thus, the presence of psychologists in the courts says that the criminal justice system is concerned about the personality characteristics of defendants and offenders, wants to implement treatment, recognizes mental illness, provides interaction with the mental health system, and incorporates psychological findings into its practices and theories (Kittrie, 1971; Szasz, 1977, 1979).

Some psychologists feel that their presence in court settings would validate a system they consider inadequate, if not immoral, and thus they do not participate. Others feel that they can be of help to a greater or lesser degree and participate to the extent that they feel comfortable. Finally, some psychologists work in the criminal justice system through the courts both by performing their functions and by suggesting, through writing, training, or consultation, major ways of revamping it.

As has become clear through these brief descriptions, psychologists are asked to perform many different tasks in court settings. The next section details the ethical issues that arise in the performance of those tasks.

Examples of Ethical Issues

Many ethical issues must and do arise in the course of psychologists' work in court settings. Some general ethical issues were mentioned briefly at the start of this chapter. In this section, using the most recent version of the *Ethical Standards of Psychologists* (1979), I consider specific ethical issues arising from the roles and functions of psychologists in court settings. These issues can be grouped under the following major headings: representations of the adequacy or effectiveness of psychological programs or services, representations of the competence of the psychologist, confidentiality, responsibility to the client, and design and use of research.

Representations of the Adequacy or Effectiveness of Psychological Programs or Services

A major ethical issue involves the usefulness of the programs psychologists support and the services they perform in court settings. For unless the assessment, treatment, and other services they provide are useful, psychologists are misrepresenting these services, and such misrepresentation is unethical. While the question of usefulness is simple, attempting to answer it is exceedingly complex.

In its broadest sense, for example, the question about the efficacy of treatment in court settings is similar to the question about the efficacy of treatment in other criminal justice settings. And since there is a lack of confirming research about the effectiveness of forced treatment (Martinson, 1974), for psychologists in court settings to represent their treatment services as adequate and effective raises many ethical questions.

Similarly, psychologists' representations of their assessment services as adequate and effective raise many problems. Some important literature, for instance, addresses the impossibility of determining psychosis at the time of the interview (Rosenhan, 1973; Wolitzky, 1973), let alone criminal responsibility at a time in the past; other literature states that the question of criminal responsibility is a matter of values and that psychologists or psychiatrists are speaking to the matter only from their own ethical and moral values and not from their purported expertise (Szasz, 1963, 1965, 1977, 1979). Still other important articles and books assert that predictions of dangerousness and violence are not within the province of psychologists or psychiatrists (Dershowitz, 1969; Monahan, 1975, 1978; Stone, 1975). If this is the case, then professionals who represent such assessments as adequate or effective are misleading the recipients of this service.

Two other problems relate to psychologists' services in assessment and treatment. One arises from the fact that psychologists may present a single service as if it were a multiple service, as in the matter of diagnosis. When various treatment or rehabilitative services are not available to defendants or offenders, psychologists will sometimes provide extensive diagnostic work-ups. Ostensibly a prelude to service, these work-ups become the only service. Even if the diagnostic services themselves were adequate and effective, their use without back-up services often constitutes indulgence in make-work on the part of psychologists.

The other problem is that psychologists may be acting illegally in a portion of their work. This issue arises especially in questions of competency to stand trial. While such questions are posed in psychological or psychiatric terms, studies have shown that the great majority of those defendants sent to mental hospitals for competency evaluations are sent for sociological, not psychological or psychiatric, reasons (Bennett & Matthews, 1968; Fersch, 1979;

Roesch & Golding, 1977; Stone, 1975; Boyer, Fersch, & Rolde, Note 2).

To the extent that psychologists participate in this process they are participating in illegal practices, whether deliberately or unknowingly. If deliberately, they are using the label of mental illness to justify the incarceration of individuals because they have no place to go, or because they are wayward, or because it is easier to provide an alternative disposition for them through the mental health system. If unknowingly, they are representing their services as adequate and effective while at the same time showing that they are not. Either way they would be acting unethically.

Some of the *Ethical Standards of Psychologists* (1979) are helpful to psychologists practicing in court settings and are discussed in the next major section of this chapter. Others, however, are not. Principle 3, Moral and Legal Standards, for example, says, in part, "As employees, psychologists refuse to participate in practices inconsistent with legal, moral and ethical standards regarding the treatment of employees or of the public" (Principle 3b, p. 2). But as has already been noted, the complex interactions between the criminal justice and the mental health systems, the use of psychological and psychiatric terminology to promote sociological and cultural goals, and the adversary nature of the criminal justice system make following this mandate quite difficult.

The *Ethical Standards* state further, "In providing psychological services, psychologists avoid any action that will violate or diminish the legal and civil rights of clients or of others who may be affected by their actions" (Principle 3c, pp. 2–3). Forcing presumed-innocent defendants to speak openly with court-employed psychologists who will report back to the courts the mental status of the defendants, and perhaps ancillary matters as well, may violate the defendants' fifth-amendment rights against self-incrimination. It may also violate the principle that defendants may have their

lawyers present while being questioned by such inimical personnel as the police. Psychologists may not see themselves as inimical to defendants, and they may not want lawyers present who will counsel defendants to remain completely silent, interrupt every question to ask psychologists what they mean by it, or invoke various privileges. But while psychologists may not see it this way, they may be taking action that will diminish the legal and civil rights of their clients.

In other words, the broad sweep of the *Ethical Standards*, while seeming to resolve these difficult issues, does not, Taken at face value, Principle 3 precludes psychologists from performing many of their most-used services in court settings. It has been argued that they *should* be precluded from performing them, and that, in effect, the *Ethical Standards* applied as written should cause a rethinking of the role of psychologists in the courts.

Similarly, Principle 4 of the *Ethical Standards* conflicts with the adversary nature of the criminal justice proceeding. It says in part, "Psychologists present the science of psychology and offer their services, products, and publications fairly and accurately, avoiding misrepresentation through sensationalism, exaggeration or superficiality" (Principle 4g, p. 4). Yet psychologists who testify in court find themselves in the position of desiring or being forced to exaggerate their testimony and its certainty in order to advance their side's case. The spectacle (and unfortunately it is too often just that in my estimation) of equally qualified psychologists or psychiatrists testifying in diametrically opposed fashions as to some defendant's mental status, criminal responsibility, or potential for rehabilitation suggests to the public at large both the inaccuracy of clinical judgments and the misrepresentation that exaggeration fosters.

Finally, Principle 8, Utilization of Assessment Techniques, states that persons tested have the right to know the test results and how they were arrived at. It provides for exceptions when they are explicitly agreed upon in advance "as in some employment or school settings" (Principle 8a, p. 6). It leaves unstated the problem arising from tests that are ordered by courts, not agreed upon in advance, and not explained to the persons tested. This principle also states that "Psychologists strive to insure that the test results and their interpretations are not misused by others" (Principle 8c, p. 6). But again, in an adversary situation, the matter leaves the control of psychologists. Try as they might, in many instances psychologists cannot avoid having their words overshadowed by those of lawyers and others who have varying views of the material and its potential use in their cases.

As already demonstrated, the representation of psychological programs and services as adequate and effective poses many important ethical issues. Many of the *Ethical Standards* are quite applicable for psychologists working independently or at least working in settings without the inherent conflicts, diversified roles, and multiple functions provided by the court setting. But for psychologists working with involuntary clients in court settings, many of the *Ethical Standards* are of little help.

Clients can, of course, exercise their free judgment however they wish. If psychologists represent that they can pick juries that stand a high chance of acquitting defendants, the defendants are free to contract for these psychologists' services or not. Consumer protection principles apply here; and lawyers are often willing, when clients can afford it, to experiment and try unusual or extreme procedures as extra precautionary measures.

The ethical problems arise primarily when the services are not wanted and are forced on persons, when the adversary nature of the criminal justice proceedings in courts sets one psychologist against another, or when psychologists are mandated by law to do what the *Ethical Standards* and another part of the law forbid them to do. Needless to say, psychol-

ogists find themselves in real binds. Increasingly, libertarian-minded psychologists and psychiatrists, civil rights lawyers, and others are pointing out these binds, increasing psychologists' awareness of them, and forcing the psychologists to make difficult choices of which they may earlier have been relatively unaware (American Friends Service Committee, 1971; Annas, 1975; Donaldson, 1976; Ennis & Siegel, 1973; Morse, 1976, 1978; Szasz, 1963, 1977, 1979).

Representations of the Competence of the Psychologist

Closely related to psychologists' representations of the adequacy of psychological programs or services are psychologist's representations of their own competence. Just as the essential question in the preceding section was how useful the programs and services are, the question here is what a psychologist can do.

But we have already seen that there are many problems relating to psychologists' representations of their competence. Researchers have examined many of the tasks psychologists perform in court settings (Saks & Hastie, 1978), and psychologists' ability to predict violence or dangerousness, to treat people under coercion, to determine competency, and to assess criminal responsibility have all been seriously questioned. Further, the dual function of psychologists in court has been discussed and the conflict between their roles as experts and their roles as advocates investigated. The question of whether their competence as experts is compromised by their abilities as advocates or even by their position as advocates has also been raised. Finally, some have questioned whether much of what psychologists profess to be their psychological competence is not really psychological at all but instead philosophical, encompassing their own sets of values and beliefs, on, for example, rehabilitation, criminal responsibility, and the desirability of a mental health rather than a criminal justice response to antisocial acts.

Principle 2, Competence, of the *Ethical Standards* deals with the problem by stating in part, "Psychologists recognize the boundaries of their competence and the limitations of their techniques and only provide services, use techniques, or offer opinions as professionals that meet recognized standards" (p. 2). Yet the latter phrase, referring to psychological standards, raises a problem, for there are times when the standards of law differ from those of psychology, and psychologists cannot meet both sets of standards. It is in these complex and shadowy areas that the true ethical dilemmas of psychologists in court settings are found.

Further, psychologists naturally want to publicize the value of scientific psychology and advance its influence. But in a setting that naturally pits some testimony against other testimony, it is difficult for psychologists adequately to draw the line between advocacy and self-aggrandizement, or between their competence as informed, capable, responsible citizens and their competence as psychologists. Ethically, psychologists ought to strive to differentiate these two important roles and to state when they are actually filling the former role although employed in the latter role. Such self-limitation can go far toward resolving the ethical dilemmas encountered by psychologists at work in court settings.

Confidentiality

The ethical issues surrounding the matter of confidentiality turn on the question of to whom the psychologist is obligated. In the typical psychologist-client relationship, the client is at liberty to retain the psychologist, and the psychologist is obligated to the keep the client's confidences with certain exceptions. If clients, for example, want to collect on insurance, psychologists will have to inform the insurance company of length of treatment, diagnosis, general progress, and related matters. Clients

knowingly waive their rights to the psychologist's confidence in this case. Of course, clients are coerced to a certain extent, for money plays a large part in such decisions. But the confidentiality is waived only to a limited extent, and the client retains control over the amount of the waiver.

Another exception is court-imposed. If psychologists learn in the course of their work with clients that the clients are about to harm some third person, they have an obligation to break confidence and to report the matter (Curran, 1975; Tarasoff v. Regents of the University of California[1]). The *Ethical Standards* reflect this legal mandate. Section a of Principle 5, Confidentiality, says, "Information received in confidence is revealed only after most careful deliberation and when there is clear and imminent danger to an individual or to society, and then only to appropriate professional workers or public authorities" (p. 4). The ethical dilemma faced by court psychologists is, of course, lessened in some ways by their readily acknowledged court affiliation. However, it is increased in other ways because studies have shown the difficulty, if not the impossibility, of psychologists' predicting dangerousness to an individual, let alone to society.

Further ethical dilemmas appear because of the uncertainty of the psychologist-client relationship. Defendants, forced to meet with psychologists and unaccompanied by their lawyers, are caught in a bind. Wishing to say nothing, defendants may perceive, usually rightly, that refusal to cooperate will be held against them while cooperating may well violate their fifth-amendment constitutional rights and may involve psychologists in an ethical violation. Section b of Principle 5 states that "every effort should be made to avoid undue invasion of privacy" (p. 4). It can be argued both that a forced interview by its very nature represents an undue invasion of privacy or that careful questioning

---

[1] Tarasoff v. Regents of the University of California, 17 Cal. 3d 425, 131 Cal. Rptr. 14, 551 P. 2d 334 (1976).

and avoidance of certain topics prevents such an invasion. Section e of Principle 5 raises a serious problem concerning publication by psychologists, for in court settings and especially with well-known cases, adequate disguising of the identity of persons is difficult.

Finally, the most serious ethical dilemma concerning confidentiality is reflected in the concluding statement of Section d of Principle 5: "The psychologist is responsible for informing the client of the limits of the confidentiality" (p. 4). In court settings there is wide variety in what psychologists actually say. Some tell defendants that they will safeguard most of what is said to them, only presenting to the court their conclusions and a bit of the actual material; others inform defendants that they keep dual files, a confidential file containing most of the material and an official file containing the reports given to the court; and others give defendants a full warning that nothing is entirely confidential.

In my view, the only ethically sound course is the latter one: Defendants must be informed that everything they say as involuntary clients can and may be reported to the court. Whether the court learns of the details of the interview or tests outright or only of the conclusions drawn from them, involuntary clients' confidences are not kept in the same way that psychologists keep those of private clients. Further, courts, while they may not question psychologists about details, can always do so. To tell defendants otherwise when the psychologist knows he or she must complete a report to the court based on psychological interviewing or testing of those defendants is to mislead them.

As is obvious, the *Ethical Standards* leave unanswered many questions concerning the complexities of court-ordered psychological interviews or tests. Psychologists working in court settings must have a far different relationship to the confidences of the persons they talk with than that of psychologists employed by individuals. It is easier for court-employed psychologists to keep involuntary clients' confi-

dences vis-á-vis the police and other agencies, for these psychologists are answerable only to the court and the defendant. But it is the conflict of interest between the court and the defendant that gives rise to the ethical problem for psychologists and the practical problem for defendants of whether and how much to cooperate.

If we assume for the moment that the defendants who are ordered to speak with psychologists are the ones who are or appear to be the most emotionally troubled, the burden on them is even greater. The individuals least able to withstand the ethical, legal, and other pressures are the ones submitted to them. Informed choice, an ethical imperative, is hardly possible under such circumstances. The question that inevitably arises is, should it be?

Responsibility to the Client

The ethical issues surrounding the matter of responsibility to the client center around the question of who the client is. The court situations most comparable to the typical psychologist-client relationship are those in which defendants have hired psychologists to provide some service to them such as testifying on their behalf, treating them, helping to pick a jury, or pointing out the unreliability of eyewitness identification. In such situations the psychologist has but one client—the defendant—and owes responsibility solely to him or her.

But in the usual court situations, in which psychologists have been called upon to assess defendants or to provide them with treatment though they want neither, psychologists in effect have multiple clients. At the least one can say that their clients are the individual defendants and the court. Because it is hard to talk about responsibility to an abstraction such as a court, however, it is easier to say that the psychologists' responsibility is to the judges or probation officers or whoever directs their work in the court. If these court personnel share a similar philosophy, then psychologists have at least two clients, the defendants (the traditional clients) and the court personnel, and psychologists' responsibilities to the two are bound to conflict at times. The ethical problem becomes more complex, however, when the various personnel within the court have differing philosophies, for this then multiplies the psychologists' clients.

The *Ethical Standards*, while usually useful concerning the matter of responsibility to the client, provide little help to psychologists in courts. Principle 6, Welfare of the Consumer (p. 5), speaks of dual relationships with clients (Section a), but not of multiple client relationships; it requires psychologists to clarify the nature of conflicts of interest and inform all parties of them (Section b); and it directs psychologists "to terminate a clinical or consulting relationship when it is reasonably clear that the consumer is not benefiting from it" (Section e). The problem however, is, that there are many consumers of psychological services in court settings. The defendant or offender as consumer may not be benefiting from the psychologist's treatment in the sense of personality change but may be benefiting by staying out of jail; the courts or judges may be benefiting from the treatment because it appears to their constituents that they have decreed suitable rehabilitative schemes for defendants and offenders; society as consumer may or may not be benefiting from the psychologist's treatment of defendants and offenders; and so on.

The *Ethical Standards* envision a consumer/client who does or does not benefit from treatment. The true situation in courts is much more complex and involves balancing the needs of psychologists with the needs of judges, defendants, and society. Even the nature of the benefits is open to dispute. While some say that the benefit to defendants of hospitalizing them is great, others say it is a violation of their fundamental rights. While some say it is a benefit to society to keep offenders out of jail, others say it is a disservice to offenders to prevent them from experiencing the consequences of

their actions. While some say it is a benefit to society to keep individuals in their communities, others say it harms society to let some individuals remain in the community. And these controversies surround the questions of benefit to society, to the court, and the the profession of psychology as well.

Principle 7, Professional Relationships, recognizes the fact that psychologists work with other professionals and must cooperate with them and support their host organizations. This principle seems to suggest that the court is a host organization as well as a client/consumer. The dilemmas arising from these different roles of the court pervade the work of psychologists in court settings.

Design and Use of Research

There are, of course, many ethical limitations imposed on the design of research in court settings. Some offenders cannot arbitrarily be found guilty nor others randomly punished more severely in order to test hypotheses. Random assignments to groups do not ethically comport with justice, either in the "just deserts" model (let the punishment fit the crime) or in the "individualization" model (let the punishment fit the criminal). Research in a setting proclaiming justice will always be bounded by the demands of ethical probity.

Further, research in court settings always raises the issue of whether there can ever be informed consent to participate in the research or whether the pressures to participate are too great to permit real choice. Principle 9 of the *Ethical Standards* raises fundamental questions: How informed can the research participants be in court settings (Section c)? How much freedom to decline (Section e) do defendants or offenders actually have and how much do they perceive they have? And how can confidentiality (Section j) be respected more fully than has already been discussed?

The problems involved in the use of research findings in courts have already been adverted to. At least three are paramount: (1) The extent to which the findings of scientific psychology undermine the commonsense psychology on which the court is based may preclude their being used in court. (2) The very essence of the adversary system is to challenge, and this method may lead to misleading conclusions and to misuse of the research. (3) The research may lead to conclusions that undermine the very work psychologists are doing in court.

We have seen that the unusual nature of the court setting continually raises important ethical and practical issues for psychologists as well as all others involved in it. Let us turn now to a number of approaches to the resolution of these ethical issues.

Approaches to the Resolution of Ethical Issues

For any ethical issue psychologists in court settings seek to resolve, three precepts are important: Psychologists must be clear what role they are performing; they must be aware of the limitations of that role and of the conflicts it raises; and they must inform all those with whom they deal of those limitations and conflicts.

We have seen that psychologists perform a number of different roles in court settings. They can be dealing either with voluntary clients or with involuntary clients, though of course there are many gradations. With voluntary clients the psychologist's role may be as an expert or as an advocate, though the two roles clearly overlap and may be the same, whether the psychologist is testifying about psychological experiments that favor the client's case or is reporting that defendants are not criminally responsible for their acts.

With involuntary clients the psychologist's role may again be that of expert or it may be as an adversary, with these two roles also overlapping or possibly being the same, as, for example, in determining that defendants ought to be incarcerated against their will in a mental

hospital as incompetent to stand trial. While this role differentiation assumes that psychologists are adversaries of unwilling clients, psychologists themselves may perceive their roles as advocates of unwilling clients. Psychologists, for example, may look at incarceration as hospitalization rather than as imprisonment, argue that it is in the client's best interests, and see themselves as allies of the clients/patients. And if the clients *want* hospitalization, then psychologists may see themselves as facilitating a desired goal, albeit for involuntary clients. In this instance the question of whether psychologists are clients' advocates or adversaries turns not on the voluntary or involuntary circumstances under which they were brought together but on the wishes of the clients. However, while the psychologist's role can turn on clients' wishes, it can also turn on defense attorneys' wishes.

Defense attorneys may view psychologists as adversaries if the attorneys are advocating liberty for their clients and the psychologists are advocating incarceration. On the other hand, lawyers faced with very difficult and seemingly mentally ill clients may see psychologists as advocates or helpers, providing an alternate disposition—mental hospitalization—for their clients. Lawyers faced with young or disturbed clients often seek such social and psychological services instead of providing the kind of legal representation they might for an accused criminal (Fersch, 1979).

However the role of the psychologist is conceptualized—as advocate, expert, or adversary—the second important precept is that the psychologist be aware of the limitations of that role and of the conflicts it raises. Thus, for example, the psychologist's role may be limited by as yet unresolved questions concerning scientific psychology. And the conflicts raised by this role may include the the dilemmas caused by the psychologist's desire to secure information and provide services and the defendant's unwillingness to deal with an adversary.

In truly adversary situations, psychologists

are faced with the necessity of permitting the clients all the protection the law affords them in such situations; if some aspects of the situation are adversary and some are not, psychologists may have the difficult task of sorting them out. In my own view, psychologists in court settings are always the adversaries of involuntary clients and ought to conduct themselves so as to protect defendants' rights. Only by recognizing the limitations of their roles and facing directly the conflicts they raise can psychologists protect clients and uphold ethical standards.

But it is not enough merely to recognize such situations; psychologists must also inform all with whom they deal—clients, courts, and attorneys—of the limitations and conflicts inherent in their roles. By clearly informing all concerned, psychologists stand the best chance of resolving ethical dilemmas.

These three precepts apply to all the roles and functions of psychologists in court settings. More specific approaches to resolving ethical issues follow.

Representations of the Adequacy or Effectiveness of Psychological Programs or Services

While it is incumbent on psychologists in court settings to fully inform the court as well as the defendant or offender, psychologists often fear that such straightforwardness will hinder their work. They generally discover, however, that once the ethical issues are confronted directly, the criminal justice system is more receptive to what they are doing.

Beyond this ethical mandate to inform all parties about the limitations of and conflicts of interest in psychological programs and services, there is a much more controversial approach to resolving ethical issues. As outlined earlier in this chapter, there are three approaches to viewing the interaction between the criminal justice system and the mental health system: the traditional, the liberal reform, and the rethinking

approaches. It is the third, or rethinking, approach that is the controversial one.

In the first, or traditional, approach, the criminal justice system occasionally called upon psychologists or psychiatrists but largely carried out its tasks by itself. In the liberal reform approach currently in the ascendancy, psychologists and psychiatrist have taken on many of the tasks formerly performed by the criminal justice system. Thus, psychologists and psychiatrists currently determine whether there is potential for rehabilitation in a particular defendant, determine whether a defendant is capable of assisting counsel, assess whether there was criminal responsibility at the time of an alleged criminal act, predict dangerousness for both mentally ill and non-mentally-ill individuals, and treat defendants diverted from trial. In these pretrial ways alone, the liberal reform approach has greatly increased the role of psychologists in courts. Similarly, as evidenced in posttrial treatment of offenders, training of probation officers, and consultation with judges, the liberal reform approach has resulted in the increasing psychiatrization of the criminal justice system (Monahan, 1975; Morse, 1976, 1978).

It is this increasing psychiatrization—combined with mounting evidence that much of it is of limited value, violates fundamental human civil and legal rights (Davison & Stuart, 1975; Gorelick, 1975), is antithetical to established principles of scientific psychology, or is socially unworkable—that has brought about the third approach that I have termed *rethinking* (Fersch, 1979, 1980).

Various scholars and practitioners have attempted to rethink the basic problems of social deviance and social control and the respective places of law and psychology in the social system. This rethinking has led them to advocate elimination of the indeterminate sentence, abolition of the insanity defense, and a return to voluntary treatment only. Such a course of action would divest the mental health system of much of its power over involuntary clients and return deliberations and power to the criminal justice system.

The procedures, for example, in determining defendants' competency to stand trial would be drastically altered. Currently, anyone—the judge, the defense, or the prosecution—can raise the question of a defendant's competency. Proceedings are then stopped, and the defendant is referred to a psychologist or psychiatrist or sent to a mental hospital for evaluation. Although, as has been noted, defendants are generally sent for sociological rather than psychological or psychiatric reasons, examiners focus on defendants' psychological states. Reforms instituted in many places have lessened the number of defendants sent to hospitals, shortened their stay, and returned more of them to court as fit to stand trial; also, some psychological examiners are being trained to understand better the requirements of the court proceedings and of cooperating with counsel.

Nevertheless, in the rethinking approach this entire procedure would be viewed differently. Let us look first at the normal situation in which a defendant wants a delay in the proceedings. Delays are sought for many reasons, and lawyers and their clients determine what is in the client's best interests. If the court wants further information before granting a delay it can seek it on its own, for example, by asking its own specialist to examine the defendant. But the decision to ask for a delay remains the defendant's and his or her lawyer's.

Further, lawyers often have difficulties with their clients that may necessitate delays in the proceedings. Some difficulties are easily resolved, such as when a defendant does not speak English and translators are used. Other difficulties such as when defendants are overly demanding, uncommunicative, or psychotic, are more difficult to resolve, but lawyers can do their best to calm their clients or sometimes translate their odd behavior by using whatever specialists are available to help. Occasionally defendants are so disruptive they have to be removed from the court, or they cooperate only in the most minimal way with their lawyers. And not all lawyers and clients are happy with each other, especially when the lawyers are appointed by the court. Yet all of these situations are considered relatively routine and are handled with the usual procedures.

The rethinking approach would argue that the suspected presence of mental illness should not change these usual procedures. Just as the suspected presence of severe physical illness or its actual occurrence might cause a delay in a trial, so might severe emotional upset or psychotic hallucinations or incoherent mumblings cause a delay if the defendant and his or her lawyer wanted one. Just because some defendants are more difficult, more bizarre, or less helpful does not mean that the criminal justice system should turn over to the mental health system the determination of such an important matter as the defendant's right to proceed with trial. The right to trial is too important to be left in the hands of psychologists, psychiatrists, or translators. It belongs with the legal profession, which understands best what capabilities the defendant needs in order to cooperate with counsel and especially with the one individual whose role is to safeguard the defendant's rights—his or her lawyer. When called on by defendants or lawyers to assist them, psychologists can of course provide services to these voluntary clients. But the overall matter belongs within the criminal justice system.

A rethinking approach, then, would eliminate the forced use of psychologists' services and leave psychologists free to continue in those roles where they simply function as willing suppliers of services to willing consumers. Thus, psychologists could continue, under this approach, to offer their advice on jury selection; they could help in plea-bargaining sessions; they could remain as expert witnesses on such matters of scientific psychology as perception and eyewitness identification, though not on such speculative philosophical matters as criminal responsibility; they could treat disturbed defendants or offenders who asked to be treated; they could be consultants to lawyers, judges, court personnel, and outside agencies; and they could conduct research as long as those being researched freely consented. Furthermore, they could explore new roles and functions.

From my training as a lawyer and a clinical psychologist and from my experience in court settings, I personally favor this rethinking approach (Fersch, 1974, 1975, 1979, 1980). It is not enough to inform courts of the limitations of psychologists' roles and functions. Psychologists must help to limit what they do. However good their intentions, however much they see themselves as humanizing influences on the criminal justice system, however positive they are that they are more accurate than research has shown psychologists to be, and however much they might wish that psychology could solve the most intractable problems of human nature and of society, psychologists must redirect their professional energies to those roles and functions in which they provide services and programs to willing clients. Voluntary, informed clients are then free to use whatever they feel will be of help to them.

At the very least, ethically, psychologists in court settings must inform the court and the defendant of the limitations and conflicts inherent in their roles and functions. At best, ethically, psychologists in court settings should endeavor to challenge the traditions and requirements that say they must perform certain roles and functions. As citizens, psychologists are free to voice their opinions on many topics; as psychologists, they should restrict their functions to those that use their expertise and protect those with whom they deal.

Representations of the Competence of the Psychologist

What is true of programs and services is equally true of professional competence. Psychologists in court settings should recognize, as Prin-ciple 2 of the *Ethical Standards* says, "the boundaries of their competence and the limitations of their techniques" (p. 2). Because this principle also says that psychologists should "only provide services, use techniques, or offer opinions as professionals that meet recognized standards" (p. 2), the most useful function of psychologists in court settings may be to help clarify standards and to lead the effort toward recognizing standards that truly make sense.

Confidentiality

Using the traditional, reform, and rethinking models, one can see three different approaches to the problem of confidentiality. In the traditional model, psychologists simply interviewed, tested, or treated defendants, realizing that the psychologists' tasks were somewhat limited, that the clients were ordered to respond by the courts, and that the psychologists were simply carrying out mandates thought useful by courts. In the liberal reform model, psychologists also interview, test, or treat. Viewing themselves as therapeutic figures, they generally do not warn clients about the problems of confidentiality. To protect the clients and to prevent misuse of information, psychologists instead put the information they gather into two different places. The more extensive material they gather remains in their own files; what they choose to tell the court goes into its files. By maintaining this double set of records and by screening what they divulge of clients' confidences, psychologists feel they are breaching confidentiality in a minimal, and therapeutically useful, way. Their aim is to get psychological help for people characterized as criminal but actually more sick than evil.

In the rethinking model, confidentiality would be respected by removing psychologists from the tasks of court-ordered preadjudication interviews, tests, or treatment. Thus there would be no determinations by psychologists of competency to stand trial (though they could assist defendants or lawyers who asked them to), no forced interviews to determine criminal responsibility, no determinations of suitability for rehabilitation prior to trial, and no diversions for treatment in lieu of trial. The rethinking model would suggest that psychological interviews, tests, and treatment be considered *after* an adjudication of guilt and then only if they meet the standard of usefulness.

However until this ideal of not providing psychological services to involuntary clients prior to trial is accepted, the rethinking position advocates a complete warning with regard to the limits of confidentiality to clients, similar to warnings now mandated for the police. Psychologists would thus have to tell defendants that nothing was in confidence, that everything could potentially be used against the defendant, and that confidentiality was such an important matter that defendants' decisions to remain silent or to refuse to cooperate with psychologists would not be held against them. Because the rethinking position views psychologists, however helpful they may ultimately be to defendants, as adversaries or potential adversaries of the defendants, it demands of psychologists what it does of other adversaries such as the police. Often, the police, in fact, turn out to be and to be seen as the most helpful agency to some defendants; yet, helpful or not, the police are viewed as defendants' adversaries and must so warn their clients/arrestees.

Responsibility to the Client

Insofar as the courts are the client of psychologists, psychologists owe them the duty of truthfulness and self-awareness. Insofar as society is the client of psychologists, psychologists owe it a clear view of what they are doing and what its effects are. And insofar as defendants are the clients of psychologists, psychologists owe them the same respect for their rights they would offer any other clients. With regard to correctional institutions, it is increasingly being argued that the decision to release prisoners on parole ought not to be predicated on the

prisoners' seeking treatment within the institution and that treatment ought to be given for its own sake. Similarly, in court settings, the disposition of defendants should not turn on their willingness to be assessed or treated psychologically, although this is the liberal reform position. One of the worst effects that psychologists have had on offenders has been encouraging them in their ability to con people by forcing them to pretend that treatment was useful in order to preclude their trial or gain their liberty.

I have proposed elsewhere that the mixing of punishment and rehabilitation in the criminal justice system is unworkable and that the process of correction ought to be divided into its constituent parts (Fersch, 1975). First, there ought to be a range of suitable punishments for antisocial acts, including restitution, service to the victim or to the community, fines, and incarceration. These punishments should be brief, follow quickly upon the offense, and be imposed only after a finding of guilt. The second part of the process should follow punishment and consist of restoration of all rights to the offender and an offer without coercion of a variety of rehabilitative services: medical, dental, financial, psychological, educational, and vocational. A final component in this process should be consideration of whether, based on their acts, offenders are so dangerous that society's protection requires they be incarcerated for longer periods of time. If this is the case, all their rights and privileges save that of liberty should be restored to them following punishment, and they, too, should be offered rehabilitative services. Psychologists' participation in the working out of the above model would go far toward discharging their responsibilities to all of their clients.

Design and Use of Research

The ethical issues surrounding research can be resolved primarily through the use of sufficient alternatives in research design to provide true choices for those involved. Just as in a university or hospital setting there is a research committee that passes on projects involving human subjects, so should there be such a committee in court settings, consisting of advocates of various groups. While this procedure might make it more difficult for psychologists to pursue their own views of research, it insures greater fairness, and adherence to ethical standards.

With respect to the *use* of research, psychologists must be alert to the possibility of misuse and attempt to correct abuses when they occur.

Questions of Public Policy

Throughout this chapter I have referred to major questions of public policy raised by the roles and functions of psychologists in court settings. Chief among them is the relation between the criminal justice system and the mental health system as both systems approach problems of social deviance and social control (Kittrie, 1971; Monahan, 1975; Monahan & Hood, 1976; Schur & Bedau, 1974; Silber, 1974; Stone, 1975; Tapp, 1976). To what extent should society view those who engage in antisocial behavior as possessing free will to choose their acts and suffer the consequences for them, and to what extent should society view such people as determined by heredity or environment to perform those acts for which the proper response ought to be some sort of psychological inquiry and treatment?

Further, what ought to be the balance among punishment, rehabilitation, deterrence, and isolation as goals of the criminal justice system (Dershowitz, 1974, 1975; Donnelly et al., 1962; Frankel, 1973; Kennedy, 1976; Oran, 1973; President's Commission on Law Enforcement and Administration of Justice, 1967; Tullock, 1974)?

Underlying all that has been said in this chapter is the view that the mental health system, whatever its benefits to willing or even unwilling clients, is always potentially and often actually the adversary of involuntary clients. What then ought to be the roles and functions of psychologists in court settings?

A related question of public policy is the role of the different branches of government in ameliorating the problems that do exist. Psychologists perform many tasks in court settings because legislatures and courts have demanded that they do so. To what extent ought psychologists to refuse to do what they know they cannot do even though mandated to do it? To what extent ought psychologists to ask their legislatures to make changes in the laws or ask their courts to interpret them differently? Unfortunately, psychologists and other professional groups often seek changes in the laws only to find that the beneficent results they envisioned as proceeding from the legislation fall far short of their expectations in actual practice. How can psychologists help bridge the gap between social theorizing and actual outcomes?

Such important questions of public policy are increasingly becoming topics for discussion among members of the legal and psychological professions as well as society at large. Psychologists in court settings have important contributions to make to such discussion.

Future Roles and Functions of Psychologists in Court Settings

With regard to future roles and functions of psychologists in court settings, if we look at the three ideological positions discussed earlier—the traditional, reform, and rethinking positions—it becomes clear that most psychologists do not support the traditional position that says they have little, if anything, to contribute to the criminal justice system. Rather, psychologists are split between the other two positions, with the far larger number favoring the liberal reform position. In concluding this chapter it is important, therefore, to view the future roles and functions of psychologists in court settings from both of these perspectives.

Both the reform and the rethinking positions would agree that psychologists can perform whatever roles and functions in courts willing clients ask them to perform, subject only to the limitations of scientific psychology. Thus, while there are questions concerning psychologists as screeners of juries or as witnesses in court, as long as defendants, their lawyers, and the courts agree that these roles are suitable, psychologists can continue in them and expand their work. The ethical standards of usefulness and truthful representation of services form the boundaries of the activities. And, after all, there are many different views of usefulness concerning psychology and psychologists, just as there are many different views concerning religion and ministers or education and teachers. The most one can hope for is clear presentation of the evidence and an informed chooser.

But the reform and the rethinking positions are in disagreement when coercion—obvious, subtle, or inherent in the situation—occurs. The reform position allows psychologists to assess or treat involuntary clients while advocating such safeguards as a greater degree of choice, a dual records system, and concern for the effects of both incarceration and therapy in psychological intervention. The rethinking position, on the other hand, would not allow psychologists to assess or treat involuntary clients, thus advocating the ultimate safeguard for the defendants—the elimination of involuntary interviews, testing, and treatment and the removal of psychologists, psychiatrists, and other mental health personnel from some of the tasks they currently perform in courts. This position would reconceptualize the psychologist's role with involuntary clients as essentially one of offering services following the adjudication of guilt, when the client, uncoerced, can decide whether or not to accept them.

Freed from dealing with involuntary clients, psychologists could then expend more effort in providing the best assessment, treatment, consultation, training, and research they could to voluntary clients—defendants, courts, and society—advising them of psychological techniques and services, retaining confidences, setting forth clearly psychologists' abilities and shortcomings, and challenging both the criminal justice and the mental health systems. In that way, the future roles and functions of psychologists in court settings would be legally and psychologically important as well as ethically sound.

Stanley L. Brodsky

4
Ethical Issues for Psychologists
in Corrections

With each breakthrough in psychological knowledge, new and profound ethical and practical problems arise. As fields of study and practice develop, they diversify. And so it is with the fields of psychology and corrections. Psychology has diversified sufficiently so that hundreds of journals, dozens of associations, and two sets of ethical standards now strive to meet the varied needs of psychologists. Even within applied fields, such as correctional psychology, a spectrum-spanning variety of conceptual, treatment, and educational perspectives exists.

Corrections also has expanded from the tiny Walnut Street jail organized by the Quakers in the late 18th century to the over 750 prisons in the United States that now house more than a quarter of a million adult offenders. An additional 140,000 adults are locked in local jails, and almost 50,000 youths are held in state and local facilities (Hindelang, Gottfredson, Dunn, & Parisis, 1977). The term *correctional facility* currently refers not only to the common Auburn-design prison of massive tiers and many inmates but also to the open, small, campus-style institution.

The contemporary sense of ethical friction in correctional psychology was not felt during the promising initial entry of psychology into

The author is indebted to Alison Nathan for her contributions to the search of the psychology-corrections literature.

prison work. Following the first World War, psychology had a new tool in hand—a method to screen and classify large numbers of persons—and corrections had large numbers of confined persons in need of screening and classifying. Thus, a working relationship was formed, and this first substantial task of screening and classifying remains an important part of psychological work in corrections today.

While psychologists come from backgrounds of scientific discipline and helping concerns, correctional administrators are a part of the justice process. Consequently, there are differences in these two groups' methods and in their understanding of the nature of human beings (Slovenko, 1973). One example of such differences can be found in the principle of advocacy. The law, from the courts through corrections, holds to the principle that truth arises from the adversary presentation of opposing views. Psychology and other helping professions assume that cooperation and collaboration are the essence of finding truth, through research endeavors and therapeutic procedures.

Psychology tends to value trust; corrections values control. Psychology cherishes expert, scientific knowledge. Law and corrections value the common man, common sense, and pragmatics. Psychology pursues objectivity. Justice accepts more subjectivity and more personal than scientific insights (Slovenko, 1973).

These differences have led experienced corrections personnel, including psychologists, to encourage graduate training programs in correctional psychology so that beginning personnel will be more realistically equipped to function in the special conditions of correctional institutions (Ingram, 1974). These conditions, which bring psychologists in contact with people of very different backgrounds and assumptions, often result in ethical dilemmas for correctional psychologists. Used to conducting research with college sophomores and practicing psychotherapy with white, neurotic, verbal outpatients, psychologists can find the tasks of research and therapy in total institutions with involuntarily confined, lower-class, minority inmates jarring and of unanticipated complexity. This chapter discusses a number of psychologists' tasks in corrections, presents some of the common ethical dilemmas involved in carrying them out, and suggests guidelines for resolving the dilemmas.

Assessment

> Correctional psychology is in a chronic state of stagnation, well illustrated by excessive overemphasis on psychological testing—most of which is either not used or misused. The operation of testing becomes an end in and of itself: numbers go into folders and there are decently interred. (Corsini, 1956, p. 22)

Intellectual assessment was the earliest type of prisoner assessment used and continues as part of psychologists' duties in corrections. The problem of the passive interral of psychologists' findings noted above, has been accompanied by reports of active interference with psychologists' work, such as wardens ordering psychologists not to use certain tests or to work at a faster pace than allowed by standardized test administrations (Corsini, 1959). Such difficulties are rare—or at least rarely reported—and the use of psychological evaluations has assumed a regular pattern in correctional settings. Assessment procedures are undertaken primarily at three times: when the confined

person enters the correctional setting, when decisions are being made about the person's exit from the setting, and at times of crisis.

Entry-level assessments typically are part of a wide-ranging classification battery from which institutional decisions are made and special characteristics of confined persons identified; psychological assessments may be included in this decision-making process. While the methods of assessment vary, a typical procedure addresses specific issues such as custody levels, choice of institution to which individuals should be assigned, and potential escape risk. In this context it should be noted that some computerized narrative MMPI printouts with prison-specific MMPI scales and interpretations have been prepared (Fowler, Note 1).

Psychopathology assessment is almost always undertaken. Indeed, two federal district courts have formally affirmed that imprisoned individuals who are psychologically disturbed have the constitutional right to be so diagnosed and then to receive treatment in the prison or be transferred to facilities where treatment programs are available.[1,2] Assessment of the depth and the nature of psychopathology thus is particularly relevant. Cumulative information about prisoner mental health problems serves to diagnose the prison system as well. That is, the nature of needed programs or service deficits is revealed by the discrepancy between prisoner needs and existing services.

Educational needs and intellectual skills are assessed with the commonly used tests of educational grade levels and intellectual ability. Increasing attention is being paid to the mentally retarded and the marginally brain-damaged within institutions, and the state of South Carolina has developed a special facility exclusively for the mentally retarded offender.

---

[1] James v. Wallace, 406 F. Supp. 318 (M. D. Alabama, 1976).

[2] Laaman v. Helgemoe, C. A. No. 75-258, U.S. District Court for New Hampshire, 1977.

In many penal settings, technician assistants and sometimes prisoner assistants are used for interviews and the administration of tests (Wilson, 1951). The choice of tests, general supervision of the group testing and scoring, and interpretation remain part of psychologists' functions. Since major security problems often exist in penal institutions, protection of records is a concern of many psychologists in such settings. Tests may be interpreted by computer printouts from actuarial data, by paraprofessionals under supervision, or by psychologists.

The reports prepared at the time of the prisoner's entry are forwarded to a classification or institutional board, usually composed of from two to five individuals drawn from custodial and other departments. The actual assignment of individuals to custody levels, work, dormitory or cell placement, educational programs, and vocational training is usually made by this board. The psychological assessment report is used along with information from case histories, FBI crime records, court records, presentence investigations, and social histories.

Psychological assessments for exit decisions are usually prepared for parole boards. Such assessment is not made routinely in most cases but in response to specific requests from parole agencies or other decision-making groups. Questions addressed include the extent to which further imprisonment would be either helpful or harmful to the person, the extent to which the confined individual poses a risk to the general population, the likelihood of recidivism, and other questions for which it is rationally (or irrationally) assumed that psychological assessment can provide answers. In some states, a psychological exit evaluation is conducted by employees of a Department of Vocational Rehabilitation. Since prisoner status in itself is considered a handicap in returning to society, the exiting prisoner who has a psychological impairment as well may be offered a number of vocational services.

Crises such as psychotic episodes, attempted suicide, and refusal to eat or work represent the third type of event at which assessments are conducted. Referrals for these evaluations are made by physicians or other prison employees, and the results are used in collaborative planning about future needs and programs for the confined person.

Three classification schemes have emerged from psychological assessment research. The I-level system of Warren (1971) uses interviews to classify confined persons in several categories along a seven-point maturity continuum, and Jessness (1966) developed a questionnaire to allow more convenient application of these I-level decisions to institutionalized populations. Quay and Parsons (1970) prepared a system classifying offenders into four behavior categories, based on current behavior ratings, past behavior histories, and a self-report questionnaire. A very recent system developed by Megargee (1977) described 10 personality types of young adult offenders based on the MMPI.

The I-level and behavior classification systems have had much wider impacts than simple assessment reports. A number of treatment programs and correctional institutions have been organized around these classifications, and a series of studies has been conducted on the interactions among offender classification and staff types and effectiveness.

While the classification systems have been practically applied, meaningful implementation of routine evaluations has frequently been absent. When they exist for their own sake, such psychological assessments can be ritualistic and pointless. In reception and diagnostic centers, these assessments have been described as boring, repetitive, and frustrating to the staff, an Edsel-like flop for the system, and a disservice and waste to resources for all involved (Brodsky, 1973, pp. 144–145).

Treatment

Here at Ohio State Reformatory, over a period of five years, I have been engaged in psychotherapy with a group of sex offenders. Approximately 30 men have passed through this group, progressed to parole status and thence to final release. Not one of those 30 has ever returned . . . (and follow-up studies have been done) no one of these individuals has been reinstitutionalized elsewhere. (Peizer, 1957, p. 13).

Since 1972, a right to psychological treatment has been defined with increasing specificity by a series of federal court rulings. The Fourth Circuit Court of Appeals recently issued this finding:

> We therefore hold that (the plaintiff) (or any other prison inmate) is entitled to psychological or psychiatric treatment if a physician or other health care provider, exercising ordinary skill and care at time of observation, concludes with reasonable medical certainty (1) that the prisoner's symptoms evidence a serious disease or injury; (2) that such disease or injury is curable or may be substantially alleviated; and (3) that the potential for harm to the prisoner by reason of delay or the denial of care would be substantial. The right to treatment is, of course, limited to that which may be provided upon a reasonable cost and time basis, and the essential test is one of medical necessity and not simply that which may be considered merely desirable.[3]

Thus the right to mental health treatment applies only to promptly needed treatment for prisoners with disorders that are both serious and curable. Mild and incurable disorders, such as chronic unhappiness, are not covered.

In July 1977, the U.S. District Court in New Hampshire ruled that prison inmates are entitled to reasonable psychiatric and/or psychological treatment when medically necessary, and that defendants are under an *affirmative duty* to provide the same.[4] The same court further held that New Hampshire inmates have

the right to be incarcerated in conditions that "do not threaten their sanity or mental well-being."

This emerging mandate has been expressed in other jurisdictions and is being litigated in still more. And it raises many complex implications for the treatment of prisoners. For example, if a prison setting produces or exacerbates pathology, how does one meet the obligation to deal with the prison-as-client? The court rulings discuss serious disorders; does this include personality disorders? What likelihood of cure rates for disorders correspond to the promise of substantial alleviation? Who judges the potential harm of treatment delay? And where is the research upon which to found these judgments? Answers to these legal-psychological questions are beyond the scope of this chapter. However, a first step in exploring these questions can be made by examining the structure of psychological treatment services.

Referrals

Treatment referrals come from a variety of sources. Some treatment settings, such as the Leon Start House in Tallahassee, Florida, and the Patuxent Institution for Defective Delinquents in Maryland, have as a goal the treatment of each confined client. The client is sent from a court or a central classification center to one of the treatment settings directed by mental health professionals. Typical referrals within prisons include the following problems and sources:

Crises

Suicide attempts and psychotic episodes often lead to evaluations and treatment for prisoners.

Ongoing Psychotherapy

These are self-referrals in which voluntary clients seek out individual, group, or problem-specific treatments.

---

[3] Bowring v. Godwin, 555 F.2d 44,47-47 (4th Circuit, 1977).

[4] Laaman v. Helgemoe, C. A. No. 75-258, U.S. District Court for New Hampshire, 1977.

Therapeutic Communities

Within single institutions, groups such as the Asklepieion transactional-analysis–confrontation programs (which originated at the Marion, Illinois federal penitentiary) may accept referrals from chaplains and officers and refer individuals elsewhere for treatment.

Parole Boards, Wardens, Work Supervisors, and Prison Physicians

All of these groups may refer offenders to specific treatment programs.

Sex Offender Referrals

As a result of legislative action, referrals from courts are now made to 23 sex offender treatment programs established in prisons and state hospitals in the United States and Canada. Several have conducted careful follow-up assessments that show evidence of lasting positive impact (Abel, Blanchard, & Becker, 1976).

Standards and Goals

National standards for offender treatment programs mandate a diagnostic report and a program plan for each disturbed offender (National Advisory Commission on Criminal Justice Standards and Goals, 1973). These standards require that psychotic offenders be transferred to mental health facilities, that special provisions be made for serious behavior disorders, and that "correctional institutional treatment of the emotionally disturbed should be under the supervision and direction of psychiatrists" (p. 374).

Goals of psychotherapeutic treatment in prisons have been divided into two categories: conformity goals and client growth goals. The conformity goals are intended to promote adaptation to the institutional environment and include particular attention to individuals who are having disciplinary problems, work prob-lems, and other prison-related maladaptive behaviors. Self-growth goals, on the other hand, include programs directed at interpersonal growth through group processes and individual psychotherapeutic efforts. A number of programs have objectives that fall in between these goals. These middle-range programs include a variety of behavioral programs in which the goals, which may include both institutional adjustment and self-growth, are specified according to an agreement between the therapist and the client. Reality therapy programs, in which responsible behavior is explicitly identified and pursued, also fall in this in-between category.

Psychotherapists who accept compliance and self-control goals for confined persons have been described as system-professionals. Psychotherapists who challenge the legitimacy of agency objectives by taking a prisoner-first, therapeutic, activist stance have been called system-challengers (Brodsky, 1973).

Methods of Psychotherapeutic Treatment

One authoritative source has suggested that the short supply of mental health clinicians in corrections and the nature of confined offenders have led to group therapy as the preferred mode of correctional treatment (President's Commission on Law Enforcement and Administration of Justice, 1967). Prominent in this treatment mode are group procedures based on mobilizing peer pressures. The Guided Group Interaction (GGI), Positive Peer Culture (PPC), and confrontation techniques are based on such intense peer pressure. Wicks (1974), in his book *Correctional Psychology*, describes the GGI procedure, noting that it is "a logical treatment approach. Not only does it conserve personnel, it also appears to be effective with the most difficult offenders—drug addicts" (p. 50). GGI leaders specifically believe that "free, frank discussion between patient and group leader and among patients is a central method of re-education: each patient's fellow deviants are agents for change" (p. 50).

Many practitioners of individual psychotherapy with inmates advocate a nonprison focus, looking at the whole behavior history of the offender. This basis for psychotherapy with offenders has an articulate spokesman in Roth (1980), who targets the preservation of therapeutic identity as the key element in the offering of such psychotherapeutic services. He suggests resolution of loyalty and conflict problems by maintaining

> a straightforward approach in dealing with both inmates and correctional officers. . . . Even when treating those inmates who are mentally ill, the correctional psychiatrist does better to focus on inmate behaviors or feelings that are presently dysfunctional or painful, and where some agreement can be reached with the inmate that the treatment is for his or her sake rather than for others. (p. 710)

Behavior modification is another widely used treatment modality in correctional settings. Wicks (1974) stated that antisocial offenders are ideal clients for behavior modification procedures, in part, because of their extreme resistance to many other treatment approaches. The prison contingency management project of Geller and his colleagues (Geller, Johnson, Hamlin, & Kennedy, 1977) however, demonstrates that even with carefully planned methodology, a program may be forced to make substantial compromises in its content and effectiveness. The START program in the federal prison hospital at Springfield, Missouri, was successfully challenged in court as being inappropriate. Yet the Achievement Place program in Lawrence, Kansas, has for several years been a source of research data on the training and use of parents and community corrections personnel in behavioral assessment and change of delinquent youth.

Confidentiality

"Can I tell you something in absolute confidence?" That kind of question is difficult for any person to say no to. It represents a compliment by the person asking it, for it suggests that the other individual is one in whom that person places full and absolute confidence. The strong interpersonal pull is to agree to the request. In professional settings, the acceptance of such a pledge of confidentiality is complex, and a diversity of opinion exists on the extent to which confidentiality may be granted. At one extreme are those who believe that the psychotherapist should be as secretive as an oyster. For example, Siegel (1976) believes that absolute confidentiality should be extended to the client and that protecting psychotherapy relationships is the clear first priority of the psychotherapist. This perspective recalls the fate of the talkative oysters in Lewis Carroll's *Through the Looking Glass* who were served in a most unplanned dinner at the hands of an equally talkative and congenial walrus.

At the other extreme are those who take the position that no confidential or privileged communication should be allowed within correctional settings. I have had to deal with a warden in a large correctional institution who took exactly that position. One psychologist in that institution had minimum privacy (her desk for counseling prisoners was located in a busy corridor). She was under orders to report in full to the warden the contents of all conversations with prisoners following the counseling or therapy sessions. This instruction was not acceptable to her and led shortly thereafter to a confrontation and some redefinitions of the roles of and the relationships between the warden and the psychologist.

This case is not an isolated instance. In prisons the warden is the unquestioned ruler of what Burns (1969) has called a miniature totalitarian state. Corsini (1957) wrote of the disastrous failure of two therapy groups with youthful offenders; the failure of one group was followed by a written memo from the superintendent of the training school.

> Henceforth the only procedure for group therapy was to meet in a school room, with the

chairs arranged class room style, proper language was to be used, and the superintendent and assistant superintendent could come in whenever they wished to hear and see what was going on. (Corsini, 1957, p. 18)

At this level of struggle between prison administration and psychotherapeutic practice, the principles of confidentiality, client relationship, and responsibility are at issue. And psychologists' responses have been unequivocal. The woman psychologist referred to, and Corsini, and others, have refused to conduct psychotherapy under such conditions.

The most frequent confidentiality dilemmas in prison come about in the course of ongoing treatment relationships. The prototypical dilemma involves the prisoner in psychotherapy who reports during a session that an escape attempt is about to take place. Following that confession, the client pleads with the psychotherapist, "Please don't tell anyone about this escape attempt. They will kill me." What should the therapist do? There is no single or simple solution.

The principle in the American Psychological Association's (1979) *Ethical Standards of Psychologists* that deals with confidentiality emphasizes the importance of safeguarding information and not communicating it. The exceptions to this are clearly specified. Information in a professional relationship may be revealed without authorization only when the client has been informed initially of the limits of the nature of the confidentiality and only to protect against a *clear and substantial risk of imminent serious injury or disease or death* to the client or another person. That is, if there is a realistic probability that serious harm will come to a person, then the implicit confidentiality in the professional relationship is not binding.

The identification of such clear and imminent danger is sometimes a vexing problem. Knowledge of an imminent plan to commit an assault apparently is a condition for violation of a confidence. A client's revelation of a past or distant criminal act poses less danger, and deciding if the confidence should be retained in this case is harder. One fundamental operating principle is that psychotherapists in prisons have a duty to maintain confidentiality and not to disclose information unless there are cogent, clear, and compelling reasons to the contrary (Foster, 1975).

Whereas the APA *Ethical Standards* identify professional ethics on this issue the statutory equivalent is the principle of privileged communication. In Pennsylvania and Alabama, for example, psychologists have the same right to privileged communications with their clients as attorneys have with theirs. Physicians and many other professionals in these states have less statutorily granted privileged communication. In addition to Pennsylvania and Alabama, 38 other states confer privileged communication on psychologists as a legal right. A state's decision to grant privileged-communication status to a profession is usually based on a relationship-justice equation. That is, the legislature weighs the injury to a relationship versus the loss to justice incurred as a result of disclosing or not disclosing confidential information (Shah, 1969).

The *Tarasoff*[5] decision identifying a "duty to warn" potential victims of psychotherapy clients galvanized the psychological and psychiatric professions, and a flurry of discussions, editorials, professional articles, and legal opinions ensued. Shah (1977) has suggested that this was an unnecessary overreaction to the implications of *Tarasoff* and that it is ethnocentric to believe that the interests and practice of psychotherapy should come before central societal concerns. "In other words, the assumption seems to be that what is good for psychotherapy is good for society," Shah criticized (p. 2). Indeed, the *Tarasoff*-defined duty to warn is consistent with the APA *Ethical Standards* on the implications of clear and imminent danger.

---

[5] Tarasoff v. Regents of the University of California, 13 C.3d 177; 529 P.2d 553; 118 Cal. Rptr. 129 (1974).

In other words, if an escape takes place and guards and prisoners are killed, a psychologist with foreknowledge could be charged with failure to warn prison officials and thus with neglect of a compelling ethical and moral duty. On the other hand, if a client is harmed because a therapist warns prison officials, the violation of confidence may have equally grievous consequences.

One lawyer-sociologist who analyzed confidentiality and privileged-communication issues concluded that the statutes governing privileged communication cannot and do not bar prison psychotherapists from reporting information learned in treatment sessions to either wardens or parole boards:

> Prison administrative decisions in parole board meetings are presumably not judicial hearings within the meaning of doctor-patient privileged communication statutes. . . . However, as in free community cases, the therapist in prison is duty bound to refrain from divulging intimate information about patients to "improper" persons, such as other inmates. (Sternberg, 1965, p. 448)

Confidentiality in correctional settings is subject to special pressures. The issue itself may be confronted frequently rather than rarely as it is in noninstitutional practice. After all, stabbings, beatings, intimidation, and other forms of real and imminent danger occur at a higher base rate in prisons than in free-world settings. In prisons, not only information revealed in psychotherapy but even the fact of being in psychotherapy, as well as other levels of information, may be used for a variety of purposes including positive incentives (Kirkpatrick, 1963). While accepting the belief that there are special pressures against full confidentiality in corrections, seasoned observers suggest that a psychotherapist may still have a meaningful relationship with clients even without the guarantee of absolute confidentiality.

However, an alternate view challenges this frequently accepted position that correctional settings present difficult and unique challenges to maintaining confidentiality. Megargee (Note 2) suggests that industrial settings, military settings, and mental hospitals present virtually identical confidentiality problems and that it is both overblown and excessive to consider confidentiality issues special or unique in corrections. Megargee similarly suggests that individuals in corrections, including clients, need to be responsible for what they do. In this vein, La Bruyère has stated, "When a secret is revealed, it is the fault of the man who confided it."

Although seeking attribution of fault is probably a fruitless endeavor, confidentiality remains a central issue that prison mental health professionals must come to grips with. Several pathways toward solution of confidentiality problems may be considered:

Definition of Client Relationships

It is important for psychologists to specifically define client relationships and the limits of confidentiality not only when dealing with individual clients but when accepting employment, when dealing with the simultaneous multiple clients present in corrections, and when specifying relationships with agency administrators or other personnel.

Written Statements

Definitions clear to one person are not always clear to another. Thus, initial development of written and personal statements of understanding by clients and psychotherapists would make these relationships and limits explicit, open to later examination, and open to revision as necessary.

Nonobvious Data

The very fact that an individual is in psychotherapy can affect a parole board's decision, the actions of a correctional officer, and other institutional events. Thus, it is important for therapist and client to deal with such nonobvious data as well as with the more obvious information actually transmitted during psychotherapy sessions.

Records

Abuses of information may come to the attention of psychologists. Often, psychological reports, case histories, and mental status exams in an individual's records are readily available to inappropriate people in an institution. In addition, the source of some information in an individual's file may be hearsay, or information derived from presentence investigations may be passed along in total when it should not be. The ethical responsibility of the reviewing psychologist is to seek to have such inappropriately transmitted materials removed (A. Brodsky, 1976).

Legal Limits

The privileged-communication status of psychotherapists should be made clear so that the legal as well as the ethical standards that govern their behaviors are explicit.

Clear and Imminent Danger

The realistic probability of events that could lead to violation of confidentiality should be clear in the mind of the psychotherapist and identified for the client.

Periodic Review

A committee of independent practitioners should periodically examine confidentiality issues with the psychotherapist. This committee, which could work informally, should discuss troublesome situations, seek to give the psychotherapist a broader perspective, and assist in protecting the multiple clientele of the psychotherapist in the correctional setting. In a 1952 speech Adlai Stevenson said, "It is often easier to fight for principles than to live up to them." Similarly, it is often easier to set up principles for dealing with confidentiality than to implement them. A committee periodically reviewing confidentiality for individual practitioners would assist in the maintenance of ethical practice.

The importance of the issue of confidentiality lies not only in the protection of clients' physical safety and in the maintenance of individual psychotherapists' integrity in correctional settings but in the essential worth and dignity of human beings. Anton Chekhov (1928), in *The Lady With the Dog*, put it very well: "All personal life rested on secrecy, and possibly it was partly on that account that civilised man was so nervously anxious that personal privacy should be respected" (p. 25).

Treatment Ethics

> Although punishment is no longer a fashionable rationale for criminal justice, the punitive spirit has survived unscathed behind the mask of treatment. (American Friends Service Committee, 1971, p. 26)

Values and Ethics

In examining treatment ethics one should begin with the observation that most psychotherapy is a vaguely defined and uncertain activity conducted in private with malleable or ambiguous goals. As Redmountain (1977) asserts,

> Even when two practitioners derive from the same theoretical tradition, what they actually do with their clients involves such a complex of language, gesture, appearance, setting, and lifestyle that there may be no discernible connection between their ultimate effects. (p. 38)

In the absence of clearly defined behaviors and goals, individuals impose their own values and belief systems. In simulated jury trials in the absence of verifiable knowledge, individuals impose their own judgments of the leniency or harshness of punishment of criminals (Kaplan & Schersching, Note 3). The same principle applies in professional activities. While Jourard (1971) indicates that a variety of subtle acts of experimental researchers may influence human subjects, the prevailing scholarly opinion is that most experimenters' roles may be well-defined and reasonably replicable. However, no such agreement as to objectivity and specificity exists for psychotherapists. A great range of possible activities and choices exists at any given response point. Some choices are dictated by the psychotherapeutic orientation of the practitioner (Glad, 1959), while others simply are responses based on individual values and communicated through differences in pitch, inflection, mood, and nonobvious levels of suggestion (LaFrance & Mayo, 1978).

Psychotherapy in correctional settings often imposes the values of the psychotherapist on both the client and the institution. This is also reciprocal; the values of the client have the potential for affecting the psychotherapist, and the prison may be affected by them as well.

> Every human act has political implications. A few are profound, and most are trivial, yet in almost every case the implications are unknown. Nevertheless it follows that psychotherapy—however we define it—does in some way affect the political climate. *How* it affects it depends upon the essential nature of the therapy: moralistic or amoral, pleasure or success oriented, patriarchal or pro-feminist. *How much* it affects the political climate is a function of the influence exerted, directly or indirectly, by the individual psychotherapist—or by an entire segment of the profession. (Redmountain, 1977, p. 38)

Treatment personnel in corrections may implicitly or explicitly accept the existence of the political implications of psychotherapy and choose to support organizational goals seeking to make persons compliant and manageable (Brodsky & Horn, 1973); this usually happens under circumstances in which "primary alle-giance and loyalty are expected and demanded toward correctional policies which are often antiquated and oppressive" (p. 73). Can psychotherapy itself ever be effectively conducted by personnel who accept this posture? If so, what does it mean for the psychotherapist and the practice of psychotherapy in prisons? Part of the resolution of these issues lies in the abilities of some psychotherapists to help and to grow and of some prisoners to transcend their immediate physical and emotional surroundings. The general question of being a psychotherapist in such an oppressed and difficult setting has been raised by Loomer (1977):

> Think of being a psychotherapist in the year of the Black Death or any year of the religious persecutions and political turmoil of the Tudors. And 1776 was awful: with women, children, and old people fleeing across America to escape genocide; towns and villages terrorized as armies fought through and around them; and new groups of displaced persons arriving in unspeakable condition with every ship from Africa. (Picture yourself as a plantation psychotherapist assigned to help these new arrivals with *their* feelings of alienation and depersonalization and to fit smoothly into their new environment without loss to their owners). (p. 4)

Loomer's resolution of the problem of oppressive settings is to state that psychotherapy deals largely with unreal dangers and imaginary catastrophes, and that the patients' reactions to true threats and stresses are unpredictable and often not relevant to treatment. From this perspective, prison oppression may be more distressing to us as therapists than it is to our clients. Loomer concludes that therapists should act in cataclysmic times and noxious settings as they would at any time or in any other place:

> seeking the fortitude to endure life's uncertainty without magical answers no matter how frightened one may be; pushing patients to look straight at themselves and their outer realities; opening up more of the rooms of

their lives; helping them to accept our ordinariness and our universal incompetence, while facing the mystery and loneliness of our uniqueness, and to glory in its adventure. (p. 5)

This is the perspective of the psychotherapist-as-psychotherapist working in the therapy hour in the therapy room with the client. Yet for the prison psychotherapist there is a continuing, inescapable involvement with multiple aspects of the correctional world. Even the part-time psychotherapist makes a number of political-professional choices. The necessity to make such choices has led to several criticisms.

Both correctional psychology and the prisons have been accused of being tools of worldwide political repression for applying labels such as evil and crazy to those who disagree with government policies and express unpopular opinions. In this view, the frame of reference is psychological-political repression. While Solzhenitsyn has provided much personal case material on this process, Goldstein (1975), an expatriate, former forensic psychiatrist for the Leningrad Commission of Forensic Psychiatry, has offered professional summary information. He examined 12,000 psychiatric patients who had committed crimes over a period of years. The crimes included expressing dissatisfaction with Soviet society, which in turn was interpreted as peculiar behavior and resulted in compulsory psychiatric examinations and treatment. Indeed, there is a special KGB (secret police) psychiatric hospital that holds many such patients. At court hearings, no opposing experts are allowed to testify. Goldstein cites a number of instances in which there was no psychiatric disease whatever identified by the evaluating expert but in which the court nevertheless ruled that significant psychiatric disorder was present because of behaviors as innocuous as "an interest in Buddhism." During a Richard Nixon visit to the Soviet Union, large numbers of persons were involuntarily confined temporarily in psychiatric hospitals, leading psychiatric attendants to describe the

syndrome as "Nixonitis." After practicing in both the Soviet Union and the United States, Goldstein rejects the charge that American prison and hospital psychiatry is primarily political and oppressive in nature. He concludes that "only Soviet psychiatry has allowed clinical analysis to be replaced by ideological speculations and people to be incarcerated in hospitals for many years because they had certain ideas on political reforms" (Goldstein, 1975, p. 20).

Further examples of such ethical-professional interfaces on this issue exist. During the middle and late 1960s, a large number of deserters and AWOL offenders were incarcerated in military stockades, prisons, and therapeutic communities. A significant minority of the deserters had left because of moral objections to the Vietnam War. Mental health professionals in these prison settings joined in offering services to "retrain" these confined former soldiers, and the highest criterion of success was successfully returning them to military duty (Brodsky & Eggleston, 1970). In this example, a number of mental health professionals accepted an ideology that was controversial in the country—that it was appropriate and desirable for well-adjusted young men to serve in the military services during the Vietnam War. And in still another related issue of international morality and prison ethics, a British forensic psychologist has urged that findings from the Korean War Chinese brainwashing experiments be applied to manipulating and controlling the social structure of prisoner groups in the Western world (Cunningham, 1970).

The concepts at hand are political influence and brainwashing; proving that one has not been politically influenced or brainwashed is like proving the existence of the null hypothesis or like proving that an individual *cannot* play the piano. Such proof can never be supplied. How and why prisoners enter psychotherapeutic programs, however, may be examined and monitored.

An alternative correctional treatment function is for psychologists to serve as mediators between opposing political forces, never taking sides but rather integrating the needs of the client and the goals of the correctional system. Sometimes, however, seeking to reconcile opposing values leaves treatment personnel caught between the administration and the inmates, unable to satisfy either group.

Psychotherapists and other correctional treatment personnel must maintain a precarious balance between their responsibilities to prisoners and their institutional loyalties. Their decisions can clearly be evaluated by the opposing sides in the adversary process. The paraprofessional treaters—the correctional counselors—are especially vulnerable to these pressures. They have much potential for achieving worthwhile objectives but not in the context of meeting rehabilitation and psychotherapeutic goals. Rather, they become particularly effective when working within the dynamics of the institution, serving as mediators, and assisting prisoners to cope with a hierarchical and structured bureaucracy (Brodsky & Horn, p. 80).

It is a measure of the acceptance of the compliance ideology that one wide-ranging study of the effectiveness of prison treatment used recidivism and prison adjustment as its main measures. The California Prison Treatment and Parole Survival Study reported that "the principal measures of treatment impact are the differences in the degree to which treatment and control subjects conform to prison and parole regulation" (Kassebaum, Ward, & Wilner, 1971, p. 15). Many find the use of recidivism as a psychotherapy criterion unacceptable, seeing it as using treatment in the service of social control and custody. "Prison mental health services should never be provided if they are utilized as an accessory to custody and punishment," Kaufman (1973, p. 257) declares.

The fundamental ethical concern here is the potential for abuse of the considerable power that exists in psychology for controlling and shaping individuals' behavior. In the juvenile courts, in the involuntary commitment of mental patients, and in the indeterminant sentencing and release of offenders from special treatment institutions, mental health professionals have played key and sometimes singular roles in determining individual freedom. Increases in the power given to those in the mental health professions have led to a situation in which mental health social control mechanisms are as potent as criminal justice control mechanisms yet without all of the constitutional safeguards. Technology is not ideology, and the sophisticated and increasingly effective application of behavior change and control methodologies presents great potential for misuse.

From this perspective, the breadth of harmlessly different behaviors in our society becomes more and more circumscribed as the reach of criminal justice and mental health social control mechanisms is extended. As part of an extensive and careful analysis of this process, Kittrie (1971) has proposed a therapeutic bill of rights for citizens that includes the following items:

No person shall be compelled to undergo treatment except for the defense of society. (p. 402)

Man's innate right to remain free of excessive forms of human modification shall be inviolable. (p. 402)

No social sanctions, whether designated criminal, civil, or therapeutic, may be invoked in the absence of the previous right to a judicial or other independent hearing, appointed counsel, and an opportunity to confront those testifying about one's past conduct or therapeutic needs. (p. 403)

Any compulsory treatment must be the least required reasonably to protect society. (p. 404)

If the protection of the rights of individuals from an oppressive and conforming psychotherapy with potential political or authoritarian ideologies is a concern, why shouldn't this protection be specified clearly in the APA *Ethical Standards*? One psychologist (Lourens, 1973–1974) has urged just that step. He proposes that it should be considered explicitly unethical for psychologists to develop any treatment program that does not involve clear and explicit permission from the clients, patients, or their legal guardians. Lourens also proposes the following principle:

> No psychologist in the employment of or working in collaboration or contract with the local, state or federal government will embark on or participate in any project or program involving clients or patients of the psychologist or his employers, which has the implicit or explicit objective of:
> a. imposing the community's norms or the social values of some particular group(s) on individuals;
> b. strengthening any particular group, political party, or social class;
> c. strengthening or establishing any doctrine or ideology;
> d. enforcing conformity; or
> e. fostering the development of a homogeneous society. (pp. 436–437)

This principle assumes first that therapy and technology can indeed be provided value-free, an assumption with which I disagree. It further assumes that a therapist has an explicit responsibility to foster the development of a heterogeneous society in the pursuit of clients' personal goals. Since these goals may include conformity, this part of the principle may conflict with clients' own wishes. Indeed, the first part of this principle seems to contradict the fourth and fifth parts. That is, avoiding the enforcement of conformity and avoiding the development of a homogeneous society seem to be the social or political values of some particular group or individual—certainly of the individual who has proposed them! Thus, it is not possible to avoid imposing individual norms or social values while at the same time imposing the values of nonconformity and of a nonhomogeneous society.

While the principle as written may be flawed, the idea offers considerable merit. That is, it should be an operating ethical principle of institutions to maintain a high degree of sensitivity

to imposing social norms or values on individuals. Since pressures for conformity from a number of institutions and society are always present, an awareness of and periodic review of one's activities in this context would be valuable.

Behavior Modification

> A strange thing happened to the behavioral psychologist on the way to the superintendent's or warden's office. For a long time after he left, the superintendent or warden cried out, "Somebody's been sitting in my chair!" That protest was not disturbing, because at that time there was a sense that psychology and the behavioral sciences were on the side of the patients, the prisoners, and justice. Then the clients themselves began howling, "Somebody's been sitting in my chair!" That also was not too distressing, because it was believed that the clients may not really know what was best for them. Finally, when the lawyers started insisting, "Somebody's been sitting in my chair, and he or she has broken it all to pieces," that was indeed disturbing, because for the first time behavioral psychologists were dealing with equally powerful and influential persons. What at first for behavioral psychologists was a brisk walk through the woods to our professional homes and seats, in the last few years has turned into a ricocheting, frantic run through a hostile forest. (Brodsky, Note 4, p. 1)

Ethical issues have swept like a whirlwind around the practices of behavior modification more than around any other treatment method in corrections. Why? There appear to be several answers.

The first is relatively mundane—there is more behavior modification practiced than almost any other treatment approach. Much more significant reasons, however, are to be found in the nature of this practice. The use of behavioral techniques is frequently accompanied by technology. While the term *behavior modification* encompasses many diverse, specific treatments, it is not unusual for a mechanical or electrical apparatus to be a central element in such treatment. The public fear of out-of-control technology has seized on this substitution of technological apparatus for the simple "talking cure."

Two media events helped sow the seeds of this fear (or perhaps were the fruits of it). The first was the popular book (and then movie), *Clockwork Orange* (Burgess, 1963), in which the icy-mannered behavioral therapist, Dr. Brodsky, replaced the protagonist's psychopathic disorder with a neurotic disorder. Alex, the protagonist, and the treatment program itself became enmeshed in political ploys.

The second media event was a widely read and cited article in *Psychology Today* by James McConnell (1970) of the University of Michigan. McConnell proposed extensive use of behavioral approaches to shape the behavior of serious and repetitive offenders against their wills. His article presents a strong case for big brotherism in correctional treatment, suggesting that it is the only effective, logical, and financially acceptable approach. This society-first, full-electrodes-ahead philosophy prompted many expressions of concern for the constitutional rights of inmates. The essence of this concern was objections to aversive conditioning. Delivery of painful and occasionally harmful stimuli to prisoners, in situations where informed consent is uncertain, has been attacked as unethical. As a consequence, law suits have been filed against aversive treatment programs, specifically those treating sex offenders.

Another substantive issue is the conversion of imprisoned individuals' rights into reinforcers for desired behavior (Wexler, 1973). In the case of the ill-fated START program, prisoners had to work in a modified behavioral economy in order to earn living conditions that they would otherwise have received routinely. This practice was criticized on the grounds that regularly available living conditions should not be removed and used subsequently as rewards. Rewards for some prisoners should not be deprivations for all others.

Three emerging ethical principles seem to be consistent with the major legal decisions of the last few years:

1. Basic prisoner rights may not be used as behavioral reinforcers in treatment or other programs.

2. The issue of informed consent is so salient and difficult that aversive treatment and conditioning may not be routinely implemented.

3. The client must be defined as a full, active, respected, participating partner in correctional treatment decisions.

The correctional milieu is changing now to permit the latter process, and, indeed, the widespread adoption of Mutual Agreement Programming (MAP) is evidence of its implementation. In MAP the inmate is a full partner, and the institution and the parole board promise that parole will be granted after certain objectives are achieved (American Correctional Association Parole-Corrections Project, 1973). Elsewhere, the same approach has been described as Promethean in the sense that power and explicit knowledge in the correctional setting are shared with the confined persons themselves (Fischer & Brodsky, 1978).

Behavior modification in prisons has been criticized severely on two paradoxical bases. First, it has been criticized because it does not work or does not work well enough (Wexler, 1975). Since it is assumed that no known technique can effectively rehabilitate prisoners and that all techniques are of as-yet-undetermined value and efficacy, behavior modification procedures are considered totally inappropriate for use with any nonconsenting prisoners.

On the other hand, the criticism that behavior modification works too well, too quickly, and too efficiently has also been made. For example, one prominent forensic psychiatrist has observed that "behavior therapies work quickly. They can be used without giving the patient the chance to contemplate the meaning of his behavior . . . or the social consequences of his treatment" (Halleck, 1974, p.

382). Some feel that behavior therapies intrinsically interfere with the expanding awareness critical to true informed consent. Because these therapies are efficient and impersonal, they eliminate the necessity of dealing "with the troubling implications of what the patient's behavior might mean" (Halleck, 1974).

Intense and vituperative criticisms have been directed at behavior therapies, and their functioning in prisons has been labeled wicked, destructive, backward, genocidal, and uncivilized (Clemons, 1975). Opton (1975) has further suggested that behavior therapies are the essence of wizardry, a fraud, a sham, and a hypocritical cover-up. Some criticisms lump all behavioral treatments together, noting for example, that "individual treatment is primarily a device for breaking the convict's will to resist . . . and is thus a means of exerting maximum control over the convict population" (Mitford, 1973, p. 117).

Behind the accusation of genocide is the belief that behavior modification approaches wrongly blame individual prisoners rather than the social and economic systems of which the prisoners are victims. This perspective views prisons and behavior modification as taking part in the same process: killing and harming those who dare to be different. Clemons (1975) considers "the new wave of behavior modification programs a concerted, genocidal attack on ethnic minorities" (p. 129) and feels that if behavior therapists and other behavioral scientists were not involved in such genocidal attack, they would confront prison administrators and direct their efforts toward eliminating the inhumanity of prisons.

Additional accusations against the *language* of behavior modification suggest that it is so abstract that it both includes and disguises the "exertion of institutional power through reward and punishment. Best of all, the language of behavior modification exorcises entirely the troublesome context of punishment" (Opton, 1975, p. 24). Opton asserts that behavior modification marvelously soothes the consciences of institu-

tional administrators, lets those who use it avoid lay judgments of decency, dresses simple ideas in esoteric jargon, and is an inevitable fraud. The fraud is that instead of a help to inmates, behavior modification is an organized method of using incentives and punishment to shape the behavior of inmates and maintain institutional power over them (Opton, 1975).

The assumptions underlying treatment methods and the choice of treatment targets are important and legitimate professional concerns. In his book, *Blaming the Victim*, William Ryan (1970) points out that it is easy to blame mental patients, prisoners, the poor, the rural, and others for being victims of wider, harmful social inequities. Without actively considering the issue, professionals often choose to utilize an offender-blame model rather than the victim-blame, situation-blame, or societal-blame models (Brodsky, 1976; Brodsky & Hobart, 1978). The offender-blame model states that an offense takes place when a person with deficits in personal-social behavior controls acts out this pathology by deliberate and overt behaviors. In the victim-blame model an offense takes place when a citizen in some way—obviously or nonobviously, consciously or unconsciously—allows himself or herself to be in an interpersonal or physical position that antecedes a criminal act. The situational blame model considers an offense to have taken place when environmental and structural circumstances, transient factors in mood or place, and crime-vulnerable parties, both offenders and victims, synergize to generate a criminal act. The societal blame model assumes that an offense takes place when accumulated cultural and societal attitudes are manifested through the harmful or illegal action of one person on another or on another's property.

The offender-blame model has an accompanying assumption of individual pathology. Even when contributing factors (such as social class) that promote certain offenses are acknowledged in the application of the therapy, the individual is still regarded as the exclusive source of his or her behavior. Two problems that result are a "more like us" judgment about treatment goals and a myopic focusing of further explanatory models primarily on offenders. If one starts with the offender, looks no further, and works backward from there in developing knowledge and decisions, one tends to ignore the other three potential places to attribute responsibility for the offense. Brodsky and Hobart (1978) report that the public tends to share this offender-blame perspective with behavior modification. Ambrose Bierce (1911) defined the word *rope* as "an obsolescent appliance for reminding assassins that they too are mortal. It is put about the neck and remains in place one's whole life long" (p. 116). The public likewise sees behavioral treatment approaches as a restricting collar and an instrument of punishment appropriate for use with offenders.

There is no simple solution to the problems caused by use of offender-blame models, for there is no single correct model. Informed professionals, however, should attempt to understand and look at any particular phenomenon from at least these four (and perhaps maybe more) perspectives. Looking only at the assailants, searching for something wrong with them, or believing that there is no shared causal responsibility, is an overly limiting and unnecessarily binding view. Discarding learned expertise about offender-blame assumptions calls for a return to fresh seeing and thinking about offenders. As Suzuki (1970) has written, "In the beginner's mind there are many possibilities, but in the expert's there are few" (p. 29).

Resolution of Ethical Dilemmas

Some of the ethical dilemmas presented here occur particularly in behavior modification in corrections. However, just as criticisms directed at behavior modification are applicable to many treatment approaches, so are the potential resolutions of these ethical dilemmas.

Thus the guidelines for resolution presented in the following sections seem to cut across the dilemmas and issues, although some have particular relevance to behavior modification.

Review Committees

A frequent solution to some of the ethical dilemmas mentioned is the use of review committees at two levels: a peer review committee to examine the professional adequacies of the procedures and a human rights review committee to look at the ethical, social, and human implications of particular treatments (Braukmann, Fixsen, Phillips, & Wolf, 1975; Friedman, 1975). Such independent review committees can provide outside and independent guarantees that treatment methods are competent and appropriate and that the rights of those in treatment are being sufficiently protected and maintained.

Goals

An alternate approach lies in the choice of treatment objectives. One psychologist in corrections has suggested that for consent to be valid in prison treatment programs, program participation must be fully divorced from all consequences within the institution. The programs themselves should be selected jointly by the inmates and the agency, and the behavior target should be *outside success* rather than intrainstitutional success (Goldiamond, 1974).

The Ayllon Guidelines

Starting with the belief that aversive conditioning should be used only as a last resort, when clear and imminent danger is present, Ayllon (1975) proposed eight ethical guidelines that have particular relevance to the behavior therapist:

1. The patient should be informed of the possible outcome of the treatment.

2. The patient should be informed of the procedure that will be used in the treatment.

3. The patient should be made to feel that he is free to choose whether or not he should partake in a program.

4. The patient should be able at any time to discontinue his participation in the program without incurring prejudice or penalty.

5. As an adjunct to the right to discontinue treatment, information necessary to make such a decision should be given the patient.

6. The patient is entitled to the treatment, rehabilitation, or education which is suited to his individual needs.

7. The patient should be given the opportunity to express his feelings, views, and attitudes toward a program.

8. Only behavioral techniques that enrich the patients' environment beyound a base guarantee of certain social and personal rights should be employed. (pp. 11–13)

The Ayllon guidelines include full optional participation in all aspects of behavioral programs, including token economies.

Constructional Solution

A constructional model has been proposed as a solution to both the ethical and conceptual dilemmas of therapeutic practice in closed institutions (Goldiamond, 1974). The constructional model refers to the construction or development of new repertoires as a solution to the person's problems, rather than the elimination of any present or troublesome repertoires. Constructional approaches are seen as the direct opposite of pathological or eliminative models of therapeutic intervention. Goldiamond (1974) points out that "the focus . . . is on the production of desirables through means which *directly* increase available options or extend social repertoires" (p. 14). Goldiamond's proposal for the constructional approach is accompanied by rating sheets, client information sheets, and detailed descriptions about different applications. The ingenious and significant part of the constructional approach is that the implications of coercion present in other approaches are much less evident. Nothing is taken away from the clients. They have exactly the same behaviors and patterns of thinking or adapting that they had before. Instead, they simply have more behavior options from which to choose. Nothing is eliminated. While this approach has yet to be implemented on any wide scale, the concept could serve as a substantial resolution of the ethical coercion problem.

Promethean Solution

Prometheus was a Greek god who shared power and responsibility with mankind. The Prometheus principle refers to an organized system of sharing professional power, knowledge, and responsibility with a client (Brodsky, 1972; Fischer & Brodsky, 1978). This system calls for full sharing with clients of all decisions and knowledge regarding professional activities. Within the prison setting it means yielding partial control of professional power to clients, including viewing of personal therapy files and access to other therapy-related information. Clients serve as active evaluators of the continuation of funding for therapy and research programs as well as review consultation and training programs and psychological assessments that affect their well-being. The Promethean approach is suggested as a way of integrating egalitarian beliefs with nonegalitarian institutional systems. The practical applications are limited so far, but reports suggest that it may be applied successfully in prisons and in other human service settings (Fischer & Brodsky, 1978).

Research Ethics

Prisons could provide an excellent setting for the investigation of crowding in humans. Prisons provide a number of advantages which, we believe, outweigh the disadvantages of employing a prison population in crowding research. (Paulus, McCain, & Cox, 1973, p. 428)

> Prisoners make splendid laboratory animals. Healthy, relatively free of alcohol and drugs, with regulated diets, they are captives unlikely to wander off and be lost to both treatment and control groups, and they are under sufficient pressure of adversity to "volunteer." (Mills & Morris, 1974, p. 60)

Availability and control: These are the components of the attraction of researchers to prison settings. Indeed, this access to subjects has produced significant results in biomedical research over a period of years. As the controversy around research involvement in penal settings is examined, biomedical research is the first focus: It is attended to because the question of potential harm is more clearly visible—as is the question of potential benefit. It has been pointed out, however, that the ethical issues raised in biomedical research apply equally well to behavioral experimentation (Branson, 1976). Although there are conspicuous examples of no significant research benefits being produced (Mitford, 1973), the research into contagious diseases and diet and disease has had important results. Thus in the course of 29 years of continuing study at the Stateville Penitentiary in Illinois, malaria has been induced in over 4,000 prisoners. Malaria is a worldwide health problem, and the Stateville investigations have led to the development of effective antimalaria drugs (Hawkins, 1976) without any reported prisoner deaths or lasting side effects.

Many confined persons actively seek and positively value participation in research studies. If we accept the statements of inmate subjects at face value, research participation is regarded as highly desirable. When the Stateville antimalaria studies were discontinued by the correctional administrators for informed consent reasons, there were loud and pained protests from many inmates.

It is freedom of choice that is the fundamental issue. The specter of the involuntary subjects of Nazi concentration camp surgery studies remains with us as a reminder of the human capacity for abusing people in the name of research. The Nuremberg Code of Ethics in Medical Research requires that the human subject be able to fully consent and choose to participate without any form of coercion, constraint, force, fraud, deceit, or duress. The discovery of the Tuskegee syphilis study provided an example in the United States of the imposition of harmful procedures on unknowing subjects. A disclosure of CIA-sponsored LSD research in prisons apparently falls in the same category ("The CIA," 1977). Thus, a study group from the United Nations has recommended that no inmates be permitted to participate in any research investigations. The conservative American Correctional Association adopted a position statement in 1976 urging that all medical and pharmacological experimentation with prisoners be ceased. The ACA concluded that the element of reward for participating is inevitably present and that full informed consent is "very doubtful." They added that "the authority which authorizes or permits prisoners to become subjects of human experimentation ignores his historic obligation as a custodian to protect" (American Correctional Association, 1976, p. 14).

Informed Consent

Cutting across all of the substantial issues relating to research with individual prisoners is the issue of free, informed, full consent. The American Psychological Association's *Ethical Principles in the Conduct of Research with Human Participants* (1973) states in Principle 5,

> Ethical research practice requires the investigator to respect the individual's freedom to decline to participate in research or to discontinue participation at any time. The obligation to protect this freedom requires special vigilance when the investigator is in a position of power over the participant. The decision to limit this freedom increases the investigator's responsibility to protect the participant's dignity and welfare. (p. 42)

An institutional context forces a compromise with the ideal notion of free consent. That is, in correctional settings, research is not a primary goal; the main work of the institution per se is the limitation of individual freedom in a number of ways. The first limit on free consent is the existence of potential or promised rewards within the correctional settings. West (1976) has pointed out that the issue is not one of coercion but rather of bribery. There have been many instances of obvious bribery and provision of incentives to participate in research. For example, in 1914 the Governor of Mississippi promised pardons to convicted persons at the Mississippi State Prison who volunteered to participate in a study on the relationship between diet and pellagra (Geis, 1972).

A variety of other incentives limits the inmate's capacity for true free choice. For example, the inmate may be offered better living conditions, food of a higher quality, more privacy, more personal-care items, or better-quality personal treatment by physicians or other staff than are offered nonparticipating inmates. Under these conditions true informed consent becomes difficult.

A parallel form of incentive is the use of inmate pay. In paying confined persons to participate in research studies, a dilemma arises. On the one hand, any payment above the very low prison wages (which may be as little as 50 cents a week in some prison settings) will strongly motivate confined persons and compromise their free choice. Thus, if research sponsors pay the ordinary outside-world rate for research participants, the incentive would be overwhelming and indeed might almost be considered to represent compulsion. On the other hand, if the inmates are paid standard prison wages, then they are being taken advantage of or exploited. That is, if they are paid 50 cents a week, or even $2 or $3 a day, and there is no difference between their wages and the wages paid for other prison activities, the charge of exploitation becomes sound (Geis,

1972). One solution to this dilemma is a full-wages prison in which all confined persons' services are paid for at going market rates. However, this solution is not possible in United States prisons. Mills and Morris (1974) have suggested that prisoners be paid what is required to attract a free volunteer to the research project and that any difference between that amount and current prisoner wages be placed in a general inmates' welfare fund.

Minority Groups

Prison populations are composed disproportionately of minority group members: Blacks, Indians, Chicanos, and other groups are over-represented in prisons. At a conference supported by the National Commission for the Protection of Human Subjects of Biomedical and Behavioral Research, it was concluded that minority groups were unnecessarily and inappropriately exploited in both behavioral experiments and biomedical research. Do proportionately more minority group members than nonminority group members serve as research subjects? While the National Minority Conference on Human Experimentation (1976) concluded that this was the case, the National Commission for the Protection of Human Subjects gathered independant data and inferred that this was not true. Indeed, they reported the exact opposite finding: White males are over-represented in behavioral science research. The National Commission suggested that this situation itself is inequitable. That is, there are a number of benefits as well as disadvantages that accrue to individuals who participate in research studies, and with fewer blacks, women prisoners, and other minorities represented among research subjects, the benefits and incentives are distributed inappropriately.

Levels of Research

One way to conceptualize ethical issues in research and to assess the risks to subjects is to consider levels of research. Thus both the National Commission for the Protection of Human Subjects of Biomedical and Behavioral Research (1977) and the APA *Ethical Principles in the Conduct of Research with Human Participants* (1973) identify three broad categories or levels of research. The first category involves evaluations conducted of institutions or programs in hopes of improving their effectiveness. This category includes research on clinical practices that have "the intent or reasonable probability of improving the health or well-being of the individual prisoner" (National Commission for the Protection of Human Subjects of Biomedical and Behavioral Research, 1977, p. 3080). The second category consists of research that is inherently related to confined persons but that may or may not affect their welfare. This level is represented by research into the nature of crime and prisoners, "studies of the possible causes, effects and processes of incarceration and studies of prisons as institutional structures or of prisoners as incarcerated persons" (p. 3080). In the third category is research that takes advantage of the availability of confined persons but that is not particularly related to their nature, activities, or dynamics. This category includes all research studies not falling into the first two categories.

The second category of research presents the fewest problems. Studies of prisoners and prisons rarely involve risk to prisoners and typically consist of questionnaires, surveys, or analyses of demographic data. More difficulty is involved in research that has the intent or reasonable probability of improving prisoners' health or well-being (the first category). The APA's *Ethical Principles in the Conduct of Research with Human Participants* (1973) notes,

> A stronger way to put this last point is that prisoners and mental patients may ethically be required to cooperate in therapeutic or corrective programs oriented toward their own rehabilitation. By extension, this argument would hold that cooperation in research for the improvement of rehabilitation might also be

required of them. A difficulty with this position is that it is too readily available as a rationalization for exploitation. On occasion, the institution in question may serve more to incarcerate and punish than to rehabilitate. Under such circumstances the argument just presented loses much of its force. (pp. 48–49)

A Moratorium on Research in Prisons

Several observers have adopted the position that research cannot legitimately be continued in prison settings because the factors influencing prisoners' decisions to participate are sufficiently controlling that no true informed consent can ever take place. Thus it has been suggested that the coercive structure itself of American prisons synergizes with the ever-present potential for injustice through exploitation. Negligence and a lack of both distributive and comparative justice in reward and risk alike are considered insurmountable problems (Branson, 1976). Thus Branson (1976) concludes that "To continue experimentation with prisoners under the present circumstances would violate and erode our sense of what we are as a society; a community constituted by mutual regard for each other's equal, intrinsic dignity" (pp. 1–28).

Some observers see imprisonment as (a) an essentially political rather than legal action, designed to oppress the powerless, and (b) as a continuation of a long American tradition of slavery and repressive racial policies. For those holding such views, prison research is an extension of colonization, racism, capitalism, and parasitical practices. Swan (1976) suggests that research conducted in prisons is a one-way process in which the subjects give time, energy, and trust and get nothing in return. On the other hand, researchers get grants, research awards, increased salary, enhanced professional status, and other personal rewards at the expense of poor and racially oppressed individuals. Swan (1976) sees researchers as inevitably taking sides with prison administrators and concludes that it is unethical for social and behavioral scientists to take sides with those who are defined by inmates as their enemies, since they see themselves in a life-and-death struggle with prison officials and the state . . . scientists cannot consider themselves dispassionate researchers without responsibilities for possible misuse of their research findings and recommendations. (p. 15-11)

West (1976), in an extension of this thinking, suggests that there should be an immediate termination of all participation by prisoners in any kind of "therapeutic" behavioral research. West further suggests that any resumption of research within penal institutions should first entail vast prison reform in order to insure thorough informed consent.

This perspective does not lend itself to either scientific support or refutation. It is more a matter of political views held on faith than a subject that lends itself to investigation or application. Certainly, a high degree of awareness of the situational factors present in research conducted in prisons is important. That is, there must be full respect for the dignity of the potential research participant, and the researcher must actively pursue his or her ethical responsibilities.

Guidelines in the Search for Solutions

Informed Consent

The Survey Research Center at the University of Michigan (Tannenbaum & Cooke, 1976) surveyed 181 confined persons in four prisons, seeking information about current research practices. It found that 97% of the research participants felt that they had been provided correct and accurate information. The prisoners viewed the research studies favorably, found it easy to decide to participate, found that the researchers were willing to answer all their questions, and participated primarily for financial reasons. Of the 175 persons who answered the question "Do you feel your participation in re-

search will help your case when it comes up before the parole board?" only 4 thought that it would, 4 more thought that it probably would or it might, 136 said no, 20 said they didn't know, 3 said it might or might not, and 8 said that it probably would not. Thus these prisoners did not regard parole as a particularly relevant incentive for research participation and felt well-informed about the research they had participated in. The survey also found that consent forms were used for research at all of the prisons.

The specific kind of consent form used is important. Grisso, Manoogian, and Kissling, (Note 5) investigated the abilities of juveniles to understand the *Miranda* warnings and identified some major dimensions and techniques for assessing the extent of their understanding. Similar research needs to be pursued on the understanding of research consent forms, particularly in view of the Survey Research Center's observation that every consent form they examined contained at least one technical or medical term.

As an ethical guideline it is suggested that a written consent form be used and that the researcher be obliged to insure the prisoner-subject's understanding of its language and meaning.

Voluntary Participation

A second guideline is that research in prisons should be independent of prison authorities and decision makers. Prisoners' participation in any level of research must be explicitly independent from decisions relating to their release, institutional treatment, housing, or other benefits, and prisoners should be made aware of this independence.

Following this guideline may result in depriving prisoners of considerable benefits that come with participation in research. For example, in the Experimental Manpower Laboratory for Corrections (Clements & McKee, 1968; Milan, Wood, Williams, Rogers, Hampton, & McKee,

1974), a large-scale behavior research program conducted at Draper Prison in Alabama, the more than 5% of the prison population that participated in the program lived in special quarters with living conditions far superior to those generally found within the inadequate environment of the rest of the prison. In its report and recommendations published in the *Federal Register* but not adopted, the National Commission for the Protection of Human Subjects of Biomedical and Behavioral Research (1977) identified 17 standards of living that it felt must be met in prisons when undertaking research of the third category (i.e., research taking advantage of prisoner availability but not about prisoners per se). These standards included single-occupancy cells available on request, a staff with a racial composition about equal to that of the prison population, adequate medical services, and working showers. While all of the National Commission's standards are desirable and indeed consistent with a number of federal court decisions, researchers should not be held responsible for improving prison conditions. This is a matter of responsibility for legislatures, prison administrators, and courts. Withholding research participation or utilizing research as a vehicle for achieving social change in prisons seem to be ineffective strategies.

The first and second categories of research mentioned earlier might include studies in which alternate and improved prison living conditions are investigated, such as in research into the effectiveness of a therapeutic community within a prison. In such a case, improved living conditions for research participants would be acceptable. However, if an elite dormitory were made available to all prisoners volunteering for a study of tolerance of severe sensory deprivation, the improved living conditions would represent an excessive incentive and be unacceptable.

Just as no favorable consequences should be used to elicit participation in most research, no unfavorable consequences should follow research participation or nonparticipation. Thus, participation or nonparticipation certainly should not become part of an inmate's permanent record. And if individuals do participate in psychological studies either of therapy or of particular environments, it is the responsibility of the investigator to minimize risks of harm or irreversible effects.

Another potential incentive for choosing to participate in research is the idleness and boring routine of prison life that constitutes the alternative choice for potential subjects. Of course, not all prison living is boring, nor is all research fascinating; nevertheless, this contrast affects many prisoners' decisions and should be considered by members of research review committees.

Research Review Procedures

Two kinds of reviews should be conducted before prison research is approved: a review of the merits of the research and a review of the protection afforded the human subjects. It is possible to have research in which the human subjects are protected very well but the scholarly work is minimal, and vice versa. The two kinds of reviews call for different committees. The review for merit should be conducted by the researcher's peers, individuals who are capable of judging the scientific value of the proposed study in the context of existing knowledge. The ethics review committee should consist of citizens, lawyers, and perhaps behavioral scientists and should address itself particularly to issues of protection of human subjects. The National Institute of Mental Health's Center for Studies of Crime and Delinquency has two sets of research review procedures and forms, one for merit and one for ethics. Although both reviews are conducted by the same committee, at least the two issues are addressed independently.

Such reviews of scientific merit and of human-subjects protection do not compose the full scope of desired and possible review procedures. Some recommend that a third review committee consisting of inmates also review research proposals. This committee could speak for peers, could give its consent on proposals involving modest and nonharmful deception, and could allow subject representatives input and participation in decisions about approval of research.

Three review committees are enough to discourage many researchers. I have agonized with colleagues and students entangled in the interminable bureaucratic labyrinths of just one review committee. Three reviews might be a blessing for inmate rights but surely a curse on researchers' motivation and a test of their perseverance. For practical purposes it would be sensible to have three review subcommittees meeting concurrently, each with veto power. They could then meet together as one committee to formulate a collective and consistent response to the research inquiry.

Review committee procedures currently exist in almost all institutions that allow research. (At the present time, according to the National Commission for the Protection of Human Subjects of Biomedical and Behavioral Research, at least eight state prison systems no longer allow organized research.) The Survey Research Center (Tannenbaum & Cooke, 1976) reported that a number of protective mechanisms exist in these review committees. All of the prisons surveyed do use review committees, and four of the five studied require unanimous committee votes to permit research. Lawyers, community representatives, and prison representatives serve on these committees. Turnover tends to be slight, and while correctional officials are not always part of the institutional review committees, at some point they do review all proposals. The review committees reject few proposals but accept very few as written. Required changes in research proposals relate to the consent forms, to detailed descriptions of the risk, and to other procedures designed to protect human subjects.

The National Commission for the Protection of Human Subjects of Biomedical and Behavioral Research (1977) proposed rules similar to the suggestions presented here. As a first step they proposed that the responsible federal agency determine the investigators' competence and the research facilities' adequacy. A second step was proposal of a human subjects review committee, composed of persons of diverse racial and cultural backgrounds, including prisoners, prisoner advocates, community representatives, clergy, behavioral scientists, and independent medical personnel. Finally, the National Commission (1977) proposed that the following criteria be considered in evaluating any research: the risks involved, the provisions for obtaining informed consent, the safeguards to protect individual dignity and confidentiality, the procedures for selection of subjects, and the provisions for providing compensation for research-related injury (p. 3081).

Although some observational and nonreactive investigations—such as questionnaire studies—may seem to have minimal impact on prisoners, the potential for both misuse of and harm to individuals exists in any study. In these studies as well as in more active manipulations of treatment conditions or offenders, it is important that consent forms, institutional reviews, and other elements of protection for human subjects be provided.

Subjects' Views

Prisoner attitudes toward research studies are overwhelmingly positive. The Survey Research Center indicated that well over 80% of prisoner subjects interviewed had strong positive feelings of support for research. Similarly, Milgram (1964) reported that only 1.3% of his subjects objected to his research on apparently harmful obedience to instructions from authority. In contrast, in a survey of eight examples of social psychological research, all of which was nonreactive field research, Wilson and Donnerstein (1976) reported that many free-world citizens do object to being research subjects. In this investigation, 174 persons, mostly non-students, were presented eight typical social psychological field studies, and a substantial minority of these persons objected to the procedures. Depending on the situation, from 18% to 47% felt that the research was unethical; from 24% to 72% said they would feel harrassed being a subject; and from 28% to 65% reported that they would mind being a subject in a particular setting (Wilson & Donnerstein, 1976).

Thus, positive attitudes toward research may well be a function of environmental and situational influences. Not only may participation in research be motivated by a reaction against boredom and other negative aspects of prison living but the attitudes expressed after participation may be colored by the context in which the prisoners are living and in which they are viewing other aspects of their lives. If these same individuals were free research subjects, it is possible that their evaluations of research participation would be more negative.

Protection of the Institutional Client

In research investigations conducted in prisons by outside investigators, there are two clients. One is the individual human subject—the confined person who more or less voluntarily participates in the study. The second is the institutional client—the administrators and the correctional institution in which the research takes place. I have noted elsewhere (Brodsky, 1977) that much alienation can occur between researchers and correctional administrators. Different language, values, and beliefs in the worth of research will lead the institutional host and the guest researcher to have very different perspectives and expectations of the research experience. To these differences should be added the potential insensitivity of some guests as well as that of some hosts. Many stories are told at correctional conventions about behavioral science researchers who conduct research and are never seen again, giving no feedback to the institution about problems of

critical concern. Even more disturbing to correctional administrators is the appearance in professional journals or the popular media, without the permission or knowledge of the administrators, of exposés or studies critical of their facilities.

One potential guideline in such research is the principle of *mutuality* (Bush, Wittner, & Gordon, 1976). When this principle is invoked, the host personnel are treated as co-investigators, and a sharing of the ideas behind and the evolution of the research is undertaken. The sense of being exploited by the researcher for his ór her personal advancement that is sometimes experienced by host institutions may also be experienced by the prisoner subject (Swan, 1976; West, 1976). One way of potentially averting this difficulty is to make use of participatory research in which the subjects as well as the host institution are active participants in the development and evolution of the research ideas.

From a similar perspective, Irwin (1976) and Susman (1976) have proposed that the concepts of bargaining power and of a rights model be implemented to ensure such mutuality between subjects, hosts, and researchers. Both Susman and Irwin begin with the position that some prisoners do have a great deal of autonomy and freedom because much of what goes on in prison settings is under their control rather than that of the prison administration. Since prisoners can thus give informed consent, it is critical that they be given knowledge of a proposed study, an understanding of the risks involved in it, and protection against possible abuse through the parity conferred by bargaining power. Prisoners must be represented, along with the administration and the review committee, in key decisions relating to approval and implementation of the research, provision for payment when applicable, and subject debriefing and feedback.

Mutuality between host personnel and researchers may be attained through similar formal mechanisms. However, the ongoing interactions between these two groups are the primary vehicle for mutual benefit and collaboration. Researchers should seek to educate the prison personnel and be educated by them, to listen well, to offer feedback on results, and to demonstrate a fundamental respect for correctional officers' opinions and experience. I am not suggesting that the integrity of the research or the protection and confidentiality of the prisoner-subjects be compromised in any way. Rather, I am suggesting that while it is urgent that prisoners' rights be protected, the rights and perspectives of agency personnel must be equally acknowledged and assured.

Research Oriented Toward Prisoner Improvement and Therapies

Much research with prisoners amounts to a search for psychopathology in the belief that something must be psychologically wrong with any individual who has committed a crime (Brodsky, 1973). Numerous researchers have been engaged in the search for this disorder. Similarly, the imposition of therapeutic programs in correctional settings is a manifestation of the same belief and assumption. In prison research, the assumption of psychological disorder has led to an overemphasis on problems, psychopathology, and negative-aspect research. This emphasis characterizes not only research in correctional settings but also much behavioral science research in general (Jourard, 1968; West & Gunn, Note 6). One way to counteract this negative orientation is to encourage the setting of minimum ratios of studies of positive aspects, altruism, and helping behavior to studies of criminality and deviance in imprisoned persons.

The introduction of open research procedures that do not use deception, that present risks openly, that require fully informed consent, and that manipulate people as little as possible may have hazards as well. A melancholy note has been sounded in a related context:

Alas, returns to grace are always somewhat chimerical. In the present case, the return to grace would at best be at the expense of the beautiful simplicity of results that characterize a number of experiments in our field and at worst be at the expense of the ability to make causal inferences from our data. (West & Gunn, Note 6, pp. 12–13)

Yet it is not necessarily a zero-sum game in which every gain for prisoners' rights and integrity represents a loss for research rigor and scholarly methodology. Rather, cooperative improvement in which both prisoners and institutions ally themselves with the goals of the research may yield more productive, meaningful, and humane findings and better serve the interests of human subjects and science alike.

Doing Well for Themselves?

The practices of psychologists in corrections have led some to view psychologists as pursuing selfish rather than altruistic interests. The ethical conflict described earlier was that of serving two masters: the individual client, and society as represented by the institution. In the present alternative perspective, the conflict is between serving both the client and society on the one hand, and the selfish good of psychology on the other. This view has been espoused by Judge David Bazelon (1973), who suggests that since offenders are fundamentally an end result of oppressive and unjust societal practices, no amount of psychological intervention or programming can fulfill the implied and sometimes explicit promise of psychology to stop crime. The conclusion Bazelon reaches from this argument is that psychologists, instead of doing good for offenders, are doing well for themselves in correctional work. Bazelon's charge that psychological explanations for criminal behavior lead to the development of programs to employ more psychologists is accompanied by his observations that there has been no significant psychological contribution to knowledge of criminal behavior, that psychological treatment programs don't work, and that hopes that psychology can resolve the problem of criminality must either arise from professional ignorance or be the product of deliberate deception.

If these allegations are true, then clearly psychology in a generic sense has been guilty of unethical behavior. Promising competence when competence does not exist and serving one's own interests rather than societal and client interests clearly violate principles of integrity and ethics.

Each of the above points raised by Bazelon has been discussed and refuted by Koran and Brown (1973); however, there is no simple answer to these charges. One experienced practitioner, in reviewing 30 years of working with criminals, asserts that character disorders have little likelihood of being cured by psychotherapy, that the potential contributions of psychology and psychiatry to corrections have been oversold, and that virtually no high-caliber psychiatric and psychological personnel are working in prisons (Thorne, 1975). He concludes that

> most of the plans for correctional reform are totally unrealistic and inadequate. The psychological and social sciences are badly oversold concerning what they can contribute to criminology. They tend to overstress behavioristic contentions that sick environments are the main cause of delinquency. (pp. 164–165)

I will not explore this issue of efficacy here, except to note that substantial literature may be mobilized to support both the position that psychotherapy in prisons works and the position that it does not work. It is just as inaccurate in discussing prison settings as nonprison settings to unequivocally conclude that psychotherapy always is appropriate and succeeds.

While the former criticisms deal primarily with efficacy, strong criticism has also been directed against the disciplinary parochialism often demonstrated by psychologists working in corrections. Putting psychology first comes from thinking of psychology first, and one responsibility for psychologists is to gain a heightened awareness of the institutional, social, legal, and related contexts within which justice and behavior problems arise and are handled. Such an awareness must include listening to those charged by society with handling these problems, must have an interdisciplinary focus, must attend particularly to issues of fairness and equity, and finally, must be founded on a broad social accountability beyond that of the psychological profession (Shah, 1978). Thus, in psychological practice in correctional settings, whenever program proposals are developed to deal with problems of confined persons, the issue of disciplinary gain must be raised and examined. The unexamined and unthinking belief that more and better psychologists will provide solutions to the problems of prisons and criminals *is* suspect. Resolution of the issue must lie in careful examination of available data and in deliberate and careful efforts to transcend disciplinary tunnel vision and look at the application of psychology to justice agencies. "When a man learns to *see*, not a single thing he knows prevails. Not a single one," don Juan has said (Castaneda, 1971, p. 194). And when psychologists see the broad context of psychology-justice activities, much disciplinary constriction of knowledge may disappear.

Class Action Suits

A new role for psychologists in corrections has emerged from class action suits. Many of these suits claim that prison living conditions are harmful to the mental well-being of inmates. Still other suits seek to establish rights of confined persons to specific numbers of mental health professionals and treatment programs. Psychologists' roles in these suits are as consultants, inspectors, and implementation agents.

Psychologists act as consultants to the civil rights lawyers planning the suit or to the state's attorneys for the defense, sharing existing knowledge, research, and standards related to the prison conditions and the complaints in the suits. As inspectors and witnesses, psychologists inspect the prisons, examine records, interview prisoners and staff, prepare reports, and then testify in court about the results of these inspections.

In one case in the Alabama prison system, psychologists assumed an implementation role at the request of the federal court. In this implementation of a court order identifying 11 constitutional rights of inmates, a university psychology department assessed and classified 3,191 prisoners according to their needs for community placement, psychological and medical treatment, custody, education, and vocational training. The state had been ordered to meet these inmates' needs once they were identified.[6]

In class action suits, psychologists work with attorneys representing either all inmates or the state. The assigned task and legal responsibility in inspection and testimony are to present impartial expert assessments of the situation. Similarly, when experts testify about the state of knowledge in general, without inspections, their responsibility is to attend to the truth and not necessarily to support or criticize particular positions. Nevertheless, support and criticize they do.

The activist functions of partisan testimony and consultation provide one reply to the accusation that psychologists are unwitting (or witting) tools of an oppressive correctional establishment and an intolerant society. For instance, psychologists who are opposed to the very existence of prisons may see their roles as Moses-like, crying "Let my people go!" They sometimes enter into cases with deep emotional investments in the outcomes, much like the Camus protagonist in *The Fall*, who said,

> It was enough for me to sniff the slightest scent of victim on a defendant for me to swing into action. A real tornado? My heart was on my sleeve. You would really have thought that justice slept with me every night. I am sure you would have admired the rightness of my tone, the appropriateness of my emotion, the persuasion and warmth, the restrained indignation of my speeches before the court . . . after all, I was on the right side; that was enough to satisfy my conscience. The feeling of the law, the satisfaction of being right, the joy of self-esteem, *cher monsieur*, are powerful incentives for keeping us upright or keeping us moving forward. (Camus, 1956, pp. 17–18)

If psychologists making expert judgments for the prisoner-plaintiffs may often exhibit scholarly righteousness, psychologists testifying for the defense often present professional justifications for the status quo. A mirror-image phenomenon appears, with each set of psychologists differing from the other and even doubting the ethical stance of the other. The current state of knowledge and research does yield a resolution of these differential perceptions. If outside parties judge the literature to be substantially in agreement with one view, then the psychologists presenting the other view are guilty of deceit, incompetence, or submerging professional responsibilities on behalf of partisan beliefs. One interpretation of the long series of decisions on prison mental health favoring the prisoner-plaintiffs is that the court—an objective outside party—found the more substantive base in the testimony of the plaintiffs' psychologists. A more compelling interpretation is that the constitutional rights of prisoners are being affirmed and that psychological issues are being swept along with the zeitgeist.

Preselection of psychologists by attorneys accounts for many differences of psychological opinion in courts. Attorneys seek to win and therefore select only psychologists whose opinions are in close agreement with their own

---

[6] James v. Wallace, 406 F. Supp. 318 (M. D. Alabama, 1976).

positions. The close consonance of psychologists' judgments with the contentions of the plaintiffs or of the defense may simply indicate how well the attorneys have succeeded at their selection tasks.

My observation of psychologists in class action suits suggests that preselection does indeed operate. The reasons particular psychologists are chosen include a combination of exceptional knowledge and expertise, good witness-stand demeanor, willingness to be involved, and strong personal beliefs (that may become stronger during the suit). A minimum ethical guideline for such psychologists is that they should explicitly attempt to sort their personal belief systems from their professional and scholarly expertise. The results of this sorting should be clear in the minds of the experts and should be made readily available to all concerned persons. This confession of beliefs is not a noxious event but rather a positive affirmation of an ability to discriminate bias from knowledge, a confession that "allows [one] to begin again lighter in heart and to taste a double enjoyment, first of [one's] nature and secondly of a charming repentance" (Camus, 1956, p. 142). What has been called "the infection of our own opinions" (Bierce, 1911) must be subjected to just such an antiseptic cleansing if psychologists are to be ethical and credible participants in prison class action suits.

A Due Process Model

A major objection to increased monitoring and enforcement of stringent ethical obligations for psychologists in corrections is that such procedures destroy the effectiveness of all mental health professionals. While it may be difficult to provide quality mental health services in correctional settings in any case, the increased safeguards and exaggerated concerns for the rights of the patient-prisoner are seen by some psychologists as making psychotherapeutic and diagnostic activities impossible and impractical.

These fears are not limited to psychological work in prison settings. The same issues apply to mental health practice in psychiatric hospitals, community mental health centers, forensic clinics, and institutions for the retarded. A skinned-knee sensitivity on the part of many mental health professionals is a reaction to being identified by civil rights lawyers as villains seeking to impose arbitrary and uncertain treatment procedures on ill-informed, unwilling, or deceived clients. Stone (1977) has been a forceful advocate of reassessing these impositions of ethical and legal standards:

> Many of the legal constraints, in my view, are based on the assumption that psychiatrists, like policemen, prosecutors, and correction officers, can and must be restrained because of the potential for abuse of their authority. Legal restraint is produced by imposing various due process safeguards on all psychiatric decision-making that the court decides infringes on the constitutional rights of the patient. (p. 273)

Stone's perspective is that these legal restraints are based on false and misconceived assumptions, that they negatively affect the delivery of mental health services, and that the psychiatrist or psychologist is forced to fill the role of prosecutorial adversary. He holds that the notion of least restrictive alternative is an anachronism and that giving a *Miranda*-type warning for clients is antithetical to dealing constructively with crisis situations. He continues this sequence of ideas:

> If one assumes that every crime is a political act and that all mental illness is an expression of political dissidence, due process safeguards seem crucial because every legal decision becomes political. The radical social science of the 1960's made just that assumption, and that has been the "radical premise" of much of the mental health litigation of the past decade . . . The legal system that adopts the radical premise and erects due process safeguards in line with that premise, will collapse of its own weight or function in the same distorted and counter-productive fashion as does the criminal justice system. (Stone, 1977, p. 274)

The alternative to implementing due process safeguards is to depend on self-policing and existing professional ethical standards. At issue are whether these standards are sufficiently comprehensive and reasonably enforced. The prior discussions of treatment and research ethics in this chapter seem to offer reasonable doubts on both counts. Several additional guidelines, ethical principles, and sets of clients' rights have been offered (Ayllon, 1975; Kittrie, 1971; Lourens, 1973–1974). The fact that state ethics committees in psychology and psychiatry and the APA Board of Ethical and Social Responsibility so rarely consider prison cases or address these issues is a sign of either immaculate practice or ineffective enforcement. The latter interpretation appears to be more valid. Such self-enforcement of standards has been criticized:

> Professional self-policing has not only failed to prevent violation and abuses in treatment, it has also failed to provide after-the-fact disapproval when those ethical issues have been recognized as violated. (Aynes, 1975, p. 458)

One must assume, then, that in any correctional setting, the potential for an adversary or advocacy relationship with prisoners is always present. Indeed, if it is not seen by the psychologist delivering the service, conducting the research, or consulting to the administrators, surely it may be visible to a person whose field of vision has been attuned to just those issues in the professional spectrum. To increase professional awareness of and sensitivity to this potential ethical dilemma, it may be useful to consider a due process model. Such a model views imprisonment as a direct extrapolation of prior legal processes based on the constitutional right to due process. A due process model in mental health services and activities would seek to afford clients in corrections the same kinds of protection that due process affords in the courts. Seven components would be involved in such a model.

1. *Assumption of the prisoner's nondangerousness unless proven otherwise.* It has been demonstrated that mental health professionals overpredict dangerousness (Megargee, 1976; Monahan, 1976). No studies to my knowledge have shown that predictions of individuals as dangerous are as accurate as predictions of nondangerousness for everyone.

2. *Assumption of the prisoner's psychological normality unless there is compelling evidence to the contrary.* The incidence of psychological disorder has been reported as ranging from 1% to 60% in different countries (Dohrenwend & Dohrenwend, 1965) and from 15% to 85% in different prison settings (Brodsky, 1973; Brodsky & Buchanan, 1971). Given the potential harm of being known as *both* criminal and disordered, a posture of special diagnostic caution is required.

3. *Opportunity to confront psychological information and accusers.* Clients must give informed consent to stay in as well as to enter relationships with psychologists, and such decisions require knowledge of the accumulating psychological information. In addition, when prisoner clients are assessed by psychologists for third parties, such as a parole board or other administrative body, the clients should be informed in nontechnical language of the psychologist's findings.

4. *Appellate review.* Assessment, treatment, and research decisions should routinely be reviewed by professional and citizen committees as a protection against problems of values-contamination, client rights, and professional incompetence.

5. *Explicit written procedures.* Explicit written procedures in understandable, lay language should be available to all clients before they give informed consent.

6. *Right to refuse treatment.* Just as full informed consent must be insured in a prisoner's decision to enter a treatment, assessment, or research relationship, so must it be obtained for a refusal decision as well. Clients should be supplied with relevant information and be given access to ex-therapy clients with positive as well as negative views of therapy, to videotaped sessions, and to summary data.

7. *Right to remain silent*. Assessment clients should be informed that they have the right to remain silent, have the right not to participate in the procedure, and have the right to have a lawyer present. Participation in psychological activities has obvious as well as nonobvious risks for the participant. That is, the very act of being assessed or of becoming a client in psychotherapy may be known to decision-making bodies or to correctional officers or classification officers, and their attitudes and judgments may be affected. In a prison with many programs in which staff are highly involved, the absence of program participation on a prisoner's record may be extrapolated to suggest negative attitudes or behaviors and thus lower potential for release. Therefore, there is a necessity to communicate to prison staff the clients' rights to be silent and to refuse treatment.

Conclusion

A friend of mine was completing an interview during which she and the interviewer had agreed that her background did not fit well with the job opening. The interviewer closed his comments with the wish, "I hope you can find a position worthy of you," to which she replied, "Oh, I intend to do much better than that."

Emerging legal doctrines of the rights of inmates in treatment and in human experimentation are not the bottom line but rather the top line, the minimum standards for the practice of psychology in correctional settings. Gerald Johnson has been credited with the remark that "to equate ethics with legality was to adopt the morals of a scoundrel," (Foster, 1975, p. 55). I have observed that psychologists who work in correctional settings are highly variable in terms of their backgrounds, theoretical postures, and actual work activities. Nevertheless, as a group, they are dedicated, aware of their multiple loyalties and roles, and often ethical to a fault. The APA Task Force Survey on the Role of Psychologists in the Criminal Justice System (see Chapter 6) indicates a high degree of sensitivity to ethical issues among psychologists who work in correctional settings. It appears that psychologists not only should find ethical positions worthy of them but indeed that many are, and all should be, doing much better than that.

Julian Rappaport, James T. Lamiell, and Edward Seidman

5
Ethical Issues for Psychologists in the Juvenile Justice System: Know and Tell

The underlying ethical issues that psychologists in the juvenile justice system face are not substantially different from those faced by psychologists in general. Nevertheless, because of its unique place in society, this system provides a context in which ethical dilemmas are highlighted for both participants and observers. Although especially problematic situations arise for psychologists in juvenile justice, these form part of a larger picture of which psychologists are often unaware. Much of what we discuss in this chapter can be placed in the context of other social systems in which psychologists work. Much of it also applies to social scientists more generally. Indeed, we sometimes use the terms *psychologist* and *social scientist* interchangeably.

As any attentive undergraduate who has taken the introductory course knows, psychology deals with the description, causation, prediction, and control of behavior. These have been the concerns of psychologists in criminal justice as well. However, the use of psychological knowledge for intervening in the lives of others constitutes an imposition of one person's or group's values onto some other person or group. Insofar as this process necessarily involves limitation of individual freedoms, it is

ipso facto ethically problematic (Kelman, 1968).

It is undeniably true that the maintenance of an orderly society requires curtailment of some individual freedoms. Even if one grants the legitimacy of this premise in the abstract, questions still remain as to *which* freedoms should be curtailed and *how*. The ethically problematic becomes the ethically pernicious when we lose sight of the fact that answers to these questions are based on values and premises that precede scientific inquiry. That is, as we shall argue in this chapter, not only the use but the very generation of our knowledge depends upon those values and premises.

This chapter is an attempt to clarify and confront the conceptions, values, and ethical dilemmas that have constrained psychologists' contributions to juvenile justice. Our hope is that by so doing, we may sensitize the reader to the fact that psychologists' work has thus far proceeded along but a fraction of the possible paths open to it and that endorsement of alternative values and ideas—social, political, and scientific—may lead to genuinely new conceptualizations of psychologists' roles vis-à-vis the "delinquency problem."

We begin our discussion with a brief consideration of the historical context out of which the functions of psychologists in juvenile justice have emerged. This is followed by a discussion of the nature of psychologists' empirical work

Preparation of this chapter was facilitated by Research Grant MH 22336-4 from the National Institute of Mental Health.

in assessment and treatment and of its ethical ramifications. Finally, we discuss the value constraints under which psychologists have operated and attempt to show how the reconceptualization of certain fundamental issues could change the face of juvenile justice psychology.

Historical Context

As is well known, the entire juvenile justice apparatus was developed as an attempt to "divert" the youthful offender from adult courts and prisons. More than anything else, the juvenile justice system has been defined in terms of its mission to prevent the development of criminal careers. As an integral component of this mission, juvenile justice practitioners have viewed as appropriate, if not necessary, a focus on the individual offender rather than on the offense (Ariessohn, 1972).

For many years it was assumed that a juvenile court would be both more humane in punishment and more effective in treatment than the adult court. Allowing juveniles to be processed by the adult system was viewed as unjust because that system itself was viewed as unjust. Unfortunately, the creation of a parallel system for youth, rather than an improved one for all, did not solve the problems it was designed to address. Instead, it created a whole different set of problems. For some of the same reasons that stimulated creation of the juvenile justice system in the first place, one hears calls today for diversion of youths from the juvenile justice system; these are, ironically, calls for "diversion from diversion" (Mullen, 1974; O'Brien & Marcus, 1976). If it is true that attention to history can prevent us from repeating the mistakes of the past, then the current call for diversion of children from the juvenile justice system may serve as a good illustration that "new" structures are not necessarily better ones. And the irony should not be lost on us as we consider the "new" diversion programs and Youth Service Bureaus that are now justified as "mental health" programs and that therefore provide dollars and employment for social service personnel but typically demonstrate little evidence of crime prevention or rehabilitation (cf. Lemert, 1974; U.S. Department of Health, Education, and Welfare, 1973; Davidson, Note 1). Such programs are classic examples of "change" that is change in name only, and the results are predictable from our past.

Given (a) the concern with nipping blooming criminal careers "in the bud," (b) the presumed desirability of focusing on the individual offender, and (c) Americans' generalized penchant for efficiency-via-rationality (i.e., science), it is not surprising that the juvenile justice system has turned to psychologists to provide many of its answers. Psychology has long proclaimed its status as a scientific discipline. Moreover, psychology has traditionally concerned itself with the description, explanation, prediction, and control of *individual* behavior. Finally, the practical needs of psychologists (e.g., subjects to treat and research, funds to support those activities, publication outlets) increased the likelihood not only that juvenile justice would turn to psychologists but also that psychologists would gleefully "roll up their sleeves" and get busy.

But what we have "gotten busy" at is a collection of tasks firmly embedded in the ideology that delinquency is an entity that exists "out there " and is therefore amenable to description, explanation, prediction, and control in the traditional scientific sense, without reference to the describers, explainers, predictors, and controllers. To be sure, the "names and faces" of those tasks have changed somewhat over the years. Dominated early by a concern with the personality characteristics of youthful offenders, the focus has shifted somewhat in recent years to a concern with socio-environmental factors. It should be emphasized, however, that at the present time, vestiges of both approaches remain both in research and in practice (Schur, 1973).

Out of this ideology, psychologists have contributed useless "diagnoses," behavioral predictions with high error rates, naive theories of prevention and rehabilitation, and ineffective treatments. Even so-called "diversion programs" may simply be bringing more children into the legal (or the quasi-legal mental health) system rather than removing those who would previously have been processed (cf. Fo & O'Donnell, 1975; Rappaport, Seidman, & Davidson, 1979; Rutherford & McDermott, 1976). All of these activities are applied with our explicit or implicit sanction because it is argued that "someone has to take responsibility" (cf. Megargee, 1976). We rarely consider alternative ways to be responsible, and that is what this chapter is about. It is not about delinquency and crime prevention per se, or prevention and rehabilitation, or punishment, or even about the juvenile justice system, so much as it is about the behavior of psychologists in these contexts. It is about our need to be honest about our values and our competence and to search for new paradigms. It is about our need to know (be informed) and tell (be honest).

Current Roles and Functions

To set the stage for consideration of ethical issues, we first need to review the general outlines of the system in which special considerations of youth and the law take place. It may be helpful, however, as we move through this description of formal roles and functions, to keep in the wings of one's consciousness three questions not often raised by psychologists but which we view as tremendously influential in determining the *latent* roles and functions of those in our profession. Ultimately, it is these latent roles and functions that pose the most

serious moral and ethical dilemmas. It is always the case that what we do today, within the commonsense understandings and assumptions of our time and place, clouds ethical issues that will later become apparent from historical hindsight. The problem for the practice of ethics is to bring these issues to awareness today:

1. *Can psychologists recognize that work in (and out of) the justice system always requires us to take value stands?* We need to know what the values that influence our decisions are, and we need to be honest about them.

2. *Can we reject entrenched paradigms and learn to heighten our moral sensibilities by saying "no"?* We must know the limits on our competence, and we must be willing to tell the public what those limits are.

3. *Are there alternatives to entrenched paradigms? Can we restate the problems, or are we forced to accept them as presented to us?* When the values and the methods we have traditionally applied are known to fail, we need to be able to free ourselves to rethink the problems with which we are dealing.

These questions and issues lie just below the surface of our discussion, and we shall return to each of them in our concluding statements.

The juvenile justice system cuts across all of the settings the adult system touches. Psychologists who enter this system may do so through law enforcement, court, or corrections agencies. They perform the same roles and functions that they do in the adult system, and more. It is therefore essential that all the issues raised in the earlier chapters devoted to these three settings not be ignored when considering juveniles.

A useful description of the criminal justice system as it relates to the mental health system has been provided by Shah (1972). He points out that criminal laws require strict and precise definition and are expected to be applied uniformly and with specified penal sanctions. Sometimes, however, and this is particularly the case with juveniles, the system is expected to be more than an agent of social control and sanction. It may be expected to predict who is dangerous, to predict who will be "delinquent in the future" (the assessment function), and to reform offenders (the treatment function). When this is the case, laws are less likely to be applied uniformly in response to an alleged violation (Monahan, 1973). This is one place where ethical questions abound, and this is also one place where psychologists are likely to appear. *Psychologists' presence is not usually justified for the purposes of social control and sanction but rather for prediction and treatment.*

In each of the three major administrative settings of the criminal justice system—law enforcement, courts, and corrections—a great deal of individual *discretion* is permitted in carrying out official duties. In the enforcement of law, police have discretion with regard to arrests, warnings, and referrals to some other (e.g., mental health) system. In the courts, lawyers, prosecutors, and judges have discretionary powers to bargain for reduced charges, to set bail at various levels, and to delay trials. If a person is found guilty, the judge usually has the power to institutionalize that person, suspend the sentence, or provide some form of probation, depending on available community programs and resources. Especially for juveniles, these decisions often involve some form of mental-health-related treatment. The apparent assumption is, "We want to get at the cause, not at the symptom." In the juvenile justice system, a common practice, regardless of the letter of the law, is to bypass formal determination of guilt and to impose judicial sanctions in the form of "treatments." Here again is where psychologists are likely to appear.

In corrections, after the convicted person serves some period of time in jail, parole may be granted at the discretion of officials. Generally, a decision is made on the basis of the judged likelihood that a person is "reformed." Again, a psychologist is likely to appear. In prisons or training schools (the euphemistic name for youth prisons), wide informal discretion is held by guards and wardens with regard to the ways in which they deal with their charges. Psychologists again can be influential.

It is at these discretionary points that a great deal of *decision-making power* is located. It is at these points that psychologists are often called upon to aid in the decision-making process. The psychologist who provides research or service at any one of the discretionary or decision-making points will do different things depending on how he or she conceptualizes the problems of concern. One useful way to view the various options in each setting is in terms of the "unit of analysis" or "level of intervention" in each setting. While research and practice are inextricably intertwined, the term *unit of analysis* is most applicable when discussing the research enterprise, and *level of intervention* when referring to service delivery or practice. As used here, both constructs refer to a focus on *individuals, organizations*, or *institutions*. Each of the settings of the criminal justice system—law enforcement, courts, corrections agencies—may be viewed at each of these units of analysis or levels of intervention. Different units of analysis or levels of intervention are employed by psychologists depending on their relationships to (or places in) the juvenile justice system and on their conceptualization of "the problem of delinquency." An understanding of the problem of delinquency only in terms of individual children will lead to different activities than will a view of the same problem as a function of organizational structures that impinge on individuals. Likewise, somewhat different activities will follow if one views the problems of individuals as a function of basic social institutions. What we are referring to here as social institutions are largely conceptual in nature—the ways in which delinquency is conceptualized, one's values and beliefs about deviance, and so on.

In deciding on a proper unit of analysis or level of intervention—individual, organizational, or institutional—unverbalized value constraints imposed by society, officialdom, and the limits of current scientific paradigms have a powerful and not always obvious effect. They combine to influence the way we see the problems we select to work on. Regardless of the setting, these constraints have insured that the most common unit of analysis or level of intervention for psychologists is the individual; and given our traditions, the most common research and practice roles have therefore been individual assessment (prediction) and individual treatment. Although organizational and institutional analysis is possible, it requires a reconceptualization of the problem of delinquency. There are a number of reasons why such reconceptualization is difficult for psychologists, some of which we will discuss later in the section titled Constraints on Our Thinking and Doing. Before discussing these constraints, however, let us review the current state of the art in psychologists' more traditional roles and functions—individual assessment and treatment—and the ethical dilemmas they raise.

The State of the Art and Ethical Dilemmas

The daily newspaper often provides clues to understanding contemporary enlightened views. Item: Dateline Chicago. The Great Mail Robbery. Mail thieves are apparently enjoying success in repeatedly opening the same letter boxes. It seems they have stolen the keys. Residents ask the post office to change the locks, but in a classic parody of social science reasoning, the postal inspector insists, "We don't want to be in the position of treating the symptom and ignoring the cause. Our first effort is to recover any keys that have been stolen" (Olmstead, 1977).[1]

Similar reasoning has been known to appear in the criminal justice system and even to pre-

---

[1] We extend thanks to Ronald Roesch for bringing this item to our attention.

dominate in the so-called juvenile justice system. It seems that the officials who operate the system are also good social scientists. They don't want to be in the position of treating the symptom and ignoring the cause. That is one reason why psychological services have been invited or welcomed. Modern, "enlightened" opinion in this century requires our presence. Moreover, the same enlightened opinion has also led us (a) to provide a specific set of services that accept "the problem of delinquency" as defined by the juvenile court, and (b) to perform the functions with which we have historically been associated—assessment (prediction) and treatment. These functions most often require that we reify negative individual characteristics of the children and prescribe ways to treat, change, or otherwise "fix" them. We sometimes attempt, in doing these things, to convince ourselves that we are changing the juvenile justice system and/or helping the child. There is little evidence for either conclusion. What we do instead is give social-science respectability to social control. This has been psychology's modal response, and it is viewed as desirable or undesirable depending more on one's politics than on one's science. We may justify our activities as legitimate state functions, but that does not necessarily justify them by social science criteria. Indeed, on the basis of acceptable social science criteria, there is little reason to believe that we are effective.

Before summarizing the state of the art in assessment and treatment research and practice, together with the ethical dilemmas raised, we ask the reader to consider the following, from the American Psychological Association's *Ethical Standards of Psychologists* (1979):

Principle 2. Competence
The maintenance of high standards of professional competence is a responsibility shared by all psychologists in the interest of the public and the profession as a whole. *Psychologists recognize the boundaries of their competence and the limitations of their techniques* and only provide services, use tech-

niques, or offer opinions as professionals that meet recognized standards. Psychologists maintain knowledge of current scientific and professional information related to the services they render. (p. 2, italics added)

Section C of this principle, as spelled out in the *Ethical Standards*, goes on to state that "Psychologists recognize the need for continuing education and are open to new procedures and changes in expectations and values over time" (p. 2).

We suggest that it is a matter of ethical responsibility for the psychologists to take seriously the spirit as well as the letter of such principles. This requires that we "know" (are informed about) the limits of our competence and that we "tell" (are honest) in "selling" our services to the public. It also requires that we be open to new ways of doing and of viewing what we do.

Assessment/Research

Many in our society—laypersons as well as social scientists—believe that, in the long run, the most efficacious means of controlling delinquency is to prevent it from occuring. Thus, the President's Commission on Law Enforcement and Administration of Justice (cited in Silver, 1968) noted that,

> In the last analysis, the most promising and so the most important method of dealing with crime is by preventing it—by ameliorating the conditions of life that drive people to commit crimes and that undermine the restraining rules and institutions erected by society against antisocial conduct. . . . Clearly it is with young people that prevention efforts are most needed and hold the greatest promise. It is simply more critical that young people be kept from crime, for they are the Nation's future. (pp. 175–175)

If we accept for the moment the assumption (and it *is* an assumption) that identifying delinquents before the fact is desirable, certain questions with important ethical ramifications are raised: On what basis shall certain adolescents be designated as those for whom intervention is indicated? How shall whatever liberties juveniles have (cf. Platt, 1969) be protected against the whims of the interveners?

It is at this point that the assessment/research role of psychologists vis-à-vis the juvenile justice system becomes salient. The best protection against subjectivity or capriciousness is objective scientific information, a product psychologists have long purported to market. As a current research-methods textbook states,

> When a (lay) person's sources of information—parents, friends, religion, teachers, and the mass media—are all in agreement, his or her ideas may be limited to a nonconscious ideology. . . . Science, by *taking as problematic* nonconscious ideologies, can go beyond their parochial culture bounds. To do scientific research, one might say, is to challenge accepted beliefs by submitting them to scrutiny through the use of demanding standards. (Selltiz, Wrightsman, & Cook, 1976, pp. 4–5)

With specific reference to delinquency prediction, then, the objectivity of psychological research could presumably serve as the needed prophylaxis against the capricious or simply erroneous selection of certain juveniles as intervention targets.

Ideally, it may be supposed, delinquency research would proceed from manipulation of certain variables thought to be associated with delinquency to observation of the effects of those manipulations on the actual occurrence of delinquent behavior. However, for obvious ethical reasons, research of this sort is not conducted (although one can find an occasional experimental analogue of law breaking—cf. Heisler, 1974). Consequently, psychological research on delinquency has been essentially correlational in nature. While correlational research has its characteristic problems, the difficulties in this case go much deeper and in any event would remain even if the research were experimental.

The ethics of proposing/initiating intervention programs on the basis of correlational findings are worth keeping in the back of one's mind, however.

Given the ethical hazards of submitting juveniles to various conditions and then monitoring the incidence of delinquent behavior, psychologists have opted for the next most straightforward approach to identifying the psychological components of delinquency. They have identified groups of people who are, respectively, delinquent and nondelinquent and then "worked backwards" in an attempt to isolate variables that discriminate those groups. Where such discriminators have been found, they have been suggested as useful bases for predicting and preventing delinquency. This process would entail (a) identifying juveniles with scores on particular variables falling within the range of scores obtained by known delinquents, and (b) availing those juveniles of treatment programs designed to shift their scores to a more desirable location (i.e., one within the range of scores found among nondelinquents).

This general paradigm, which conforms quite closely to what is known in personality assessment circles as the "contrasted groups" methodology (Wiggins, 1973), is the sine qua non of psychological research into factors associated with delinquency. Of 20 studies bearing on the identification of delinquency correlates and published between 1967 and 1977 in the *Journal of Abnormal Psychology* and the *Journal of Consulting and Clinical Psychology* alone, every one employed this strategy.

Of course, the specific variables investigated have differed somewhat. Some authors have focused on personal characteristics/attributes, including personality traits and demographic and socioeconomic factors (Bixenstine & Buterbaugh, 1967; Cantor, 1976; DeMyer-Gapin, & Scott, 1977; Kantor, Walker, & Hays, 1976; Kirkegaard-Sorensen & Mednick, 1975; Newman & Pollack, 1973; Smart & Jones, 1970; Stein, Sarbin, & Kulik, 1971).

Others have focused on cognitive factors such as verbal mediation (Camp, 1977), ego development (Frank & Quinlan, 1976), problem-solving ability (Levenson & Neuringer, 1971), discrimination-learning ability (Schlichter & Ratliff, 1971), and future time perspective (Stein, Sarbin, & Kulik, 1968). Still others have studied some combination of the above (Alexander, 1973; Ganzer & Sarason, 1973; Hetherington, Stouwie, & Ridberg, 1971; Jurkovic & Prentice, 1974; Kulik, Stein, & Sarbin, 1968; Roberts, Erikson, Riddle, & Bacon, 1974; Smith & Lanyon, 1968).

All of these studies involved a comparison of scores obtained by a group labeled "delinquent" with scores obtained by a group labeled "nondelinquent." Moreover, in nearly all of the published articles, some reference was made to the implications of the findings for predicting/preventing delinquency. Some specific examples of this thinking are provided below:

> Training in use of self-guiding verbalizations appears to be effective in improving the cognitive performance of impulsive and/or hyperactive children . . . and in achieving control over phobic and text-anxious behavior. . . . It remains to be seen whether a similar relation between self-verbalizations and control of aggressive behavior can be demonstrated. (Camp, 1977, p. 152)

> The authors would like to underscore two conclusions. The first is that a self-report checklist of antisocial behavior has demonstrable utility for establishing types of persons. The second is that it is possible to differentiate among the artificially homogenized members of that class of persons vaguely called "delinquents." These conclusions are saturated with implications for future research, among them the relative ease of acquiring information so that differentiations can be made early for treatment and prevention programs. (Kulik, Stein, & Sarbin, 1968, p. 382)

> Perhaps it can be hoped that children who are identified early as being at high risk for the development of sociopathic patterns in later life may, with proper management during formative years, be effectively socialized by being taught to satisfy their needs for stimula-

tion in ways that are socially acceptable. (Whitehill, DeMyer-Gapin, & Scott, 1976, p. 104).

The essence of these passages is quite simple: The authors are maintaining that certain factors have been isolated that by virtue of their correlation with a measure of delinquency, may be useful as bases for predicting, preventing, and thus controlling delinquency before the fact (or at least that future research along the same lines will permit the realization of this goal).

In considering the ethical ramifications of this work, it is necessary to keep firmly in mind its implicit or explicit promise: to facilitate the prevention of delinquency before the fact (assumed to be a justifiable endeavor in the first place) while *simultaneously* eliminating (or at least minimizing) the capriciousness to which such an enterprise would be subject if it were not done "scientifically." The question, then, is, To what extent can we "deliver" on this two-pronged promise?

The level of discrimination actually achieved in our research is typically quite small. While statistically significant differences between "delinquents" and "nondelinquents" on various and sundry dimensions may indeed be obtained, it is not at all clear that the *magnitude* of those differences is such that the predictors could safely be employed in actual practice.

In the absence of prediction schemes that *perfectly* discriminate "delinquents" and "nondelinquents" (and no such scheme has even been approximated to date), the danger of identifying "false positives" is ever present. That is, the actual employment of a less-than-perfect discriminator would result in the indentification of some intervention targets who in fact—if left alone—would never become delinquent.

The general issue involved here has been discussed by several authors with reference to the prediction of dangerousness or violence (Livermore, Malmquist, & Meehl, 1968; Megargee, 1976; Monahan, 1976; Monahan & Cummings, 1975) but seems equally applicable to the pre-diction of deviance in general—including delinquency. By substituting the terms *delinquency* and *delinquent* for *violence* and *violent* in the quotation below, the issue is crystallized:

> Violence is vastly overpredicted whether simple behavioral indicators are used or sophisticated multivariate analyses are employed, and whether psychological tests are administered or thorough psychiatric examinations are performed. . . . We are left with the central moral issue. . . . How many false positives—how many harmless men and women [and children] are we willing to sacrifice to protect ourselves from one violent individual? (Monahan, 1976, p. 21)

This matter is particularly crucial as it pertains to the prediction of delinquency (Schlesinger, 1978). Because juveniles, in the eyes of the court, have been viewed as possessing diminished rights (Platt, 1969), it is much easier to overlook the sacrifices of innocents resulting from inaccurate predictions.[2]

The contemporary "enlightened" view is that "someone must make these predictions" (cf. Megargee, 1976). The matter is quite debatable, of course, and its resolution depends on whose side one is on. From the *system's* point of view, the errors to be minimized are false negatives, in which case the assertion that "someone must make these predictions" is *obvious*. But from the juveniles' point of view, the errors to be minimized are false positives, in which case the "enlightened" assertion is not only not obvious but patently absurd.

Unfortunately, it appears at the present time that activities that follow naturally from alignment with the system are viewed as scientific,

---

[2] More recently, Monahan (Note 2) has argued that the justice system has shied away from actuarial prediction in juvenile justice because it would make it very clear that the "best" predictors are demographic, rather than psychiatric or psychological, characteristics. To rely on race, sex, and age as predictors would be socially frowned upon as a means for differential disposition; consequently, the psychologist and psychiatrist enter the scene as "middlemen" who provide clinical justification.

while those that follow (equally naturally) from saying "no" to the system are regarded as political. In fact, either decision is political, and it is time psychologists recognize this.

But regardless of where one's politics lie, the simple fact remains that any identification of intervention targets based on currently available scientific findings cannot be regarded as reducing capriciousness to any large degree. At best, such efforts must now be viewed as a substitution of psychologists' capriciousness for practitioners' capriciousness. Such a state of affairs can hardly be regarded as "delivering" on the implicit or explicit promise mentioned earlier.

In view of this, perhaps it is time for us to get out of the prediction, intervention-before-the-fact enterprise altogether. Perhaps, after all, such predictions do *not* have to be made in order to protect society, and indeed, with high error rates they may actually hurt society—*especially if one includes as a part of society those who end up as false positives*. In any event, for those who deem this alternative inadvisable, we regard it as an ethical necessity that continued attempts to predict be explicitly acknowledged as, by all available indicators, empirically bankrupt endeavors.

Apart from the error-of-prediction issue, a second, more subtle matter perhaps deserves more of our attention. This matter concerns the nature of the criterion against which our prediction schemes are "validated" in the first place. The question is, Whose values have been adopted for the purposes of distinguishing the criterion groups—"delinquents" and "nondelinquents"—in our research?

Given the promise of reduced capriciousness through science, this question becomes extremely important. The actual use of our scientifically generated prediction schemes can not possibly be any less capricious than the values involved in defining the criterion against which these schemes were validated. It must be emphasized that this is true *regardless* of the predictive accuracy achieved.

Any distinction between delinquents and nondelinquents relies on a set of norms that are ultimately and irreducibly subjective. Social scientists have recognized this fact for decades (Douglas, 1971), and that recognition is reflected in the contemporary axiom that deviance of any kind must be conceptualized relativistically (see, e.g., Sagarin, 1975). However, while subjectivity cannot be totally eliminated from a distinction between delinquents and nondelinquents, conventional wisdom has it that subjectivity can be *minimized* by employing norms endorsed by wide popular consensus. Thus under these conditions, interventions in the lives of juveniles are justified not on the basis of some "neutral" distinction between delinquents and nondelinquents but on the basis of a non-neutral distinction that has been generally accepted instead of formulated arbitrarily by a select few.

By far the most preferred technique for distinguishing delinquents from nondelinquents in psychological research is reliance on official records. In 16 of the 20 studies cited earlier, delinquents were operationally defined as juveniles who had been labeled by the state as such, and nondelinquents as juveniles who had not been so labeled. Thus, it is *officialdom's* values that underlie the criterion in the vast majority of our empirical studies. And it is by no means clear that all of those values are widely shared.

It is certainly true that for some juveniles (e.g., those guilty of assault, burglary, or rape), the designation of "delinquent" would probably be widely regarded as appropriate. However, for others (e.g., those guilty of running away from home or other "status" offenses), the designation of "delinquent" might be regarded by a substantial proportion of the populace (including psychologists) as inappropriate. For still other juveniles, the appropriateness of designating them delinquent cannot even be determined, because their "offenses" are not meaningfully defined.

For example, a juvenile may become an official delinquent by being labeled as a "person in need of supervision," a designation that could result from such offenses as habitual truancy, incorrigibility, and ungovernability (Kassebaum, 1974). Now, even if it could be shown that wide popular consensus exists regarding the appropriateness of classifying truant, incorrigible, and ungovernable adolescents as delinquent (which is doubtful, cf. Schur, 1973), there is absolutely no reason to assume that all authorities (let alone people in general) define these terms in the same way. Quite to the contrary, juvenile authorities have intentionally been given wide discretionary latitude on such matters (Barton, 1976; Kassebaum, 1974). In effect, these offenses mean whatever those empowered to make decisions say they mean.

To complicate matters further, adolescents who are delinquent by virture of these ill-defined "offenses" are not normally distinguished in our research from those who are delinquent by virtue of more explicit and generally agreed-upon offenses (Kassebaum, 1974). Thus, any sample of delinquents based on official records is very likely to contain a substantial number of persons the appropriateness of whose status as delinquent can by no stretch of the imagination be regarded as "generally agreed upon." Stated otherwise, when our criterion is defined on the basis of official statistics, it is *itself* influenced to some (usually unknown) degree by subjective and sometimes capricious judgments.

Strictly speaking, all that can safely be said about criterion groups identified on the basis of official records is that one group (the delinquents) is composed of individuals whom agents of the state have disapproved of and that the other group (the nondelinquents) is composed of individuals who have not (yet) been so disapproved. In turn, all that can safely be said about a prediction scheme validated on the basis of this distinction is that it is capable, to some (usually low) degree, of *reproducing that distinction.*

There is a large gap indeed between empirical findings that can accomplish this (even if the reproduction were perfect) and the assertion that those findings justify interventions in certain individuals' lives. When we, as psychologists, make such an assertion, *we are functioning as advocates of the decision strategies employed by those individuals who created the official distinctions.* The use of our scientific finding in this way is, in fact, no less capricious than the judgments that created the criterion on which those findings are based.

This is a rather curious state of affairs for a discipline presumably in the business of "challenging nonconscious ideologies," for not only are the ideologies (nonconscious or otherwise) of juvenile justice authorities left unchallenged by our research, they are, for the most part, left undefined. We simply accept the categories of "delinquent" and "nondelinquent" as they are presented to us, and as though they were scientifically meaningful, and proceed from there. In the words of Douglas (1971), we commit "the cardinal sin of science [by] not critically, systematically [investigating] the nature of the information [we are using]" (pp. 46–47).

In light of our discussion up to this point, it is apparent that psychology is in no position to deliver on the implicit or explicit promise of its research. On strictly empirical grounds, we are ill-equipped to reduce capriciousness in the selection of intervention targets because our predictive accuracy is low. But more fundamentally, we have argued that even if predictive accuracy were high, a closer inspection of the criterion we attempt to reproduce reveals that it is *itself* capricious to a large extent. Paradoxically, if we *could* accurately predict this criterion, we would be perpetuating rather than reducing or eliminating capriciousness!

If we are to be consistent with the ethical principle cited at the beginning of this section, then it will be necessary for us to recognize (know) and acknowledge (tell) that our ability to fulfill the predictive function is extremely limited. Moreover, to the extent that we are able to predict, it is imperative that we recognize (know) and acknowledge (tell) exactly what it is we are doing. Let us speak no more of "delinquency" and "delinquents" in our professional writings, as though we all knew and agreed upon the referents for those terms. Rather, let us speak of "acts and people that/whom certain powerful individuals either approve or disapprove of." Let us dispense with titles of the general form "Psychological Characteristics Distinguishing Delinquents from Nondelinquents" and use instead titles such as "Psychological Characteristics Distinguishing Juveniles Approved of and Disapproved of By Certain Powerful Individuals."

Let us make the same substitution at all places in the texts of our articles and books where we have heretofore referred to "delinquents" and "nondelinquents." Such substitutions would surely generate cumbersome prose but by our own "rigorous" scientific standards would be infinitely more appropriate given the operational characteristics of our criterion.

Again, if we are to be consistent with the ethical principle cited earlier, then it is incumbent on us to seek out new paradigms for research on delinquency. One general framework for accomplishing this is discussed later in this chapter. For the present, however, let us consider the state of the art and the ethical ramifications in the area of treatment.

Treatment/Research

The treatment of adjudicated juvenile offenders is markedly unsuccessful. "There is general agreement that over half the persons released from juvenile training facilities will be reincarcerated" (Dean & Reppucci, 1974, p. 874). The same is true for more enlightened forms of treatment, almost all of which are based on an *individual* level of intervention or on an organi-

zational unit of analysis that attempts to create more efficient *individual* socialization.

Davidson and Seidman (1974) surveyed over 60 research reports on the use of behavior modification with problems of juvenile delinquency and concluded that claims of success are largely unsupported. They found that 82% of the studies did not use an equivalent no-treatment control group and that only 18% reported follow-up data on the long-term effects of behavioral treatment. Only 3 of 20 studies in institutional settings collected follow-up data. Positive results achieved by children in treatment programs have not been shown to generalize or to reduce later delinquent behavior. This is true even for the relatively better-known programs with children who are far from "hard-core" by anyone's criteria (cf. Hoefler & Bornstein's [1975] review of Achievement Place). Fo and O'Donnell (1975) even found that applying a behavioral treatment program to youths who had committed no prior "major offenses" actually *increased* their delinquent behavior compared to that of control youths.

Martinson (1974) and Klapmuts (1973) both concluded in reviews that milieu treatments and other forms of institutional care are no more effective than various forms of community treatment. While this has been used, quite reasonably, as an argument for community treatment (because it is a least restrictive alternative), it is clearly an argument by default. In fact, *no* treatments have proven effective for "delinquents" in general.

It may be that the following question posed in psychotherapy is a good way to ask about treatment outcomes in the criminal justice system as well: "What treatment is effective for what persons, under what circumstances?" The overriding answer today must be that most treatment programs now operating are effective for only a limited class of youth and under very limited circumstances. Although a number of individual programs for juvenile offenders (generally aimed at reduced likelihood of recidivism) report their own success (e.g., Baron & Feeney, 1976; Baron, Feeney & Thornton 1973; Davidson, Rappaport, Seidman, Berck, Rapp, Rhodes, & Herring, 1977; Goldenberg, 1971; Klein, Alexander, & Parsons, 1977; Palmer, 1971, 1974; Seidman, Rappaport, & Davidson, 1976), recent comprehensive national reviews of juvenile justice programs more generally are quite uniformly negative in their evaluations of outcomes (see, e.g., Lemert, 1974; Rutherford & McDermott, 1976; Scari & Hassenfeld, 1976; Vinter, 1976). Indeed, the most consistent conclusions are that programs for juveniles are unsuccessful, including those that emphasize diversion, and that diversion programs are probably dealing with children who would actually be released if it were not for the program, while those who would enter the system continue to do so (see, e.g., Klein & Teilman, 1976). As Vinter (1976) has put it, in such programs, diverse human beings are arbitrarily and nonrationally distributed; administrators think that their programs "work," and they are not skeptical. However, despite what program administrators believe, great disparities exist between the program realities and the program aims. Indeed, the staff and the children often agree with the evaluators' conclusions rather than with the program administrators'.

Many of the reviews cited above are national studies. Such studies tend to tell us what is normative or what the average program one would expect to find in a given jurisdiction might create. While this gives us a realistic description of things as they are, it does not tell us how things can be. For that purpose, one must take a closer look at the "best" programs, or those with the best reported results, and at those in which the details reported are adequate to allow us to know exactly what was done. We must recognize, of course, that such a closer look will produce a very biased set of data, collected under conditions of experimental attention and enthusiasm, with all of the ad-

vantages that this brings in the short-run evaluation. Such studies represent a very small sample of the programs actually conducted and share a number of characteristics that limit their generalizability to other jurisdictions. Nor do they necessarily have implications for the operation of such programs over a long period of time, after their "experimental" nature has been depleted (cf. Rappaport, Seidman & Davidson, 1979).

Close examination of some of even the "best" programs does not clearly reveal that they necessarily accomplished what the orignal reports say they did. The work of the California Youth Authority (Palmer, 1971, 1974), for examṕle, may be interpreted as at best doing no worse than sending children to corrections institutions (Klapmuts, 1973). The outcome data reported may be seriously biased by the way the study was conducted (Robison & Takagi, Note 3), and some of the differences reported between experimental and control youths appear to be a function of methodologically inappropriate comparisons (Rappaport, 1977a).

The major characteristics shared by the relatively successful programs[3] listed above (Baron & Feeney, 1976; Goldenberg, 1971; Klein et al., 1977; Seidman et al., 1976) are (a) a carefully designed research plan (which includes all the close monitoring, postive excitement, and expectations that are so difficult to maintain when the program becomes routine), and (b) an emphasis on work with significant others in the child's life (especially in the family and the school, and sometimes in the work setting) rather than with the individual child. These programs have tended to be concerned with mobilization of resources for the children in their natural environment as well as with avoiding involvement in the criminal justice system per se

---

[3] *Successful*, as used here, refers to programs that (a) employed a research design that satisfied generally acceptable standards, and (b) included follow-up data contrasting experimental and control children.

and avoiding labeling the child with a mental health diagnosis or as a criminal.

It would be mistaken to conclude that any of this handful of programs are likely to "solve the problem of delinquency." Rather, each represents an alternative to the more common methods of treatment found to fail in the national evaluations. Each program demonstrated some utility with particular kinds of children and under a particular set of circumstances. While this is not the place to detail the "fine-tuning" of such programs, it is important to emphasize that given the diversity of so-called "delinquents" it is a mistake to place "all our chips" on any one program of treatment or any single method of prevention. As Mullen (1974) has pointed out, family counseling (emphasized in each of these programs) may not be the treatment of choice for everyone, and we need to recall that the category of "delinquent" may have no meaning in terms of what a particular situation or a particular child requires. What we might reasonably conclude is that it is possible to provide some useful services for some children in difficulty and that there may be various ways to do this without involving children in the criminal justice apparatus.

On the other hand, we must not forget that we are discussing a handful of evaluated and successful programs in the context of national evaluations and large-scale reviews that have shown most programs to produce negative outcomes. Also, it is somewhat striking that when outsiders evaluate programs, the results seem to turn out much worse than when the evaluators are also the program developers. Whether this is a result of positive "bias" on the part of the committed researcher, or a "real" effect of careful evaluation and enthusiasm, or an effect of the program specifics per se is not certain, but in any case, the general conclusion that most treatment programs for adjudicated juveniles are unsuccessful while only a handful of those for nonadjudicated youth are successful seems correct. This should not be particularly

surprising to anyone familiar with psychological treatment research more generally, particularly since juveniles are not often demographically like the population for whom our psychological treatments are most successful.

Despite the overwhelming failure of most individual psychological treatments to accomplish their aims with so-called "delinquents," as a profession we continue, both in assessment and treatment, to view the problems in the same ways and to provide the same services (often dressed up with a new vocabulary) that we have always provided. We seem unable to change, despite logic or data. We continue to perform individual assessment and treatment functions at a rate not justified by their payoff in terms of research understanding or practical utility. We have a difficult time rethinking the problem of delinquency in a way that would enable us to try different kinds of research and practice. At the same time, as a profession we often seem to be either unaware of, or unwilling to tell the public of, the limits on our competence to predict and treat. This situation raises a number of ethical dilemmas.

If one takes seriously the ethical principle of competence cited earlier in this chapter, the ethical dilemma posed is severe. We are undeniably overstepping the bounds of scientifically demonstrated competence in most of the individual treatment programs offered to youth in trouble with the law. While we may justify such activities in terms of the need for social control or the need to try to do something helpful, we can not ethically justify them on the basis of competence as judged by scientific criteria. Ignorance of the research is no excuse; we have an ethical responsibility to "know" (be informed) and to "tell" the public what the limits on our competence are. If psychologists want to reject the existing data because they feel that they can treat better than others, it seems reasonable to require psychologists to collect and present data to that effect.

That these demands are not unreasonable is

attested to by the fact that officials in the criminal justice system are beginning to impose such competence demands on social scientists. It now appears that prediction and treatment will eventually be taken out of the official justice system (see the next section). Ironically, the very same activities involving the very same people may very well remain in the *functional system* nonetheless. The distinction between official and functional systems is crucial in considering ethical questions raised by psychologists' work with juveniles. The legal profession is probably about to find its way (and rightly so, we feel) out of the business of prediction and treatment for juveniles in general and certainly for juveniles involved in behaviors not illegal for adults. The legal profession is more willing to act on the data than we are, perhaps because we have more to lose. This fact will ultimately lead to a crossroads of choices for psychologists and other mental health professionals, who will then be faced with even greater responsibilities and moral questions. That crossroads is the place where we will have the opportunity to create a new functional system or to continue to carry out the roles of the past official system with a new name.

The Dilemma We Are Headed Toward

It is now apparent that in political and legislative reality, as well as in theory, the adult criminal justice system is moving toward criminal sanctions based on punishment as a function of the seriousness of the crime, with definite sentences, and away from a prediction and treatment orientation with individualized sentences and release contingent on "rehabilitation." This movement is due, at least in part, to the overwhelming evidence for the failure of prediction and treatment to pay off. The legal profession, if not our own, seems to accept this evidence. At the same time, the entire juvenile justice system remains *based* on prediction and treatment. Without this conceptual underpinning, the system has no rational basis.

Sanford J. Fox (1977) has recently argued that this paradoxical situation must ultimately lead to the end of the juvenile court. In the absence of operative concepts of prediction and rehabilitation, "the era of captive audiences for penal treatment programs comes to a close" (p. 22). The trend is already clear. There is a widespread call in criminal justice circles for the elimination of status offenses from the domain of the court (IJA–ABA Joint Commission on Juvenile Justice Standards, 1976; Lemmert 1974; McCarthy, 1977; National Council on Crime & Delinquency, 1973; Rubin, 1977; Scari & Hassenfeld, 1976). Yet today, one third of the reform schools and pretrial detention facilities are populated by status offenders. Recent data from a national study by Scari and Hassenfeld (1976) indicate that 70% of the juvenile cases brought before the court are screened out before reaching a judge. Offenses against the person account for only about 6% of juvenile crimes. As Fox (1977) has argued, and as the Institute of Judicial Administration–American Bar Association Juvenile Justice Standards Project (IJA–ABA Joint Commission, 1976) has suggested, *the issue now is not a matter of diversion but a need for a limitation of court jurisdiction.*[4]

If these trends are correct, we should ultimately see the legal community acting to reduce the misconceptualization of most acts of childhood misbehavior as crimes instead of as questions of parent and community responsibility. The problems will then be redefined as outside of the criminal justice system. This is both a realistic and a desirable trend. It is not only logical but pragmatic as well, since it will reduce the caseloads of probation departments and lessen the problems of mislabeling as criminals many children who have never done anything

---

[4] The IJA–ABA Juvenile Justice Standards Project is still controversial and continues to stimulate much discussion (cf. *Boston University Law Review*, 1977, *52*, July). However, as of this writing, 17 of the 23 volumes have already been approved by the membership of the American Bar Association.

different from most other children. The detrimental effects of "overkill" in identification, which may actually create an increased likelihood of crime, will be eliminated.

But this movement raises a set of very difficult questions for psychologists engaged in work with the same population of youngsters, whether called criminals or not. The legal profession will come out of this cleanly. They will wash their hands of the situation, claiming it is not under their jurisdiction. And they can even afford to be humanitarian—to wit, the suggestions of Fox and others that society "offer services," presumably through mental health or other social service agencies, when faced with problem children. That would, after all, be giving the children the benefit of the doubt. According to the letter of the law, this would be a responsible postition. It recognizes the need of some children for help and the mistake of calling such children who need help criminals. But in fact, it will functionally change nothing. It will target the same children for the same treatments presently imposed, ostensibly for their own good and not as punishment, but by means of a different social system, be it mental health, social services, or whatever. Presumably, children will not be forced to participate, but they really will be, given the demand characteristics, the social sanctions, and the informal powers that will be brought to bear.

What then is our responsibility? If prediction and treatment do not work when called juvenile justice, can we expect that they will work any better when called "mental health"? If status offenses leading to treatment do not result in positive outcomes because the treatments don't work, neither will what is now called legal misbehavior relabeled as "mental health problems" or as "community problems" likely be dealt with any more effectively by existing individualized treatment and control programs. What we as psychologists must recognize is that the removal of juveniles from one system to another is not sufficient. We instead need to

redefine the problem so that we can do different things. But to do so is very difficult. Despite our data and our desire to "do good," we are controlled by a number of constraints that make it very difficult for us to escape from this ethical dilemma and to reconceptualize the "problem of delinquency."

In the next section we separate and analyze the multiple interacting and convergent forces impinging upon the psychologist to form what we have labeled *constraints on thinking and doing*. These constraints on our ability to conceptualize problems can be seen to predetermine the way in which questions are addressed. More specifically, such constraints predetermine the unit of analysis for the researcher and the level of intervention of the practitioner.

The major categories of constraints are *dominant societal values, officialdom, and paradigm constraints*. The extent to which a given psychologist understands each of these constraints on his or her ability to reconceptualize problems, do research, and create new interventions may be related to how closely he or she resembles Brodsky's (1973) "system professional" or "system challenger." Brodsky's distinction between these two types of psychologists centers around the sense of responsibility to the offender, the agency, one's self and the profession, and society. Sense of responsibility, however, implies a more conscious process than what we mean by constraints. Sense of responsiblity suggests that the individual psychologist has a great deal of both awareness of and control over choices and actions. While this it true to some extent, and Brodsky's distinction has heuristic value, many psychologists are not aware of the more subtle paradigmatic and societal constraints that limit their ability to rethink the problems of the criminal justice system. For example, many of the 203 psychologists who answered the task force questionnaire described in Chapter 6 (sent to 349 psychologists identified as working primarily in the criminal justice system) did admit to (a) inadequate tools for accomplishing their goals, (b) role confusion that leaves them feeling helpless, and (c) awareness of the danger of inadvertently accomplishing ends they do not seek. Nevertheless, they did *not* view research and problem conceptualization as posing major ethical dilemmas. *It is our contention that the ways in which we conduct research and conceptualize "the problem of delinquency" are constrained by a number of preconditions that in turn force constraints on our thoughts and actions and ultimately become the basis for the ethical dilemmas that surface around more specific issues.* These constraints may be the real reason we are unable to change despite our awareness of the negative outcomes of individual prediction and treatment and the ethical dilemmas they pose.

Constraints on Thinking and Doing

It is simply unarguable that very basic values and premises influence what we as psychologists do and how we do it. Psychologists' contributions to juvenile justice are no exception to this state of affairs. However, the constraints on our thinking and action are sometimes less than obvious and often quite invisible. Under such conditions, these constraints may result in what Seidman (1977) has called an "error of conceptualization." That is, certain unrecognized pressures may impinge on a researcher or a practitioner in such a way as to force acceptance of a given way of viewing and doing. These pressures thus limit—before the fact—the research paradigms one considers "reasonable" or the intervention strategies one entertains as "possibly useful." In turn, the results of our research and the consequences of our interventions are to some extent determined before they are ever conducted or implemented.

The error of conceptualization has been discussed by other authors in the context of both research and practice. Watzlawick, Weakland, and Fisch (1974) view it as the reason that apparent change generated by "innovative" treatment programs is often change in name

only (first-order change) rather than genuine (second-order) change. They note that change of the latter type, which requires a fundamentally new way of viewing the problem, is very rare.

For example, if one views "the problem of delinquency" to be a function of individuals in need of individual treatment, it matters little insofar as a solution to the problem is concerned if "modern" behavior modification techniques are substituted for more "archaic" psychodynamic therapies. Such change is merely first-order in the sense that the underlying conceptualization of delinquency as a problem inherent in individuals remains unchanged. The possibility that one technique may be more "successful" than the other in individual cases (which has not been demonstrated, cf. Davidson & Seidman, 1974) is of less importance than the fact that the change would not substantially affect our basic understanding of the delinquency problem.

On the other hand, reconstruing delinquency as a *social process* rather than as an individual problem would constitute second-order change. Under such a reconceptualization, the need to clarify and critically evaluate the policies that *define* delinquency would become "obvious," while interventions of any sort based on the concept of the treatment of individual "sicknesses" would be rendered a bit curious (cf. Schur, 1973).

In the context of research, Mitroff and Turoff (1974) have referred to the error of conceptualization as a Type III error, by which they characterize research limited, before the fact, by the way in which the problem has been conceptualized. One would be hard pressed to find a better example of this than in the delinquency research discussed earlier, which has been enormously (if unwittingly) constricted by prevailing conceptions of what it means to conduct scientific inquiry. For example, if one seeks the correlates of delinquency in individual personality measures, one is likely to find some. If one conceptualizes delinquency as an individual problem, then one is likely to arrive at certain facts in research and to do certain things in intervention as a consequence of the problem definition per se. The choice of research strategy or problem definition is often inadvertently determined by dominant societal values, officialdom, and paradigm constraints, which in turn may lead us into the ethical dilemmas mentioned earlier.

Dominant Societal Values

Sjoberg (1975) has noted that social scientists have too often accepted the power structure's definition of what is right and what is wrong. These societal values constrain, often without our awareness, our ability to formulate a problem. For example, the notion of individual motivation and responsibility has always been a cherished, dominant, and pervasive value in this society. It is at the root of our legal and constitutional structures. It has led to what Caplan and Nelson (1973) and Ryan (1971), among others, have referred to as a person-centered causal attribution bias, or a "victim-blaming" ideology. This bias refers to the tendency to find individuals responsible for their own problems despite antecedent and contextual economic, social, and political factors. It is part of a larger set of social processes in which our institutions work toward the socialization of almost everyone to a "single standard" and in which those who fail to behave in conformity with the norm are labeled deviant in the negative sense of the term (Rappaport, 1977a; Ryan, 1971). This position ignores the fact that "deviance" may also be viewed as a social judgment process. Such a viewpoint, as we shall see later, would lead to somewhat different research and practice alternatives. However, it would also place the psychologist in the position of opposing dominant societal values, a constraint on our thinking that is difficult to avoid. Neither the scientist, the decision maker, nor anyone else is immune to such values and biases.

The psychologist often accepts without question the same myths about "delinquents" that the general public believes. Perhaps we even create the myths. Our traditional emphasis on testing, classification, prediction of criminal behavior as a function of individual characteristics, and individual treatment is a major preoccupation. Reinforced by studies such as the Glueck and Glueck (1951, 1971) reports, we have paid almost exclusive attention to the idea that there are personal differences between delinquents and nondelinquents rather than to the data or to the usefulness of the paradigm as a means to enhance understanding or practice.

The general nature of the "blaming the victim" paradigm is classically described by William Ryan (1971):

> The formula for action becomes extraordinarily simple: Change the victim. All of this happens so smoothly that it seems downright rational. First, identify a social problem. Second, study those affected by the problem and discover in what ways they are different from the rest of us as a consequence of deprivation and injustice. Third, define the differences as the cause of the social problem itself. Finally, of course, assign a government bureaucrat to invent a humanitarian action program to correct the differences. (p. 8)

The premise that the individual juvenile is not only the culprit but also the proper focus of change (level of intervention for the practitioner or unit of analysis for the researcher) is central to research and practice in delinquency (and of course in psychology more generally). This premise may have more to do with dominant societal values than with what is usually meant by objective scientific data. It is only *one way* to conceptualize the problem of delinquency. Moreover, as justice system professionals (if not psychologists) are beginning to admit, such a conceptualization, which is the basis for individual prediction and treatment, has had precious little practical success.

Officialdom

Most research funding comes through some governmental agency. "It seems obvious that if social science is to have a practical short-run application, a given research problem must be defined in terms which are familiar to public officials" (Green, 1971, p. 15). In fact, Galliher and McCartney (1973) have recently demonstrated how funding patterns have affected the use of certain research strategies and methods as well as the emphasis on individuals in the sociological literature on juvenile delinquency. Moore and Nay (1977) provide similar documentation for research in the social sciences more broadly conceived. A special issue of *The Annals* of the American Academy of Political and Social Science, entitled "Social Science and the Federal Government" (Lyons, 1971), was devoted to an extensive discussion of this general topic. It is not difficult to imagine the ramifications of governmental funding patterns on the formulation of problems for study by social scientists. For example, at the technical level one may accept governmental statistics, definitions, and categories of criminal behavior. This is precisely what has occurred with regard to social indicators research; that is, government agencies such as the Law Enforcement Assistance Administration have requested scientists to make use of the data banks the agencies have compiled (e.g., victimization surveys and Uniform Crime Reports) for policy analysis. The results of such investigations can only support inherent biases already existing in the agencies' definitions and categories of criminal behavior. As long as we allow funding agencies to determine the type and formulation of research problems we address, we are bound to continue making errors of conceptualization.

This problem is far from an impersonal one. The stated goals and values of an organization for the enhancement of justice usually are concerned with improving social welfare, equity, etc. These goals may be expressed in attempts to adequately or efficiently achieve certain program objectives, but it is implicitly assumed that the attainment of such objectives will in no way bring about the end of that agency. This is not hard to understand in that the entertainment of such a possibility threatens the very people who have, to say the least, a vested interest in maintaining their jobs, status, and power. The question of how an agency can attain its lofty objectives usually means, "How can we more adequately or efficiently, by doing what we already know how to do, attain these objectives and maintain, or better yet increase, the quantity and quality of our jobs, status, and power?"

In the case of psychology's official position, with the exception of a relatively small number of psychologists, there is likely to be little opposition to proposals that would essentially eliminate the juvenile court (as proposed by the IJA–ABA Joint Commission on Juvenile Justice Standards, 1976, which rejects both status offenses and the prediction and treatment rationale). This is because few psychologists work in such settings per se and because such proposals are likely to be tied to maintaining the same functions for psychologists in different (i.e., mental health) settings. Rather than being provided with true alternatives, the children will likely be dealt with by psychologists doing what they have always done, under the mental health rather than the legal system's sanctions. This is a prime example of first-order change, a change constrained by both dominant societal values and the needs of officialdom. Such constraints limit our ability to redefine the "problem of delinquency" and to test out new approaches despite the failure of the old. We insure old wine in new bottles.

Paradigm Constraints

Perhaps the most difficult of all constraints on problem formulation for the social scientist to recognize are those rooted in the scientific models subscribed to by most contemporary social scientists. Maruyama (1974) delineates the structures of reasoning, or as he labels them, "paradigms," that lie beneath different cultures, professions, and disciplines. Scientists and others seem unaware of these structures of reasoning. Maruyama (1974) explicates a dimension of paradigms ranging from a unidirectional causal paradigm to a mutual causal paradigm. The unidirectional causal paradigm is essentially a traditional "cause and effect" model. This paradigm appears to be uncritically employed most often by social scientists in an apparent attempt to emulate the physical sciences. It is heavily based on a classificational logic.[5] Following are the assumptions of this classificational logic:

1. The universe consists of material substances (and, in some cases, also of power substances).

2. These substances persist in time.

3. They obey the law of identity and the law of mutual exclusiveness, except that the power substance may penetrate into things.

4. The substances are classifiable into mutually exclusive categories. The classification is unambiguous. The categories persist in time and space. (The categories are believed to be uniformly and universally valid.)

5. Categories may be divided into subcategories, and categories may be combined into supercategories. Thus, categories are a hierarchy.

6. The categories can be constructed *a priori*, i.e., they can preexist before the things are to be put into them. They have their reality independent from things, and higher than things. (Maruyama, 1973, p. 136)

From a different perspective, Watzlawick et al. (1974) have commented on the negative consequences of such classificational logic:

For instance, the handling of many fundamental social problems—e.g., poverty, aging, crime—is customarily approached by separating these difficulties as entities unto themselves, as almost diagnostic categories, referring to essentially quite disparate problems and requiring very different solutions. The next step then is to create enormous physical and administrative structures and whole industries of expertise, producing increased incompetence in ever vaster numbers of individuals. We see this as a basically counterproductive approach to such social needs, an approach that requires a massive deviant population to support the raison d'etre of these monolithic agencies and departments. (p. 159)

Coming from a different, but somewhat similar, vantage point, Mitroff and Turoff (1973, 1974) describe how different methodologies stem from different philosophical premises or inquiring systems (Churchman, 1971). These different inquiring systems (e.g., Lockean, Leibnizian, Kantian, Hegelian) may be ill-suited to the conceptualization of a particular problem but are employed without a thorough analysis of their fit and concomitant constraints on problem definitions, methodology, and outcome.

Seidman (1978) has recently summarized the problem of constraints on the thinking and actions of both researchers and practitioners:

To buck the tide of the societal, funding agency, university and discipline-based underlying rules, premises, pressures and assumptions described above would seriously jeopardize an individual investigator's understandable striving for academic and material success. Nevertheless, not to at least question them, forces the researcher into a number of predetermined actions which are taken for granted, and may inhibit desirable social changes. This is not meant to imply that most researchers do not also exhibit a genuine quest for knowledge, but rather that social scientific activities have multiple determinants, not all of which are encompassed by the search for "truth." Furthermore, all of these determinants commingle in a complex fashion with those of the host organization to form a mutually beneficial exchange relationship. The frequent but unwitting consequence may be an error of conceptualization or the investigation of the "wrong" problem. Paradoxically, the "real" problem goes unaltered and is, in fact, often perpetuated. Successive phases in the research process are subject to similar determinants, but the selection and formulation of the problem is most critical.

---

[5] Lest the reader suspect that this discussion is esoteric, it is interesting to note that a recent issue of *Criminal Justice and Behavior* (1977, *4*[2]), the official publication of the American Association of Correctional Psychologists, was devoted entirely to the development of a scheme for classifying types of criminals.

Unfortunately, the social scientist's acceptance of preselected and preformulated research problems adds credibility and legitimation to the values inherent in such conceptualizations. Individually and collectively social scientists must take a much more active role in the process of problem selection and formulation, and institute mechanisms, to the largest extent possible, to maximize diversity in the conceptualization of research problems. (p. 189)

Alternatives for Psychologists In (And Out of) the Juvenile Justice System

In this section we propose a number of steps that might be taken by psychologists in dealing with the ethical dilemmas perpetuated by the constraints discussed above. It is worth stating explicity that what we are calling for is a *multiplicity of problem definitions, research, and intervention strategies*. While we suggest a number of specific research and intervention activities designed (a) to provide roles beyond those of supplying individual assessment and treatment, and (b) to expand our unit of analysis or level of intervention beyond the individual child, it is not our intention to reify as the "solution to crime and delinquency" any of these specific activities. Indeed, were we to do so, we would find ourselves back in the very same ethical dilemmas.

The Overarching Ethical Issues: Know and Tell

We assert that it must be explicit in the ethical standards of any profession that its members be well informed on the state of their art. For psychologists, the responsibility to "know" must include knowing both the value bases of our conceptions and the outcomes of our interventions. Psychology is a *social* science and, as discussed above, is unavoidably influenced by the constraints of contemporary social history. As Gergen (1973) Cronbach (1975), and Riegel (1972) have recently made clear, "basic" as well as applied psychology is very much influenced

by current (and changeable) social values, politics, and economics.[6] Because both our research and our interventions are subject to these influences, it would be less than honest to say that we are simply objective scientists dealing only with "facts." Rather, the very facts we *choose* to collect, interpret, and deem worthy of attention are often decided *before* we ever engage in the practice of what we usually think of as science. This is unavoidable, and we are not suggesting that psychologists stop doing this (we couldn't, even if we wanted to). Rather, we are arguing for what, in popular terms, might be thought of as "consciousness raising." We need to *continually* engage in *active* consideration, and reconsideration, of the values that influence us. We need to recognize that differing values may lead to differing ways to do research, differing kinds of data to collect, and differing interventions to try. What this requires, *before* problem formulation, research designs, and interventions are peformed, is a multiplicity of viewpoints that may be formally contrasted with one another because we are willing to be open to the possibility that differing ways to view the problem will lead to different answers, each of which may have scientific merit. This aspect of "knowing" means knowing that we are influenced by value constraints and being willing to try to explicitly contrast differing values. It implies that we are also willing to "tell" the public that this is the case, rather than hide our value choices in social science jargon.

A second aspect of the problem of "knowing," which is as difficult for the researcher as it is for the practitioner, involves knowing about the *outcomes* of our research and our interventions. While most researchers will assert that practitioners need to do evaluation and outcome research to know if they are really accomplishing what they think they are (and of course we agree), researchers are much less

---

[6] For a full debate of these issues, the reader is referred to the *Personality and Social Psychology Bulletin*, 1976, *2*(3).

prone to understand that knowing the outcomes of their own "basic" research, in terms of its implicit implications, is equally important. That is, researchers who accept problem definitions and currently socially acceptable paradigms for their research are to the extent that this acceptance, limits their vision of alternative paradigms and reifies current ideology as the only scientifically acceptable form, not dealing well with the problem of knowing. Indeed, the basic researcher often reifies the way in which the applied researchers and practitioners view the problem. As long as basic research in psychology continues (a) to focus on the contrasted-groups research design as the predominant (only?) model for understanding "delinquency," and (b) to emphasize, to the exclusion of other approaches, the discovery of individual characteristics of "delinquents" per se, the implication for applied research and practice is that such ways of viewing the problem are not only consistent with dominant societal values but are also the only scientifically acceptable way to view the problem.

In both applied and basic research, the problem of knowing about outcomes is again followed by the problem of "telling." To be ethically responsible, we need to tell the people who are the targets of our research, and the public, exactly what outcomes they might expect. We also need to tell them that there are other ways to "view and do" that can be just as "scientific" as those that are currently acceptable.

Given the constraints discussed above, knowing and telling is quite a difficult task. How can we begin to deal with it?

Seidman (1978), in the context of law and social policy, has recently suggested a set of guidelines for what he calls "value conflict generating mechanisms" as a means to apply a conscious effort to avoid errors of conceptualization or of accepting problem definitions as given. He cites Maruyama's (1966, 1974) notion of "demonopolarization" as a necessary first step—that is, rejection of the notion that there is *one* truth, one correct theory, one right way. Seidman endorses Johnson's (1975) notion of "criticism" as a formal step in public policy evaluation. This means examining and advocating alternative policies that can be directly contrasted to existing policies and problem definitions. It involves what Watzlawick et al. (1974) call "reframing the question," or placing the "facts" within an alternative conceptual framework. While the facts would remain the same, the new context would change their meaning.

One important implication of this strategy is that reframing often requires one to look at the pattern of transactions between units of analysis. For example, one begins to ask about juvenile misbehavior questions such as "How would viewing these facts at the institutional level differ from viewing them only at the individual level?" The result, of course, is that one ends up asking questions about the *process* of defining social deviance and how that process affects individuals. One also begins to ask if the social values represented by this process are acceptable or questionable. In the context of juvenile justice, Schur's (1973) classic statement on "radical nonintervention" did exactly this. Seidman (1978) has added to Schur's comparison of individual treatment, liberal reform, and radical nonintervention, a number of comments that are presented in Table 5-1. Reading through the table may help to make concrete how framing the question in different ways can lead to considerably different methodologies, social policies, and long-range effects on the "facts." If at this point the reader finds our argument for reframing to be unconvincing, we strongly suggest a closer look at Table 5-1. Table 5-1 is not presented to focus on radical nonintervention per se so much as to illustrate the way in which *contrasting conceptual systems* and *opposing problem definitions* can be helpful in highlighting the implicit values and assumptions of each. Such an exercise should make it easier for psychologists to know and to tell.

Table 5-1 *Conceptualizations of Delinquency and Their Consequences*

Issue	Facts: Youth violating social rules. Oftentimes, the rules violated are those that apply solely to youth, that is, status offenses.			Comments
	(A) Individual Treatment	(B) Liberal Reform	(C) Radical Nonintervention	
Social science orientation				These are ideal types; they are not mutually exclusive. They also represent a historical progression from A to C.
Basic underlying assumption (conceptualization)	Offenders are *different* from nonoffenders, and differences are assumed to be a function of *individual* variables.	Offenders are *different* from nonoffenders, but differences are assumed to result from *social conditions* to which they've been exposed.	*Reactions* to certain behaviors largely determine their social meaning (i.e., "deviance") and consequences (i.e., further rule violations).	Orientation C's frustration with the lack of efficacy of orientations A and B's policies led to reframing the basic underlying research problem (or error of conceptualization) of A and B. A and B are basically similar because of the common assumption of or concern with differences. A and B are heavily influenced by dominant societal values.
Favored research methodology and focus	Comparison samples of delinquent and nondelinquent youth matched on demographic and other social variables. Thus, social system variables are held constant and *personological-like factors are free to vary* (∴ the focus).	Comparison of rate of rule violations in different social classes, neighborhood settings, group and subcultural contexts. In a sense, holds constant individual variability, leaving *social and cultural variables free to vary* (∴ the focus).	Self-reports, observations, and legal analyses focused upon *pattern of interactions between* "deviants" and social control agents.	In A and B, one or the other is the focus (individual or social system variables), while the focus for orientation C is on the pattern of interactions between the two. Reframed conceptualization of C leads to a different methodology and focus.
Implicit causal perspective	*Unidirectional causality;* individual difference variables, by the nature of methodology employed, are "set up" to be the cause of rule-violating behavior.	*Unidirectional causality;* environmental or social parameters, by the nature of methodology employed, are "set up" to be the cause of rule-violating behavior.	*Mutual causality;* pattern of interactions, by the nature of methodology employed, is "set up" to be cause of rule-violating behavior.	A and B's causal perspective is similar in attempting to emulate the physical sciences. The reframed conceptualization of C implies a different causal model than A and B.
Social policies created (or implied)	*Treatment and rehabilitation of "deviants";* agents of social control must act on behalf of the violators' "best" interests.	*Treatment and rehabilitation* of "deviants," with increased attention to social factors and causes.	*Narrowed scope of juvenile court jurisdiction.* Decriminalization of status offenses. Treatment only on a voluntary basis.	Social policies stem directly from prior issues.
Long-range effect on the "Facts"	Increased numbers viewed as "deviant" and in need of treatment or rehabilitation. Problem has reached crisis proportion.	Increased numbers viewed as "deviant," and need for social reform is emphasized. However, functionally is translated to increased services. Problem has reached crisis proportion.	Increased tolerance of diversity. Fewer individuals viewed as problematic.	The manner in which C reframes the basic assumption of A and B leads to drastically different long-range consequences.

Note. Adapted by Seidman (1978) from Table 1 (p. 20) of Schur (1973). From "Justice, Values, and Social Science: Unexamined Premises" by E. Seidman. In R. J. Simon (Ed.), *Research in Law and Sociology: An Annual Compilation of Research, Vol. 1* (Greenwich, Conn.: Jai Press, 1978). Copyright 1978 by Jai Press. Reprinted by permission.

114

Questions resulting from a reframing or nega-tion of the original problem have no greater priority on truth or justice than those tradi-tionally posed. . . . What is imperative is that we *examine the premises underlying the selec-tion and formulation of research problems, generate alternative conceptualizations, eval-*uate each empirically, and thoroughly examine their respective intended and unintended social consequences. (Seidman, 1978, p. 193, italics in original)

Seidman (1978) goes on to list, following Mitroff and Blankenship (1973), several guide-lines to force the *generation of value conflicts.* These suggestions include bringing to bear on the formulation of a research problem at least two "radically distinct" philosophical models; or contrasting two radically distinct disciplines; or conceptualizing research by bringing together people with radically different points of view; or bringing into a research team someone who "walks with only one foot in our camp." This last notion is similar to what Sarason (1972) has called "the outside critic."

Two other suggestions that deserve close consideration are also offered. The constituents, participants, or ultimate beneficiaries (or vic-tims) of the research should be considered in the selection and formulation of the research problem, and autonomy from the organizations and institutions being evaluated and/or served should be maximized. These latter points de-serve far more space than we give them here, and we are not unaware of the difficulty in im-plementing such strategies. The point to be em-phasized, however, is that while these guidelines may be viewed as "impractical," we must not sidestep their importance simply because they are not foolproof. Rather, we need to view them as ideal directions to move toward. Below we offer some suggestions for making concrete the spirit of these guidelines, which we feel allow psychologists to confront more directly the ethical issues that are unavoidable in doing their jobs.

Assessment/Research

Earlier we argued that the implicit or explicit promise of psychological assessment/research vis-à-vis the juvenile justice system has been to facilitate the prevention of delinquency through the identification of intervention targets using objective, scientific, noncapricious procedures. An overview of articles published in the past 10 years in two of the better-known psychology journals led us to conclude that (a) due to low levels of predictive accuracy we are presently incapable of making good on this promise, and (b) given the nature of the criterion normally employed in our work, fulfillment of the promise would be doubtful even if predictive ac-curacy were high. We have further argued that continued attempts by psychologists to function in this manner demand forthright acknowledg-ment of these limitations. For those of us who do not wish to continue to function in this way, however, the need for *genuine* alternatives be-comes prepotent.

At the conceptual/theoretical level, social scientists have argued for decades that delin-quency and other forms of deviance can only be understood relativistically (Douglas, 1971). The argument is that it is impossible to construct a taxonomy of delinquent acts and/or people without some reference to a set of (ultimately value-based) norms. If psychologists were truly interested in achieving an understanding of de-linquency, one would expect to find their re-search organized within a general paradigm such as that diagrammed in Figure 5-1.

In Figure 5-1, the Ps represent people whose status (delinquent or nondelinquent) is in ques-tion. Each P may be described with reference to a set of behaviors and/or personal characteris-tics (Sagarin, 1975). The Ns refer to different normative systems subscribed to by powerful individuals or groups, against which the be-haviors/characteristics of the Ps are evaluated.

To illustrate the sort of information that this paradigm could be expected to yield, the cells in

Normative Systems

People	N_1	N_2	N_3	...	N_n
P_1	d	d	d	...	d
P_2	n	n	n	...	n
P_3	d	n	d	...	n
⋮	⋮	⋮	⋮	⋮	⋮
P_p	n	d	n	...	d

Figure 5-1. Schematic representation of a relativistic research paradigm.

the matrix have been filled with *d*s or *n*s, which represent, respectively, "delinquent" and "nondelinquent." Thus, in the hypothetical cases described, P_1 and P_2 are shown to be, respectively, delinquent and nondelinquent across all normative systems assessed. Thus, they represent the genuine possibility that popular consensus may exist regarding the status of certain individuals. In contrast, the status of P_3 and P_p changes as a function of the normative systems. P_3 is shown to be delinquent under Normative Systems 1 and 3 but nondelinquent under Systems 2 and *n*. Just the opposite is shown for P_p.

The most noteworthy aspect of the paradigm shown in Figure 5-1 is that *it is capable of generating relativistic empirical data*. That is, it is capable of illuminating changes in the status of single individuals as we move across normative systems.

It may be merely gratuitous to point out here that psychological research on delinquency has *not* been structured within such a paradigm. Instead, the constraints discussed in the preceding section have all contributed to our heavy reliance on a paradigm of the sort depicted in the solid portion of Figure 5-2.

The solid portion in Figure 5-2 represents that portion of the relativistic research paradigm (Figure 5-1) that is actually considered in empirical research. The dashed portion of Figure 5-2 represents that segment of the relativistic paradigm that is typically ignored.

Again, the Ps in the figure represent people whose status (delinquent or nondelinquent) is in question. However, in contrast to the paradigm considered earlier, it is obvious that the paradigm shown in Figure 5-2 could not *possibly* generate evidence that the status of any P as delinquent has anything to do with norms. On the contrary, because variance in the normative parameter has been eliminated, the only *possible* source of variance in the criterion that can be investigated is people. And this is precisely where psychologists have looked for the correlates of delinquency.

The single normative system that has underlain most of our empirical research has been, as we have seen, the *official* normative system. There are a handful of studies in which this has not been the case. Of the 20 cited earlier, four relied on distinctions between "delinquents" and "nondelinquents" formulated by the investigators.

These four studies provide clear examples of what we referred to earlier as first-order change. One may recognize that reliance on official statistics for distinguishing delinquents from nondelinquents in research is hazardous. One may then proceed to substitute some other basis for this distinction—that is, some other normative system. But so long as a *single* normative system is employed, it is clear that

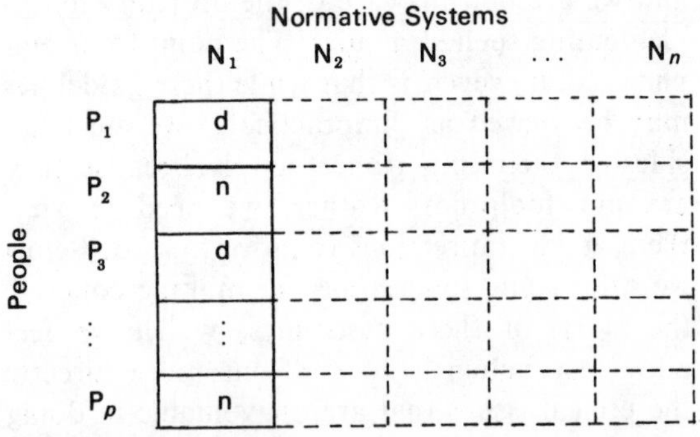

Figure 5-2. Schematic representation of the prevailing research paradigm.

one remains within the solid portion of Figure 5-2 and that the dashed portion remains obscured. While the specifics of the single system (in this case, a research paradigm) may well have changed, the paradigm itself remains unchanged; this may be thought of as a first-order change.

In contrast to first-order change, second-order change refers to a situation in which the fundamental rules, assumptions, and premises of the system itself are challenged (Rappaport, 1977a; Seidman, 1978; Watzlawick et al., (1974). In the context of delinquency research, second-order change could be accomplished by working within the paradigm depicted in Figure 1, where delinquency is explicitly construed as an *interaction* of, or confrontation between, behaviors/characteristics and normative systems.

Adoption of such an alternative paradigm becomes quite reasonable when one recognizes that delinquency research to date has been, for a variety of reasons discussed earlier, constrained to one of many possible research paradigms. More specifically, we have labored under the belief that scientific knowledge pertaining to delinquency can be generated and used within what Mitroff (1974) has described as a Leibnizian/Lockean inquiry system. The mode of inquiry that transpires in such a system may be characterized as the study of *relationships between entities that are themselves well-defined*. Traditional experimental designs (or their correlational counterparts where ethically necessary) involving the formal testing of well-defined hypotheses are the prototypes of the Leibnizian/Lockean inquiry system.

All of the studies cited earlier have been conceptualized within such a system. They all begin with operational definitions of the variables under investigation (i.e., personality, demographic, socioeconomic, and cognitive factors on the one hand, and "delinquency" on the other). They proceed to explore the relationships between those variables and conclude with some discussion of the practical and/or conceptual significance of those relationships.

The specification (measurement) of the variables themselves is *not* regarded as problematic and is discussed, if at all, only at a descriptive level.

The problem, of course, is that the definition of at least one of the variables is quite problematic. The terms *delinquency* and *delinquent* do not admit of any precise definition, and as we have seen, attempts to formulate such definitions generate serious ethical (not to mention empirical) problems.

It appears, then, that juvenile delinquency falls into a class of problems that Mitroff (1974) has described as *wicked* or *ill-structured*. He distinguishes these from *well-structured* problems in the following way:

> Well-structured problems are problems about which enough is known so that [research] problems can be formulated in ways that are susceptible to precise analytic methods of attack. The biggest problem connected with ill-structured problems is to define the nature of the problem. Ill-structured problems have an elusive quality that seems to defy precise methods of formulation. Most social problems seem to be of this type. (p. 224)

Mitroff (1974) goes on to argue that a Leibnizian/Lockean inquiry system is

> best suited for working on well-structured problem situations for which there exists a strong consensual position on the nature of the problem situation. If a strong consensual position does not exist, or if the consensual postion is suspect no matter how strong it might be, Kantian and Hegelian inquiry systems may be called for. (p. 228)

Viewed from this perspective, it is possible to see how a major problem associated with our current research strategies (i.e., the problem of truly reducing capriciousness) results from an attempt to force the delinquency problem into an inquiry system for which it is ill-suited. Our entire argument has been, in essence, an exhortation to suspect any delinquency research that relies on some single normative system. If this exhortation is justified, and if Mitroff's

(1974) analysis of scientific inquiry systems is cogent, than it is apparent that the study of juvenile delinquency would more aptly proceed within a Kantian/Hegelian rather than a Leibnizian/Lockean inquiry system. While a complete exposition of the former is beyond the scope of the present discussion, it is nevertheless possible to briefly discuss what is involved in such a Kantian/Hegelian inquiry system and some of the questions that might be raised within it.

The essence of a Kantian/Hegelian inquiry system is that it incorporates multiple definitions of the problem. Thus, within this system, the study of delinquency would entail not only the assessment of individual differences in the behavior and personal characteristics (e.g., sex, race) of juveniles but also individual differences in the judgment policies of various individuals with legal power over juveniles. Delinquency would thus be construed not as an *entity* inherent in certain acts or people but rather as a *process* defined by the confrontation of certain individuals' behaviors/characteristics with other individuals' judgments. In short, the use of a Kantian/Hegelian inquiry system would create a research paradigm such as that shown in Figure 5-2 above. It should be reemphasized here that the relativistic paradigm in no way precludes the possibility of popular consensus. Rather, the framework suggests that consensus is but one from among many possible outcomes that might be observed. Stated otherwise, whether or not consensus exists is an empirical question in Figure 5-1, while it is an a priori assumption in Figure 5-2.

How might a relativistic inquiry system be "brought to life?" Recent work by Lamiell (Note 4) illustrates one possibility. In this study, variance in normative structures was defined in terms of individual differences among high school teachers in the judgment policies they employed for evaluating the behavior patterns of high school students. Lamiell obtained preliminary evidence that those teachers with similar points of view tended to agree in their ratings of the relative deviance of actual adolescents, while teachers with a different point of view tended to disagree with these ratings. Thus, whether or not a given adolescent was "good or "bad" depended not only on what he or she did *but on who was making the judgments*.

By conceptualizing the "delinquency problem" as a *process of confrontation* between behavior and judgment, rather than as an *entity* inhering in people (or their backgrounds), one is led in very different directions, both in terms of research *and* "treatment." As regards research, for example, questions such as the following are raised: Where is there disagreement among various powerful people (e.g., parents, teachers, police officers, probation officers, juvenile court judges, correctional personnel, social scientists) regarding who is and is not delinquent? Given some agreement on who is delinquent, where is there disagreement regarding the appropriate disposition of cases (e.g., psychiatric examination, probation, incarceration)? Where disagreements exist, whose policies tend to be followed and whose are overridden? How consistent are particular decision makers in the exercise of their policies over time? Given that many judgments pertaining to juveniles are based on perceived risk of future delinquency (Scarpitti & Stephenson, 1971), how valid is a particular decision maker's policy, given his or her own or someone else's definition of delinquency?

New questions regarding "treatment" are raised by the simple fact that a factor (a) necessary for the very existence of delinquency and (b) existing *outside of* the "delinquents" is under consideration. More specifically, since delinquency would be seen as partly attributable to judgment policy, it would follow naturally that one means of dealing with the problem would be to change the policy rather than the "delinquent." This approach is perhaps the essence of Doleschal and Klapmuts's (1973) "consciousness III criminology" and Schur's (1973) "radical nonintervention."

It is worth noting that what would *not* follow from this perspective is treatment in the conventional sense of the term. It is obvious that in struggles between juvenile behavior and adult judgment policies, the latter will not (and should not) always give way. But construed in this manner, the enforcement of a judgment policy (through, for example, punishment) would be regarded as *just that and nothing more.*

Alternative Intervention Strategies

Rappaport (1977b) has suggested that the sources of our intervention strategies are implicitly tied to our social values and goals. Psychologists who focus exclusively on individual change strategies aimed at identified delinquents tend to view the values and goals of our current social policies as their own. The problem for applied behavioral science (it is said) is to help as many people as possible adjust to the norms of the society, to be "adaptive," and to "fit in." The exact content of the "treatments" varies with the specific conception of human behavior, but all are focused on changing *individual* identified persons to fit into available environments.

Other psychologists argue that social problems are the result of interpersonal difficulties within *primary groups*, including family, peers, and work groups. Deficits in the group rather than in its individual members are emphasized. Communication skills are often implicated as problematic. Family and group therapy are common strategies of intervention.

Still other psychologists have focused on the failure of settings such as schools and police and welfare organizations to accomplish their socialization tasks. This has led to the study of *organizations* and to intervention strategies such as organization development that have required conceptions focused on organizational (rather than individual) processes.

Underlying each of these viewpoints is a basic agreement on social values, that is, that "problem people" should be made to fit into the society. It may be that individual people need to be "helped" directly, or that the agents of socialization need to be bolstered, but in either case the goal is the same. While such a position is exactly congruent with the *constraints* discussed above, it is not necessarily right or wrong. It simply accepts current values unchallenged. While the outcomes of such interventions may be submitted to scientific verification (indeed, as we have argued, they *must* be if we are to meet the ethical standard of competence), the underlying values/goals themselves cannot be.

If one were to adopt an *institutional* unit of analysis or level of intervention, a different perspective would be necessary. One might assert that social problems are a function of social policies, values, goals, and political/economic ideology. If this is the case, then rather than simply taking current values as given, different value systems can be contrasted. Suppose one substitutes for dominant societal values those supportive of diversity and alternative pathways to success based on autonomy, respect for differences among people, support for people's strengths rather than identification of their deficits, cultural relativity, and the right to resources. Under such a value system, to *limit* interventions to those that enhance the ability of organizations, small groups, or individuals to socialize others and to distribute resources on the basis of conformity to a single standard of "competence" would be folly.

When one is willing to step outside of the constraints and consider value conflict generating mechanisms (as discussed earlier), the possibility for coming up with new approaches is enhanced. To the extent that one's values/goals require institutional rather than individual, small group, or organizational change, different conceptions, strategies, and tactics must be considered. For example, the strategies and tactics of community organization and social advocacy and the creation of autonomous settings may begin to make as much (or more) sense than individual treatment. These are strategies new to psychology. They require different sets of conceptions and a search for new paradigms.

Willingness to engage in strategies at the institutional level does not necessarily preclude a willingness to engage in any others. Often, levels and strategies can be combined in practice. Multiple levels of study and intervention are desirable. What we must keep in mind, however, is that unless each of us is willing to openly state our basic values/goals to ourselves, our professional colleagues, and our colleagues in the communities we serve, we may be violating our own ethical standards. We must recognize that we cannot justify our values as science, and this we must know and tell.

As already noted in our review of "the state of the art," most methods for individual treatment of delinquency, values aside, are simply failures for most children. However, some methods have been shown to be helpful for some children. Programs described by Baron and Feeney (1976), Klein, Alexander, and Parsons (1977), Seidman, Rappaport, and Davidson (1976) and Davidson et al. (1977), with children, their families, and significant others, are probably worthy of further exploration as *one way* to view childhood misbehavior. They are among only a handful of programs that have presented convincing empirical data. Voluntary involvement of some children and their families in such programs probably has its place. There are probably children who would benefit from the kind of communication skills, behavioral contracting and individual advocacy conducted.

Davidson and Rapp (1976) have detailed a number of concrete steps for conducting advocacy programs. In reframing the question, they have taken an environmental resources conception of "delinquency" and suggested that rather than view the child as functioning with a personality disorder, one can help the child to develop strategies for obtaining resources from his or her local community. This sometimes involves changing significant others in the child's life rather than changing the child. More recently, Davidson and Rappaport (1978) have suggested that the advocacy model may apply to strategies for change at. the administrative (organizational) as well as the policy (institutional) level. Table 5-2 presents examples of an advocacy approach that may be applied in a number of different styles. The specific problem it is applied to in Table 5-2 is truancy, common among so-called delinquents. Depending on the situation, an advocate may take a *positive* approach, in an attempt to gain the good favor of significant others in the child's life, or a *neutral* approach, often referred to as consultation or provision of information, or a *negative* approach, by means of criticism.

Table 5–2 presents nine different ways in which an advocate may work for children viewed to be in need of resources. Each form of advocacy is determined by the "style" and by the level of intervention—individual, administrative, or social policy. What needs to be emphasized here is that this way of viewing the problem of concern (e.g., truancy) is not in terms of individual personality or intrapsychic characteristics but rather in terms of the provision of environmental resources. This viewpoint gives the psychologist greater latitude in seeking to assist children. It does not require that all problems be seen as due to characteristics of the individual child (although some may be), but rather, it allows one to apply, where appropriate, a variety of tactics aimed at changing organizations and institutions. It also allows one to act at *multiple* levels of intervention simultaneously by means of a sequence of problem-solving strategies:

> In contrast with other approaches, the environmental resources conception does not concern itself with the eradication or amelioration of differences in individuals or target groups. At the very heart of the environmental resources conception is the notion that a wide variety of differences do exist in this society. From a statistical standpoint, given two comparison groups of sufficient size, there will be differences observed on a multitude of indi-

Table 5-2

Alternative Advocacy Strategies

Style of advocacy	Focus of advocacy		
	Individual level	Administrative level	Policy level
Positive approach	I. Advocate identifies individual teachers and seeks their agreement to make adjustments in classroom curriculum more conductive to the individual educational needs.	II. Advocate would contact educational administrator with a proposal for drafting an application for educational innovation funds to generate additional curriculum alternatives.	III. Advocate would lobby with state legislators to alter the state-wide curriculum requirements.
Neutral approach	IV. Advocate provides information to individual teachers concerning the educational goals and needs of the target youth.	V. Advocate would present information to the pupil personnel services concerning the rates of educational attainment among the target group and ensure that such information was made available to the media.	VI. Advocate would present state board of education and state superintendent of schools with dropout rates and preferences for educational alternatives and would highlight the right of all students to public education.
Negative approach	VII. Advocate would have the local media cover the story about a young person's being denied a quality education due to irrelevant classroom rules.	VIII. Advocate would initiate a class-action suit against the school district for failing to meet its legislative mandate to educate all youth in the district.	IX. Advocate would enjoin a legislative committee to investigate the educational agency mandated to provide educational alternatives.

Note. From "Toward a Model for Advocacy: Values, Roles, and Conceptions From Community Psychology" by W. S. Davidson and J. Rappaport. In G. H. Weber and G. J. McCall (Eds.), *Social Scientists as Advocates: Views From the Applied Disciplines* (Beverly Hills, Calif.: Sage Publications, 1978) p. 79. Copyright © 1978 by Sage Publications, Inc. Reprinted by permission.

vidual and environmental variables. Finding problems such as crime, poverty, etc., disproportionately represented in various social groups has in the past led to the conclusion that to eradicate the observed differences, the major characteristics of the groups or individuals had to be altered. Within the environmental resources conception, group differences are viewed as the assests of a pluralistic society *and* such differences are to be supported rather than used as a basis for exclusion from resource availability. Some (Triandis, 1977), have even suggested that the special assets of "out groups" should be taught to the majority as a means for creating a true multi-cultural society.

The environmental resources conception takes a universalistic rather than an exceptionalistic approach to social problems (Ryan, 1971). The universalistic approach assumes that the variety of unmet needs displayed by various groups in our society are not exclusively housed within those identified groups and individuals. It is recognized that the very process of identification of "problem groups"

often sets in motion a series of events which exacerbate rather than remedy the situation while placing responsibility for failure on the individuals in question. The alternative suggested by the environmental resources conception is that all people of this society have a right to have their collective and individual needs fulfilled. The vehicle of advocacy is suggested as a means of focusing intervention efforts on resource stimulation and generation rather than on individual repair. (Davidson & Rappaport, 1978, p. 76)

The work of the Massachusetts Advocacy Center is an example of the application of advocacy to problems of childhood. The center grew out of the experience of a group of Boston citizen-advocates known as the Task Force on Children Out of School. In 1973 the group received a Ford Foundation grant and became the Massachusetts Advocacy Center. The early development of the original group has been described by Peter Edelman (1973) in the *Har-*

vard Educational Review. It is an interesting story in its own right. In that article, Edelman describes the involvement of Hubert Jones and Larry Brown, who brought to the attention of the people of Massachusetts the large number of children being involuntarily excluded from school because of discipline problems, pregnancy, physical and emotional handicaps, or language problems. These are children who are often labeled "delinquent." Jones and Brown organized a task force of lay and professional people who put together a report on the problem. The task force was composed of "nonestablishment" people together with agency professionals who would have to respond to the report. It included, from the outset, those who lived in the neighborhoods most directly affected as well as those who were less likely to be advocates but who were both influential and willing to examine the facts. In the process, all of the task force members became convinced of a need for change, and they were able to support the report's widespread dissemination, which led to specific changes in public school policy and programs throughout Massachusetts.

In 1974, a law went into effect in Massachusetts calling for every school system to provide education, for *all* children, aimed at whatever the individual needs of a child happen to be. This is the law that has served as a model for similar national legislation. The people at the Advocacy Center view one of their roles to be a monitor of *implementation.* They established citizen monitors in 280 of the state's 351 school systems and provided the monitors with checklists of substantive issues to examine. The monitors collect data and follow up on schools not complying with the law. They train parents, as well as other case advocates, to assure that all children receive the full and intended benefit of the law (Massachusetts Advocacy Center, 1975).

In the context of describing the early work of the Advocacy Center, Edelman (1973) and Davidson and Rappaport (1978) have pointed out several "rules" or tactics useful when engaging in the advocacy strategy. Although this is not the place to detail such specifics, it may be worth noting the general style adopted by the Advocacy Center. After clear documentation of a difficulty and the dissemination of a report through the media directly to legislators and other citizens, a climate is created that allows the advocates to follow through. This means that much of the actual implementation is at the *administrative level* and that advocates can begin with positive or neutral tactics (see Table 5–2) when working in each school district. Negative tactics, including adverse publicity, use of the courts, and pushing for legislative change, are not excluded, but it is often the case that laws already exist and enforcement is the issue. What is often required is public attention to a difficulty *and* people who accept the responsibility for follow-through. These then are the key elements in the approach: (a) *public attention* that sheds light on a *general* problem; (b) people who keep the pressure on *specific* responsible agencies by providing specific and constructive change suggestions; (c) implicit or explicit threats to focus the attention from the general difficulty to a specific setting in question; and (d) quiet negotiation with agency administrators, backed up by a potential for publicity that has already been demonstrated.

What Edelman refers to as *administrative advocacy* is not litigation, nor is it ideology. There is no formula or ritualized way to proceed. Flexible reaction to a local situation and persistence are required. The exact content and style must differ from one locale to another. At the same time, various researchers and activists (Alinsky, 1971; O. M. Collective, 1971; Fairweather, Sanders, & Tornatzky, 1974; Rappaport, 1977a; Rothman, 1974) seem to arrive at very similar suggestions for social change activities.

The Massachusetts Advocacy Center has now implemented its model in multiple problem areas and has issued formal reports on topics such as "The Politics of Mental Health in Massachusetts"; "An Education Handbook for Students, Parents and Professionals"; "Childhood Lead Paint Poisoning"; "Hunger in the Classroom"; Special Education in Boston"; "The Drugging of Children"; and the "Juvenile Court." The Center's staff (with a budget as of 1975 of $120,000 provided by various foundations) expanded to eight full-time people and over 30 part-time volunteers, including attorneys, social scientists, educators, and students. Staff continue to see their role as initiators of others into action. In its 1975 *Annual Report*, the Advocacy Center describes itself as "monitoring the administrative process . . . to direct attention of policy makers, the public, and community/professional organizations to the unmet needs of Massachusetts citizens, particularly children." The staff do not focus on one area such as delinquency, education, or mental health but rather on the view that law is not enough and that the rights of children must be functionally translated into administrative action in various social systems. They seem to have "reframed the question."

The environmental resources and advocacy conception is only one of a number of possible alternatives for intervention once we begin to free ourselves from constraints on thinking and doing and begin to apply attempts to "reframe the question." For example, it was suggested earlier that the participants (or victims) of our research be included in its formulation. One such program was developed by Goldenberg (1971), who created an autonomous alternative setting for hard-core delinquent youth. The major characteristics of the setting were very different from those of most corrections programs and emphasized a horizontal organizational structure in which the youths and the staff were freed from a "one-up, one-down" relationship. Goldenberg attributed the success of this program in keeping the youths employed and out of legal difficulty (compared to a control group) to an experience that altered the nature and pattern of transactions between the

"treater" and the "treated." It is not possible here to describe in any detail the atmosphere created, but Goldenberg (1971), in *Build Me a Mountain*, does it very well, and this project serves as an example of the possibility for effective collaboration between professionals and target people.

The number of other possible alternatives, once we begin to break from the constraints of the past, may be limited only by our creativity. Some worth mentioning here have been discussed in more detail elsewhere (Monahan, 1976; Rappaport, 1977a).

In the realm of juvenile corrections, it may make sense to follow the general plan toward which the adult system seems to be heading, one that will base punishment on the crime and leave treatment a voluntary matter with no effect on the punishment (Morris, 1974). If we do move in this direction, perhaps it will be possible to unconfound punishment and treatment goals. Punishment seems appropriately "sentenced" on the basis of the crime (especially if, as the IJA-ABA Joint Committee on Juvenile Justice Standards (1977) suggests, there is repeal of all special offenses for juveniles, decriminalization of certain private offenses, and a tailoring of criminal law to the special situation of juveniles). On the other hand, once we begin to move away from viewing childhood misbehavior as a personality disturbance contained *in* the children, the "sentencing" of treatment is a bit absurd.

Without belaboring this point, which has now been made in enough places to be generally well understood in the case of adults, treatment probably should be limited to voluntary clients. While it is *possible* to do this, what it requires of us—if it is to be *truly voluntary*, and if we are to be *honest* about its likely outcome and its goals—is a completely different relationship between clients and treaters (cf. Goldenberg, 1971). Falling short of this will merely produce another example of first-order change in which children and their families will, perhaps more subtly, be coerced into the same treatments.

To satisfy these criteria, programs will need to be evaluated carefully (so we will know). In addition, whether programs aim to change the volunteers' personalities, communication skills, and styles, or to make resources available to them (as in advocacy), honesty requires that we tell these volunteers what the goals are and/or set up mutually agreeable goals before they enter our programs.

If people are not to be coerced, and if we are honest about our evaluations and our aims, a *multiplicity* of genuine alternatives will probably be required, since all people in trouble are obviously not the same. For example, it seems likely that programs such as Goldenberg's or programs of advocacy, which reject a victim-blaming ideology, are more likely to be viewed as sensible to many of the target people than are the psychotherapy or family counseling offered in other programs. If voluntary treatment is the ethical answer, then it must be truly voluntary. No one program is likely to be chosen by everyone, and what we now need to do is make available more options that are genuine alternatives for people in difficulty. True voluntary involvement requires a *genuine choice* between conflicting ways to view problems and to solve them.

We have already suggested that assessment research in consultation and in work with the courts requires a new face. Viewing crime and delinquency as a judgment process may lend weight to the possibilities for decriminalization of certain crimes without victims, and to the extent that this view of crime is a valid one for social scientists, it can help to challenge constraints on our thinking.

There are clearly other kinds of contributions psychologists can make to the courts. Research on jury decision making as well as consultation on program evaluation techniques are but two that come to mind, and the point, once again, is that being responsible does not require doing the same things we have always done.

Working with local police and providing them with alternatives for dealing with children in trouble (e.g., crisis intervention techniques; see Bard, 1970) is another way psychologists can be helpful. It may make even more sense to do this *indirectly* by helping to develop independent crisis centers staffed by local non-professional people (cf. McGee, 1974) in order to make resources and people outside of the official legal system available to children in difficulty. Such centers, of course, might end up merely dispensing transplanted versions of the same old methods; but if we do not insist on having these centers controlled by the mental health establishment, they *could* offer services based on the kind of genuinely new relationship discussed above (Rappaport, 1977a).

Conclusions

We conclude with a very brief set of answers to the questions raised at the start of this chapter:

1. Can psychologists recognize that work in (and out of) the justice system *always* requires us to take value stands?

We must; and we must acknowledge these values rather than pretend that they are scientifically justified. Furthermore, we can, by means of various value conflict generating mechanisms, actually study and take values into account so as to consciously use them to help generate new ideas.

2. Can we reject entrenched paradigms and learn to heighten our moral sensibilities by saying "no"?

We must: and we must acknowledge the limits on our competence and tell the public what these limits are. This will require careful evaluation of the things we do and a willingness to discard what does not work.

3. Are there alternatives to entrenched paradigms? Can we restate the problems or are we forced to accept them as presented to us?

There are alternatives, and we must learn to restate the problems in order to find them. The method we have suggested—reframing the question and searching for a multiplicity of alternative strategies with varying value bases—is presented as one way to deal with the inevitable ethical dilemmas in which we find ourselves.

A Final Note

Although we have emphasized comparison of contradictory value systems and alternative intervention strategies, it should be clear that we ourselves subscribe to some very definite biases. Our values suggest to us that those who would label children "delinquent" are as responsible for the existence of delinquency as are the children they label. The "problem of delinquency" cannot be understood without reference to the judgment policy of the labelers. Further, we believe that more can be accomplished by changing the significant others in the lives of those children who become entangled in the juvenile justice system than by trying to change the children themselves. Finally, we suggest that those who would intervene provide service as advocates who know their limitations and tell their clients of them.

W. Glenn Clingempeel, Edward Mulvey, and N. Dickon Reppucci

6

A National Study of Ethical
Dilemmas of Psychologists
in the Criminal Justice System

Is there any real viability or fullness for a [clinical] psychologist in a criminal justice system? To me the answer is "no." The breadth and depth of what a psychologist is is significantly reduced and translated into what court administration wants. It's like trying to help change significant, multiply-determined problems from within a dark closet with a flashlight that is running on 20-year-old batteries.

Although the sense of frustration depicted in this quotation is somewhat dramatically expressed, it represents the predominant tone of the ethical dilemmas reported in the 1976 APA Task Force Survey on the Role of Psychologists in the Criminal Justice System. Although the actual dilemmas reported varied considerably in their situational components, many common features and similar precipitating circumstances emerged from analysis of the data. This report is an effort to examine several of those common features.

Although the general area of ethics in psychology has been addressed directly (see APA's *Ethical Standards of Psychologists*, 1979), very little concern has been specifically directed at the ethical problems of the psychologist working in the criminal justice system. What little attention has been paid appears to focus on specific issues such as the use of behavior modification in correctional settings (Franks & Wilson, 1976) or the intricate relationship

between the law and psychological treatment (Szasz, 1963). Recently, Brodsky (1972) and Robinson (1974) have commented upon the daily ethical problems of psychologists in criminal justice settings; while these authors have shown considerable insight, they have presented little or no data. We hope the data presented here will serve as a first step in the analysis of the personal ethical dilemmas of the psychologist in the criminal justice system.

During the summer of 1976, the 349 psychologists who had stated in the APA 1975 Manpower Survey that their primary employment setting was related to the criminal justice system were contacted by the APA Task Force on the Role of Psychologists in the Criminal Justice System. Two hundred three (58.2%) of these psychologists responded to a questionnaire concerning ethical considerations (see p. 152). These individuals represented a wide range of justice-related backgrounds and roles. Two thirds had PhDs, and one third had MAs. They had a mean of 10.9 years of post-degree experience. The sample was predominantly male (82.8%) and overwhelmingly white (98.4%). The median percentage of the sample's professional activities related to the criminal justice system was 98.6%; the median percentages of their professional activities related to adults and to juveniles, respectively, were 84.8% and 10.1%. Thirty-four percent taught courses concerned with psychology and the criminal justice system at the college or graduate level, and another 26% taught courses at police academies or other settings. Most of the sample offered direct or indirect services to correctional institutions (70.0%), followed by courts (46.3%), probation departments (40.9%), parole agencies (31.0%), community correctional agencies (25.1%), and police agencies (17.2%). The most frequently provided services were psychological assessment of offenders (75.4%) and their psychological treatment (73.9%). Other significant services included consultation to administrators (53.2%), training personnel (52.7%), and screening personnel (21.2%).

The questionnaire focused on several potential ethical issues encountered in working in the criminal justice system. Certain questions addressed specific issues such as right to rehabilitation, right to refuse rehabilitation, indeterminate sentences, effectiveness of treatment, and prediction of violence, while others gave the respondents an opportunity to relate much more of their personal concerns (e.g., "What are the three major ethical issues confronting psychologists in the criminal justice system?" and "Give examples of personal ethical dilemmas you have confronted."). These latter questions provided the most valuable information for a phenomenological understanding of the issues. The great majority of those responding (81.8%) had personally encountered an ethical problem in their work in the criminal justice system. Overall, these psychologists indicated that they were troubled by a wide variety of ethical "tight spots" in which they regularly found themselves. The most personally troublesome ethical dilemmas appeared in the responses of psychologists working in correctional institutions, while the least distressing ethical conflicts resulted for psychologists in agency consultation roles (e.g., to halfway houses and police agencies).

At least two limitations of the data should be noted. First, as investigators, we had no way of clearly discerning the exact employment setting of each psychologist and of separating the data accordingly. However, given the high percentage of respondents working with or in correctional institutions, much of the following discussion inevitably focuses on psychologists employed in these particular settings. A second limitation inheres in the qualitative approach used. Examination of the content of qualifying responses to certain questions revealed that the alternative response categories given in the questionnaire were often ineffective in differentiating response content. Respondents making different categorical responses many times supported their positions with nearly identical justifications. Thus, after realizing that response categories in themselves would be fairly meaningless, we decided that careful, qualitative analysis would be most effective in communicating the richness of the data (200 single-spaced, typed pages!) as well as in providing some framework for future role considerations. As a result, our own outlooks may have shaded the categories somewhat, but we cautiously attempted to adhere to the data.

We begin discussion of the data by focusing on two overriding concerns—"custody versus treatment" and "Who is my client?"—concerns that were reflected throughout the responses to all of the questionnaire items. We then address more specific issues. First, we consider three problems of psychological assessment and treatment: the indeterminate sentence, the prediction of dangerousness, and behavior modification in corrections. Next we examine the twin issues of right to receive and/or to refuse treatment. We then discuss in some depth the predominant issue of confidentiality. Finally, we attempt to delineate three sources of these ethical dilemmas. Our goal in this attempt is not to formulate guidelines or to offer solutions, but to explicate as clearly as possible the ways in which psychologists in the criminal justice system perceive and deal with the most prevalent ethical dilemmas.

One last note—we have not addressed ethical dilemmas arising from research in the criminal justice system in this report because few of the responding psychologists cited research as an area of major ethical concern. Only three respondents cited research-related problems in the question regarding personal ethical dilemmas. Each of these cases involved the issue of confidentiality of research data, and the threat of research results being misused appeared very real. Moreover, the extent to which a researcher is responsible for program implementation of a study's findings certainly deserves further consideration. However, the sparsity of responses precludes discussion of these issues in the present report.

Two Overriding Issues

Custody Versus Treatment

While the conflict between custody and treatment is certainly neither new (Irwin, 1974) nor entirely unique to the criminal justice system (e.g., maximum security wards of mental hospitals experience it), its effects permeate every niche of the criminal justice system, often with intensity and high frequency. Moreover, the psychologist may very well be a focal point for this conflict. Even though only 10% of the responding psychologists directly cited custody versus treatment as one of their major ethical concerns, it was crystal clear that many of the ethical dilemmas cited were inextricably linked to or directly shaped by this conflict. Much of the national debate regarding value issues inherent in the custody versus treatment conflict has centered on the level of policy formation (Clark, 1970; President's Commission on Law Enforcement and Administration of Justice, 1967), but it is the concrete effects of this conflict that are confronted daily by the psychologist in the criminal justice system.

Since the criminal justice system has multiple and often conflicting goals, such as punishment, deterrence, rehabilitation, and restitution, the psychologist must try to balance all of these in the performance of assessment and treatment

duties. Consequently, the psychologist is the one who is often responsible for making supposedly therapeutic decisions while being constantly aware of the security implications of any such therapeutic moves. The following example from the survey may illuminate this point:

> I was assigned full time as a clinical psychologist at a girls' rehabilitation center. Individual girls were referred to me for counseling. On several occasions, when I called to see a particular girl, I was told she was confined to her room and inaccessible to me. Many confrontations with administrative staff over similar types of situations occurred to me over a ten-year period. I'm sure that the controlling staff perceived my actions as undermining their control system. For the most part, however, there was cooperative give and take between my role and that of the administrative staff. But for me, in this setting, treatment and accessibility had a higher priority than control and punishment.

One of the continuing problems in this decision making is that the "environmental press" of an institution does not always allow for a clear definition of either custody or treatment. Although psychologists' training and general orientation clearly direct them toward providing treatment for the sake of rehabilitation, the security pressure of an agency or institution often encroaches upon this role. Ethical dilemmas arose for some psychologists when custody-oriented activities were thrust upon them directly. For example, one psychologist was expected to carry a firearm, and another was instructed to participate in a search and shakedown. While these examples are blatant cases of the infringement of custody values on the psychologist's treatment role, most dilemmas result from more subtle factors affecting the psychologist's preconceived role.

The influences of institutional status, priorities, and language many times confuse the security and rehabilitation functions and force psychologists to define these functions for themselves. An example of this phenomenon frequently cited in the data is the prisoner who enters therapy for the purpose of gaining a positive parole recommendation. While rehabilitation is the ostensible goal, the real decision given to the psychologist is determining whether or not to recommend continued custody.

Any attempt to resolve this nagging difficulty by selectively applying custody or treatment goals seems to prove troublesome for psychologists. Brodsky (1972) has posited that most psychologists assume either a "system challenger" or "system professional" role as a resolution to this conflict. System challengers generally leave the criminal justice system after a short period of time and a number of confrontations, while system professionals stay on in a continuing effort to make difficult decisions in an educated manner. While this formulation may be a useful conceptual tool, our data seem to indicate, to the apparent dismay of much of our sample, that the marginal position between system professional and system challenger is the one that most of them view themselves as occupying.

Decisions regarding custody or treatment appear to hinge not on a single, clear ideological stance but rather on a variety of interrelated factors such as assessment of the seriousness of past or planned crimes, assessment of the potential risk of society, and the prognosis for the client given the current or a potential treatment program. Although some of these issues have received serious attention from social science researchers, it should be clear that no precise formula for weighing or quantifying these factors exists. The result is that the psychologist in the criminal justice system is forced to rely in large measure on personal values as well as specific expertise in making decisions regarding custody versus treatment. Politicians, policy makers, and administrators openly discuss the incongruities of rehabilitation and custody values and often make decisions based on subjective morality, conceptions of civil liberties, or political or economic realities. In contrast, the psychologist is generally viewed as

the professional in the analysis and prediction of human behavior. Supposedly, then, expertise and not values is the basis for the psychologist's recommendations and decisions. Judging from our data, this is a myth. The issue of values has not been purged from the psychologist's role because of any fund of scientific knowledge, even though psychologists and the world at large might wish this to be the case. In reality, the psychologists's role in the criminal justice system can be seen as a focal point for the inevitable conflict of custody and treatment goals and values.

Who Is My Client?

For our sample, the question "Who is my client?" is complicated by two major issues. The first is the difficulty of conflicting allegiances to the offender, the institution, and the society when making individual treatment decisions that would affect more than just one of these potential clients. The second is the determination of the level of intervention appropriate to the particular situation. The "client," therefore, is rarely the same across situations but may change with each new intervention strategy and set of circumstances.

Responses to many of the questions indicated a perceived powerlessness to effect genuine institutional or individual change. Frustration and despair with the pitfalls of organizational or individual program implementation in an institutional setting were commonplace. Under such circumstances, the issues of to whom or to what system (i.e., offender, court, institution, police force, or society) the psychologist is committed and under what conditions these commitments change become paramount. Consider the following. In response to the question "Have you personally encountered an ethical problem in criminal justice work?" 18 of the 109 psychologists who described incidents cited decisions regarding incompetent line staff, psychologists, psychiatrists, or administrators, and another 14 cited the problem of how far to pursue an issue when specific recommendations were disregarded by courts or administrators. Further, in response to the question "What are the three major ethical issues confronting psychologists engaged in criminal justice work?" 12% of the respondents directly stated "Who is my client?" and many others implied it.

The issues raised in these data go far beyond the simple question of the institutional status of psychologists in various settings. Instead, the psychologists in our sample seem to be raising a straightforward, but nonetheless ethically complex, question of just who qualifies as their primary client when working in the criminal justice system. To take the society or the institution as one's only client may imply a willful disregard for the welfare of the offender. On the other hand, choosing the offender as the sole client may imply no obligations regarding the protection of society. The difficult position of compromising these potentially conflicting ethical allegiances is occupied by a large number of our respondents.

Resolution of this ethical quandary obviously depends on a wide variety of situational and personal variables, and no consistent, quantifiable decision rules could possibly be deduced from our data. Three examples reveal the complexity of this sort of situation:

One particular problem emerges all the time. . . . In my position I am responsible for making recommendations to a parole board on men I have in psychotherapy. Naturally, I know more about my patients than the official record reflects, and I know that the things I tell the parole board will largely determine whether or not the man is granted parole. The philosophy of the board is conservative; I'm a liberal humanist. Where do my responsibilities lie? To the patient I'm treating or to the board that employs me? Most often I decide in favor of the patient and keep from the board information which I feel would hurt the patient. Implied in this also is my responsibility for the protection of society. There are simply no easy answers.

A child was placed in seclusion for fighting in an incident which, in my judgment, was pro-

voked and inadequately handled by a staff member. I issued a memorandum in support of the child which was squelched by the administration. I subsequently campaigned for more thorough and fair disciplinary procedures. The campaign was to no avail. My professional reputation was compromised so that this incident has ethical implications for treatment of staff as well as inmates.

Is the psychologist working in a correctional setting always a psychologist first, or is he a correctional worker first? Correctional settings are unique in that they clearly define *security* as the first responsibility of *all* employees and this frequently conflicts with the psychologist's role. My position is that I am first a correctional worker, and though I try to avoid conflicting situations, there are occasions when my job is similar to the correctional officers, e.g., shakedowns, riots and disturbances, disciplining inmate infractions, etc. My observation of many correctional psychologists' failures is that they see their institutional role as quite different from other employees and gradually they lose credibility and the confidence of fellow employees.

As these examples suggest, offender, criminal justice system, and society are simultaneously clients, but with necessarily varying priority status. The offender's motivation, the efficacy of the treatment program, and the potential danger to self or others are obviously mitigating factors in the ordering of client allegiances. The gravity of one of these circumstances (perceived dangerousness or truthfulness, for example) can change a psychologist's position from confidentiality to disclosure or from institutional compliance to advocacy.

Another more basic factor often affecting the structuring of priorities, however, is the clarity of the psychologist's role in the setting. Some would even contend that clarity of role is the only issue worth consideration:

There are no major problems of ethics, there are only problems that tend to be encountered in any therapy relationship. The effectiveness of correctional psychology cannot be improved upon by creating additional standards of ethics. The problem lies in the psychologist and in the administration failing to establish the role of the psychologist properly.

Whether role clarity is the panacea for all ethical dilemmas is obviously open to debate. What clearly emerges from our data, however, is the fact that the psychologist's role in the criminal justice system is usually multidimensional, and often ambiguous. Since a vast majority of the people in prison or in contact with the criminal justice system do not have a readily treatable mental disorder (Brodsky, 1972), the psychologist is faced with treating individuals whose progress from verbal therapy is often minimal. Environmental modification may be a more effective intervention stance, but the psychologist choosing this route inevitably becomes involved in organizational and institutional change as well as individual therapy. Thus, the level of intervention that could prove most beneficial in many instances may require an understanding of psychological functioning at the group, organizational, and/or institutional level as well as at the individual level.

In concluding this section, we view discussion of these two general concerns—custody versus treatment and who is the client—as a necessary backdrop for productive discourse regarding more specific ethical issues. We see no need to impale ourselves on the horns of either of these dilemmas by providing categorical answers that are at best oversimplified and at worst simpleminded. The most reasonable approach seems to be one acknowledging (a) that *at different times and with varying priorities* (Monahan, Note 1), the goals of both custody and treatment are legitimate and ethical, and (b) that both the offender and the criminal justice system are the clients of the psychologist working in that system.

Psychological Assessment and Treatment in the Criminal Justice System: Problems from the Psychologist's Perspective

As previously mentioned, the most frequently provided services of psychologists in the criminal justice system are the psychological assessment (75.4%) and treatment (73.9%) of offenders. This prevalence of psychologists in assessment and treatment roles provides a focal point for discussion. The responses of these psychologists to the following three questions and our subsequent categorization of their qualifying comments into common themes served to illuminate some of the sources of ethical dilemmas that arise in the performance of assessment-treatment roles. Following are the three questions and the percentages of psychologists providing comments in reply: Should the indeterminate sentence be maintained or abolished? (63%); Are psychologists and psychiatrists accurate in predicting whether an offender will be dangerous? (65%); What is your view of the use of behavior modification in corrections? (78%).

Should the Indeterminate Sentence Be Maintained or Abolished?

The majority of psychologists (83.7%) indicated that indeterminate sentencing should either be modified (37.8% suggesting "maintain but modify" and 19.9% suggesting "drastically modify") or completely eliminated (26%). Only 8.7% indicated "maintain as is," and 7.6% expressed "no opinion." Consequently, our analysis focuses on those comments of psychologists advocating changes in existing indeterminate sentencing procedures.

Four interrelated problems in indeterminate sentencing were identified as dilemma-engendering: (a) the inadequacy of treatment and assessment methods, (b) the lack of clarity in release criteria, (c) institutional abuses of procedures, and (d) the contamination of client/treatment-agent relationships by conflicting organizational goals. The major themes to emerge focused on the potential for abuse of indeterminate sentencing and the difficulties in determining when or if an offender has been "rehabilitated." Since indeterminate sentencing procedures are predicated upon a direct relationship between length of sentence and judgments of rehabilitation, the very essence of the system is undermined by inaccurate judgments. Furthermore, this inaccuracy sets the stage for widespread abuse. The psychologist as a, if not *the*, primary treatment agent is often required to deliver direct treatment services to offenders, to evaluate their progress, and, consequently, to make significant contributions to these rehabilitation judgments. As psychologists have become aware of the problems vitiating such judgments, ethical dilemmas have emerged. Moreover, these dilemmas are exacerbated by the recognition of the serious consequences of judgment errors.

Regarding the inadequacy of treatment and assessment methods, a substantial number of psychologists acknowledged that the absence of efficacious treatment techniques and validated assessment methods precludes the just administration of indeterminate sentencing. For example, one psychologist remarked, "Until assessment and treatment methods are better validated, a convicted man should have the right to a firm and definite sentence." Along similar lines another psychologist commented, "Our state of knowledge doesn't permit highly accurate prediction or evaluation, and therefore a determinate sentence is preferable to an open-ended one." Following similar reasoning, many psychologists asserted that indeterminate sentencing should be employed only when efficacious treatment programs exist and there is a high probability that an individual offender will be rehabilitated. The psychologists's dilemma emerges from his or her focal position, as a designated expert on treatment and behavioral prediction, in a "crucial-decision/inadequate-tools" predicament.

The lack of clarity in release criteria was a related problem area that surfaced in two kinds of comments, including (a) those in which psychologists suggested the development of explicit release criteria as a modification to indeterminate sentencing procedures, and (b) those in which psychologists acknowledged the frustrations of offenders kept in limbo about the length of their sentences. The majority of the modifications in indeterminate sentencing proposed by psychologists were aimed at combating the ambiguities and inconsistencies in release criteria. The following comment is quite typical: "Concrete, objective criteria should be specified as establishing eligibility for parole with inflexible minimum and maximum sentences—and the possibility of early release." Furthermore, psychologists recognized that the lack of clarity of release criteria engenders an extremely frustrating situation for offenders—one in which they neither know what is expected of them nor when they will be released. One psychologist remarked, "I've seen too many prison officials dangle a sentence before a man like an ice cream cone. Most inmates would prefer to be in control of their own sentences." Another psychologist responded, "Too much room for inequality with indeterminate sentencing. It is also frustrating for the offender who has to keep questioning, wondering, and worrying about when he will be released." Irwin (1974) analyzed rehabilitation from the convict's perspective in the California Correctional System and concluded that offenders suffer greatly from the perceived hypocrisies and whimsical nature of indeterminate sentencing. Moreover, indeterminate sentencing resulted in longer sentences (Irwin, 1974).

Another problem area focused on the organizational abuses of indeterminate sentencing procedures. One psychologist who had worked with these procedures for six years commented, "[I] see it as very subjective and subject to all the abuses and biases of staff making the decisions." In many comments, such as the following, parole boards were singled out as mechanisms of abuse: "Currently parole boards are perverting [indeterminate sentencing] procedures to keep individuals in custody for extended periods or are applying it arbitrarily." For the psychologist, the dilemma is often accompanied by a feeling of helplessness in the face of these perceived abuses. Witness the following example from the personal dilemma data:

> I discovered in the course of a program evaluation in an institution for delinquent youths that the data system on which the indeterminate sentence system operates was purposefully manipulated by staff to generate positive or negative parole board reports on the basis of personal subjective appraisals rather than actual prisoner performance. Staff also knowingly permitted the falsification of data and token economy pay by prisoners. I reported my findings in an open report to a top administrator. I have often found that problems of this sort trouble persons associated with them, but are allowed to continue because of social or organizational pressures against rocking the boat, or confronting co-workers with their ethical weaknesses.

Finally, an obviously very problematic area for psychologists centered on the contamination of offender/treatment-agent relationships by conflicting goals. Linking length of sentence (i.e., punishment) to judgments of treatment progress presents a very peculiar assessment-treatment problem; namely, the offender may not want treatment per se but may choose to participate in an effort to manipulate the system and gain an early release. Although length of sentence is often determined by institutional factors such as the minimal required sentence and the earning of "good time," it is an open secret among prisoners that a psychologist's recommendation is often the most powerful factor in parole decisions (Heinz, Heinz, Senderowitz, & Vance, 1976; Irwin, 1974). The fact that the psychologist is often viewed as an *evaluator* for purposes of punishment may insure that the trust and confidence usually considered important in treatment relationships are not attained. The psychologist is thus presented with the almost impossible task of distinguishing true rehabilitation from "pseudorehabilitation" and game playing from genuine interest in treatment. Watzlawick, Weakland, and Fisch (1974) label these difficulties the "paradoxical contamination of conflict-

ing goals." Following is their lucid portrayal of this dilemma:

> Whether the setting is a maximum-security prison or merely Juvenile Hall, the paradox is the same: the degree to which the offender has supposedly been reformed by these institutions is judged on the basis of his saying and doing the right things because he has been reformed, and not because he has merely learned to speak the right language and to go through the right motions. Reform when seen as something different from compliance inevitably becomes self-reflective—it is then supposed to be both its own cause and its own effect. This game is won by the "good actors": the only losers are those inmates who refuse to be reformed because they are too honest or angry to play the game; or those who allow it to be apparent that they are playing the game only because they want to get out, and are therefore not acting spontaneously. Humaneness thus creates its own hypocrisies, which leads to the melancholy conclusion that in this specific sense it seems preferable to establish a price to be paid for an offense, i.e., a punishment, but to leave the offender's mind alone and thereby avoid the troublesome consequences of mind-control paradoxes. (p. 69)

Are Psychologists and Psychiatrists Accurate in Predicting Whether an Offender Will Be Dangerous?

Only a small percentage of our sample felt that psychologists or psychiatrists were either "very accurate" (2.6%) or "very inaccurate" (5.2%) predictors of dangerousness. Instead, a middle-of-the-road posture characterized the majority of responses, with 43.8% indicating "fairly accurate," 18% indicating "don't know," and 30.4% indicating "fairly inaccurate." The difficulty of the decision-making process is illustrated by the following example from the personal dilemma data in which two psychologists using identical assessment techniques with the same individual reached totally opposite conclusions:

> I did a diagnostic evaluation of an individual who had stabbed another to death (and two weeks later shot a member of his own family

nonfatally) using Rorschach, DAP, TAT, etc. As usual during the Rorschach inquiry I did testing of the limits on color. My conclusion was that here was clear need for psychotherapeutic help. Within three weeks another psychologist repeated the same tests (with my report in hand), obtained the demonstrated responses, and concluded the opposite. *As a result we now have what I regard as a highly dangerous individual at large.*

Regardless of which psychologist was accurate, this example can be used to illustrate the two possible decision errors—the identification of false positives or false negatives—that are clearly the focus of both the prediction problem and the resulting ethical dilemmas. If the psychologist commentator was right, then a potentially dangerous person was predicted not dangerous (i.e., a false negative) and was released, thereby creating an unsafe situation. However, if the psychologist commentator was wrong and the recommendation had been carried out, then a nondangerous person would have been predicted dangerous (i.e., a false positive). Such a prediction may have resulted in incarceration and thus been an injustice.

It is this latter problem, the identification of false positives and the resultant overprediction of dangerousness, that emerged from the comment analysis as the most salient issue. One psychologist, for example, responded, "I think we are perhaps fairly accurate only because we tend to overpredict dangerousness. This conservatism identifies a lot of dangerous people, but it also mislabels a large number of nonviolent individuals." Still another psychologist commented, "[We] can isolate many; but there is an 'overkill' and pressure to be sure and safe which leads to overidentification." As these and many similar comments suggested, the essence of the prediction-of-dangerousness dilemma focuses on determining the proper tradeoff between the two decisional errors. Put in its usual context the central question becomes, "How many false positives should we tolerate to protect ourselves from one false negative?" The nagging difficulties in the weighing of decisional costs are

rather dramatically reflected in the comment by this psychologist: "But is the good done by a correct prediction that an offender is not likely to repeat violence outweighed by the harm when a small number of predictions are wrong and a released offender then commits a child rape-murder?"

The problem of overprediction is intensified by the current state of the prediction art. Recent reviews have attested to the deficient reliability and validity of dangerousness predictions and the strong tendency to err on the side of overprediction (Monahan, 1975; Morris, 1974; Von Hirsch, 1972). Furthermore, Monahan's (1975) review dramatically revealed that the percentage of false positives ranged from 54% to a phenomenal 99%.

While a significant number of psychologists acknowledged the overprediction problem, many others posited factors likely to improve the prediction process. Witness the following representative comment: "Prediction based on previous behavior is quite accurate. Social histories and criminal records are essential for this sort of prediction." Other psychologists stressed the importance of combining traditional methods of psychological assessment with social history data: "I know that psychological methods of doing it are very inaccurate but they can be effective in conjunction with additional life history data." Still other psychologists suggested the importance of assessing situational-ecological factors: "Situational/contextual/environmental factors are just as significant as intrapsychic factors. Just assessing the individual is fraught with errors." All of these assertions accentuate the often voiced concern that psychological data alone are not sufficient (e.g., Mischel, 1968, 1973; Moos & Insel, 1973; Wenk & Emrich, 1972). Megargee (1970), in his extensive review of the effectiveness of psychological tests in predicting dangerousness, confirms this concern and concludes that no psychological tests are effective predictors in the individual case. There is also evidence, however, that even the combining of a multitude of predictions, using sophisticated multivariate analyses, is inadequate (Monahan, 1975).

In spite of the generally dismal findings of studies on the prediction of dangerousness, the current demands on the criminal justice system to make such predictions cannot be overlooked. In an apparently pragmatic response to these demands, several psychologists raised the annoying question "If not us, then who else?" While acknowledging both the limitations of existing prediction instruments and the wide variability in the prediction skills of mental health experts, these psychologists contended that they (as a group) were the professionals most capable of making dangerousness predictions. One psychologist, for example, after circling "fairly accurate," went on to comment "[The judgment of psychologists and psychiatrists is] a good deal more accurate than the judgment of the legal and judicial personnel who are usually called upon to make these decisions." Another psychologist remarked, "Not the question that should be posed. Rather ask, since the courts must make this type of decision, is anyone better qualified or more accurate?" Moreover, and not surprisingly, some who raised this question also argued for psychologists' general superiority over psychiatrists in dangerousness predictions. Witness, for example, this rather pessimistic comment: "I would trust about one of 20 licensed clinical psychologists to do this, and about one of 50 psychiatrists. No one else is going to exceed them in accuracy." Thus the sentiment that psychologists are the best, albeit inadequate, predictors of dangerousness surfaced in different forms in a variety of qualifying comments.

As reported earlier, psychologists acknowledged the "pressures to be safe" in their comments on overprediction of dangerousness. The following statement gives us a hint of possible contingencies beyond the concern for community safety that may underlie these pressures: "Since these professionals often do not wish to take the risk and the responsibility of calling potentially dangerous behavior to others' attention—especially since it is often difficult to predict whether violent thought will lead to violent behavior for the particular prisoner, few wish to put their professional necks on the line." As suggested by this comment, a threat of aversive consequences for the psychologist underlies errors in predictions of dangerousness. The emphasis on "pressures to be safe" rather than "pressures to be just" suggests different consequences for underprediction and overprediction errors. While overprediction may result in unjust incarceration, the errors are quite conveniently concealed from public or professional scrutiny. Therefore, significant negative consequences for the psychologist are unlikely. Underprediction, in contrast, could have several negative effects upon the reputation of the psychologist. A murder committed by a released offender who was judged to be not dangerous by the psychologist could result in public and political condemnation for the criminal justice agency and the psychologist. Given the equivocal attitude of psychologists toward the accuracy of dangerousness predictions (and the different personal consequences of the two types of error), it is no surprise that overprediction proliferates.

In conclusion, the prediction of dangerousness poses dilemmas, especially as the psychologist is often conducting assessments to facilitate administrative-judicial decision making about incarceration rather than individual treatment prescription. Moreover, the tools for making such assessments are viewed as woefully inadequate. Personal ethical dilemmas thus emerge as psychologists develop an awareness of both the "crucial-decisions/inadequate-tools" predicament and the consequences of overprediction errors for the individual liberty of false positives.

What Is Your View of the Use of Behavior Modification in Corrections?

A mushrooming legal concern for protecting the rights of individuals in closed institutions (Friedman, 1975; Wexler, 1973, 1975), combined with horror stories of flagrant abuses of alleged behavior modification techniques with prisoners (*Knecht v. Gillman*[1]; Mitford, 1973; Opton, 1975; Reppucci & Saunders, 1974), has made the use of behavior modification programs in corrections a controversial public issue (Saunders & Reppucci, 1978). As the professionals most often advocating and/or overseeing such programs, psychologists often find themselves immersed in this controversy and having to grapple with a host of ethical dilemmas.

In response to the survey question regarding behavior modification, 75.8% of the psychologists indicated that they were "in favor" (19.2% "very much in favor"; 56.6% "in favor with qualification"), while only 15% were opposed (5% "very much opposed"; 10% "opposed with qualification"). The majority of qualifications were concerned with potential abuses, and therefore, our analysis focuses on these.

One major theme of the responses was concern that the rights of prisoners not be violated by behavior modification programs. The psychologists felt that the doctrines of right to refuse treatment, informed consent, and complete voluntariness needed to be guaranteed. However, given the nature of correctional institutions—where one group has almost total power over another, where punishment and custody are priority values, and where treatment participation is linked to release—the difficulty of assuring these rights and the potential use of behavior modification to accomplish nontreatment functions were ostensibly troublesome to many psychologists. Several psychologists voiced doubts that true freedom of choice can exist in correctional institutions. As one psychologist put it, "I do not feel that a person in an institution actually has an option of participation.. The possibility that such participation may influence parole—or be perceived that way by the inmate—eliminates true freedom of choice." For the most part, the issue is not whether behavior modification should be used, but rather, whether a given inmate is voluntarily seeking treatment or is coerced into treatment.

In their comments, the psychologists outlined a number of specific rights that should not be violated by behavior modification programs: (a) a clear statement of treatment goals, (b) a clear statement of methods to be used to achieve those goals, (c) periodic statements of progress in treatment, (d) professional expectations regarding outcomes of treatment and nontreatment, (e) knowledge of alternative treatment approaches, and (f) withdrawal from treatment at any time without penalty.

In addition, lay and professional monitoring committees were mentioned by several psychologists as mechanisms to assure adherence to these rights. Furthermore, the distinction between "absolute" and "contingent" rights was implicit in many comments but explicit in the following one: "All prisoners should have certain basic rights and privileges that should not be tampered with—rewards should be above and beyond these." This assertion has been discussed previously (Davison & Stuart, 1975; Wexler, 1973) and affirmed by legal mandates (*Wyatt v. Stickney*[2]).

Another dilemma-engendering concern was the process of selecting goals, with a focus on the following question: "For whose benefit (i.e., inmate, psychologist, institution, or society) are the goals selected?" For example, one psychologist remarked, "While behavior modification techniques as one part of a total program have been effective, they are not justified in the interest of good housekeeping." Another stated, "Criterion performance should be more reflective of what situation the inmate will face when he is released." These comments are representative of many that expressed the opinion that behavior modification should not be used for the benefit of the institution in

---

[1] Knecht v. Gillman, 488 F.2d 1136 (8th Cir. 1973).

[2] Wyatt v. Stickney, 344 F. Supp. 373 & 387 (M.D. Ala. 1971), aff'd sub. nom., Wyatt v. Aderholt, 503 F.2d 1305 (5th Cir. 1972).

assuring compliance, docility, and maintenance functions but rather should only be used to accomplish goals related to effective functioning in the community. However, this choice of goals is not as straightforward as it may appear at first glance. Several psychologists acknowledged that the problem of differentiating these goals is complicated by the paucity of behavior modification research demonstrating generalization of behaviors learned in prisons to community situations. Ostensibly "appropriate" goals might therefore have uncertain long-range relevance and, in fact, serve nothing more than "keep-busy, temporary-control" functions.

A third set of concerns converged on the theme that behavior modification is not a monolithic procedure but represents an array of potentially therapeutic techniques, some more useful or dangerous than others. The major qualifications derived from this theme were recommendations that certain techniques not be employed (e.g., aversive conditioning) and that specific techniques be matched to individual needs. The issue of abuses that often result from uniform applications of techniques appeared to underlie these concerns.

A related issue is the egregious limitation of resources for accomplishing the tailoring of procedures to individual needs. Most often mentioned were the shortage of well-trained psychologists to effectively coordinate programs, the shortage of trained staff to carry out such programs, and the overall absence of accountability. As an example, one psychologist remarked, "The programs must be controlled by well-trained ethical clinicians. The giving away to other professions and disciplines of psychological techniques has led to serious abuses." Another psychologist who was "very much in favor" commented, "They should be used but only with adequate supervision and training of staff." Taken as a whole, the comments suggest that a "sense of powerlessness" may be a source of ethical dilemmas for psychologists involved with behavior modification in corrections. Psychologists may feel "power-

less" either to provide quality programs to meet individual needs or to remediate abuses stemming from limited resources.

Referring to behavior modification procedures, Skinner (1971) stated, "Such a technology is ethically neutral. It can be used by villain or saint. There is nothing in a methodology which determines the values governing its use" (p. 150). An overriding problem for psychologists with regard to the use of behavior modification in corrections appears to focus on determining "the values governing its use." Many psychologists acknowledged in their comments that behavior modification can be used in the service of punishment and institutional control as well as in the service of enhancing individual competencies and/or the likelihood of adjustment to the community upon release. However, the question "In the service of what (treatment or control) is behavior modification being used?" is not ordinarily an easy one. The source of difficulties in determining "the values governing its use" in correctional institutions seems most skillfully captured in the following psychologist's comment:

> Again these are double-edged swords which can be used as immensely helpful therapeutic adjuncts or as instruments of control and, yes, as abuses of power. In any situation where one group of humans has been provided with power over another, there is the spectre of abuse. The setup is an adversary one by definition, and the mental health expert inevitably gets caught in the crossfire. *The most insidious concern with respect to behavior modification is the confounding of intentions—such as control vs. treatment.*

The "confounding of intentions" phenomenon suggested by this comment is reflected most clearly in the very language of corrections. Medical metaphors (e.g., calling what the prisoners refer to as "the hole" an "adjustment center") are quite pervasive and are examples of how language can obscure the values often served by behavior modification programs. Several comments by psychologists opposed to behavior modification in corrections argued that the jargon disguises the actual goal of institutional control by wrapping it in the ceremonial robes of treatment. One psychologist who was "very much opposed" expressed this sentiment quite lucidly: "It is cosmetic and highly related to control inherent in prison. As soon as a prisoner is released all hope of treatment is lost. Behavior modification in prisons is a fancy name for institutional control."

In conclusion, it should be recalled that despite the concomitant ethical dilemmas, the vast majority of psychologists were "in favor" of the use of behavior modification in corrections. Furthermore, it appears that this majority also believes that with appropriate steps taken to guard against abuses, behavior modification techniques can serve positive treatment goals in prisons. Only a very small percentage of our sample argued that the mixture of behavior modification and corrections is necessarily abusive chemistry.

The Prisoners' Rights Dilemmas: More Problems from the Psychologist's Perspective

The debates on prisoners' rights have focused attention on the complexities of a more pervasive conflict—the right of individuals to be deviant versus the right of society to protect itself from this deviance. While society's rights are assumed to be legitimate, a growing array of court cases have greatly expanded the rights of involuntarily confined individuals (*Wyatt v. Stickney, Rouse v. Cameron*[3], *Holt v. Sarver*[4], *Donaldson v. O'Connor*[5]). This expansion of rights has instigated much needed reform, but it has also raised difficult questions for those professionals employed by closed institutions. Once again psychologists in the criminal justice

system find themselves caught in the crossfire of these recurrent debates. In an attempt to extricate the related issues most bothersome to psychologists, the following questions were included in the survey: Should a right to rehabilitation exist in prisons? Should a right to refuse rehabilitation exist in prisons?

Approximately 60% of the psychologists gave qualifying comments to the right to rehabilitation question, while 55% commented on the right to refuse rehabilitation. As in previous sections, we have organized these qualifying comments into major content themes, which constitute the primary focus of analysis.

Should a Right to Rehabilitation Exist in Prisons?

Legal support for the right to treatment for persons committed to psychiatric hospitals was first provided in *Rouse v. Cameron*. Since this landmark decision, subsequent court rulings have strengthened this doctrine for involuntarily confined mental patients (*Wyatt v. Stickney, Donaldson v. O'Connor, Lynch v. Baxley*,[6]). Furthermore, the right-to-treatment doctrine has been extended to a right to rehabilitation for imprisoned offenders (*Holt v. Sarver*). This right-to-rehabilitation doctrine has spawned considerable polemics on the legitimate goals of prisons and the difficulties of providing rehabilitation services in prison settings.

In response to the survey question "Should a right to rehabilitation exist in prisons?" 81.5% of the psychologists gave affirmative answers (49% "definitely yes"; 32.5% "qualified yes"). Opposition to a right to rehabilitation was voiced by 16.5% (10.5% "definitely no"; 6% "qualified no").

Even though a great majority of the sample clearly favored increased rights for prisoners in regard to their treatment options, the qualifying comments indicated caution about designation

---

[3] Rouse v. Cameron, 343 F.2d 451 (D.C. Cir. 1966).

[4] Holt v. Sarver, 309 F. Supp. 362 (E.D. Ark. 1970).

[5] Donaldson v. O'Connor, 493 F.2d 507 (5CA 1974).

[6] Lynch v. Baxley, 386 F. Supp. 378 (D.C. Ala. 1974).

of rehabilitation and/or treatment as a human right. There was a clear preference for the existence of the *opportunity for* rather than the *right to* rehabilitation in prisons. Witness the following comments across response categories:

"definitely yes"—Although some may not want such services, [they] should at least have the opportunity available to [them].

"qualified yes"—Provided and encouraged to use services, but not coerced.

"qualified no"—Prefer to see "opportunities," rather than rights.

"definitely no"—Some don't want and can't use [them] meaningfully.

One major theme of the qualifying comments was that a genuine motivation for rehabilitation services should be a necessary prerequisite to a right to rehabilitation. In a substantial number of comments, psychologists emphasized the motivation of the prisoner as an important consideration in the implementation of right-to-treatment doctrines. For example, one psychologist remarked, "Such a right presumes a genuine desire by the client plus the psychological wherewithal to benefit from professional help." Another psychologist commented, "Some services should be provided, but a great number of inmates do not need or want psychological services." This issue also emerged when psychologists suggested screening systems to identify genuinely motivated individuals. One psychologist, for example, qualified his support of the right to rehabilitation with the comment, "[I support it] if two or more professionals certify to the prisoner's serious wish for help." However, while screening mechanisms may provide some assistance, an abundance of responses extending across all survey questions testified to the extreme difficulty, if not impossibility, of reliably differentiating the good actors from the genuinely motivated.

A related theme concerned the fear of widespread abuses by prisoners if a right to rehabilitation was mandated. This concern was captured most lucidly in the following comment:

The right to rehabilitation must recognize that some inmates use service as nothing more than to receive credit on their record for parole and make no effort to change as individuals. I resent inmates dictating to me that I will see them regularly and they make no effort to help themselves when I could be working with someone perhaps more motivated. Let's not become a victim of inmates' manipulative skills because of a law.

Some even felt that a guaranteed right to rehabilitation would create a bureaucratic, legalistic monster:

Whatever is declared a right of the prisoner usually becomes a nightmare of unending demands from sociopathic types . . . [the] psychologist working under such an edict would soon find himself inundated with work, much of which is totally useless.

Thus, a right to rehabilitation was seen by some as a solution that would create more problems than it would solve. Prisoners would still be unmotivated and services would still be lacking.

A final concern focused on the overall relevance of psychological services in prison rehabilitation efforts in conjunction with the inefficacious quality of these services. Many psychologists qualified their affirmative responses with comments such as the following:

All sorts of things operate under the umbrella of rehabilitation services. Many of these do not do the job. If real rehabilitation were possible, I would give an unqualified Yes.

The general tone of the comments suggested that psychological services were not always necessary or relevant for prison populations. One psychologist put it well: "I'm certainly not going to fall in the trap of saying that it has to include the services of a psychologist until I see it demonstrated that a psychologist has unique services to offer." Another remarked, "The rehabilitation services needed will not always require the services of a psychologist. The use of a psychologist should be selective and not routine." In essence, psychological services should be available if relevant but not exist as a blanket right for all.

In a somewhat different but clearly related fashion, some respondents implied that the right to rehabilitation should be reframed as the right to "effective" rehabilitation. Note the following remark: "Only if some progress can be documented. Considering the lack of evidence that such programs have been very effective, I feel we first need more innovative programs and good evaluation research." Others went so far as to suggest that the misrepresentation of ineffective services as effective was unethical. Witness the following comment: "We haven't yet developed demonstratively effective rehabilitation techniques. Pretending expertise where none exists is at least unethical."

In summary, these psychologists in the criminal justice system expressed a preference for the opportunity for rehabilitation services rather than the right to rehabilitation. Consequently, they argued that legal mandates should ensure the availability of services but that such mandates should not force services on prisoners who do not want them or are not likely to benefit from them. Moreover, given the lack of efficacious treatment strategies and the egregious shortages of treatment resources, they acknowledged that rehabilitation on a broad scale is, at best, a chimerical notion.

Should a Right to Refuse Rehabilitation Exist in Prisons?

The vast majority of psychologists (85.3%) were in favor of a right to refuse rehabilitation (51% "definitely yes"; 34.3% "qualified yes"). Only 13% were opposed (6.5% "definitely no"; 6.5% "qualified no"), and 1.7% had "no opinion." The qualifying comments, however, revealed a variety of stipulations for the right to refuse rehabilitation.

A key issue was adherence to the doctrine of informed consent. The major concern was that the prisoner be given all relevant information, especially in regard to the consequences of refusing rehabilitation, in an effort to insure an educated choice between accepting or refusing treatment. For example, one psychologist commented, "[The right to refuse rehabilitation] should go hand in hand with the prisoner's getting the information about what this refusal may do to him/her in terms of parole." Several psychologists also voiced support for the broader conditions of informed consent, including a clear specification of treatment goals, methods, and professional expectations regarding outcomes and risks. In addition, the salient issue of whether true informed consent is even possible in prisons was often raised. These comments focused on the contingencies of coercion that influence a prisoner's choice to accept or to refuse treatment and on whether, or in what cases, a refusal of rehabilitation should have adverse effects on the prisoner.

The national debate on informed consent has focused on such cases as *Kaimowitz v. Michigan Department of Mental Health*[7], in which the court ruled that an involuntarily confined mental patient's decision-making abilities were affected by institutionalization to the extent that voluntary consent for psychosurgery could not be obtained. It has been argued that an extension of this ruling to less intrusive treatment approaches would rob the prisoner of self-determination in the decision to accept or reject treatment, since any treatment of involuntarily confined individuals would be considered coerced (Friedman, 1975; Wexler, 1975). The comments of the respondents reflected the complexities of these discussions.

---

[7] Kaimowitz v. Michigan Department of Mental Health, U.S.L.W., 42, 2063 (C.A. 73-19343-AW, Cir. Ct. Wayne County, Mich., July 10, 1973).

Many psychologists expressed the right of society to protect itself and therefore to impose longer sentences for treatment refusal. As one psychologist remarked, "Public needs protection—right to refusal in some cases should mean continued imprisonment." Others, however, asserted that the right to refuse treatment should be reframed as "the right to refuse treatment without adverse consequences." The view here was that any consent to treatment would necessarily be coerced and that voluntary decision making would be bastardized. Nevertheless, the comments implied that the amount of coercion, and therefore the extent to which voluntariness should be encroached upon, is variable and contingent upon at least two factors: (a) an evaluation of the dangerousness and concomitant risk to society if the prisoner is released without rehabilitation services, and (b) the degree to which the treatment services are proven effective in remediating deficiencies in the prisoner directly related to estimated dangerousness. In essence, while the importance of informed consent was stressed, coercion (in the form of longer incarceration for treatment refusal) was regarded as at least legitimate, if not desirable, as a means of fostering the protection of society from dangerous individuals.

A second major theme revolved around those exceptional circumstances in which the right to refuse rehabilitation might be abrogated. The mental competence and age of the prisoner and the nature of the psychopathology and/or offense were cited as three major factors involved in such circumstances. In cases of questionable mental competence, several psychologists suggested that the right to refuse treatment should be overridden by the right of the state to impose treatment in the "best interests" of the prisoner and society. One psychologist, for example, who had given a "definitely yes" response, commented, "The only exception would be in cases of severely ill persons who need treatment to be able to have a human existence, and who

are incapable of making rational decisions on their own behalf." The troublesome question of legal age for refusing treatment was also raised by a few psychologists. While there was no consistent answer in the data regarding the exact age necessary to refuse treatment, there was consensus that juveniles could not always make meaningful decisions regarding certain treatment options. Overall, the tone of the psychologists' remarks implied agreement with recent discussions (Friedman, 1975; Wexler, 1975) asserting that while the state lacks sufficient justification to force treatment on unwilling competent persons, it does have the right to impose treatment in the "best interests" of unwilling, incompetent clients.

Several psychologists clearly stated that the nature of the psychopathology and/or offense should be a consideration in determining whether the right to refuse rehabilitation should be denied. A major theme of these comments was that individuals considered dangerous to themselves or others may be legitimately prevented from exercising a right to refuse rehabilitation. For example, a psychologist giving a "qualified no" response commented, "[Right to refuse rehabilitation should] not [exist] if a direct link between psychopathology and the offense can be established, e.g., sex offenders." Along similar lines, another psychologist remarked, "[Right to refuse rehabilitation should exist] except for inmates with a demonstrated potential for assaultive behavior. Society has a right to modify the behavior of overtly aggressive individuals." Even in cases of clearly dangerous individuals, though, most psychologists maintained that the application of drugs should constitute a clear limit to forced treatment. As one psychologist put it, "If a prisoner is a psychotic he should be treated by medication, but have the right to refuse psychotherapy, shock treatment, psychosurgery, etc., especially if he/she is a danger to himself or others."

A final theme evolved from numerous comments suggesting that forcing "treatment" would necessarily render it ineffective. Psychologists maintained that rehabilitation is ultimately a self-instigated process that is doomed to failure if coerced:

> It is impossible to force rehabilitation on anyone. Any rehabilitation efforts including testing and evaluation must have the cooperation of the prisoner. If he doesn't want to cooperate, dealing with him in this way is a waste of time.

> Treatment, as I view it, requires the active motivated participation of the client if it is to be effective. I doubt if people can be forced or coerced into rehabilitation. Forced rehabilitation is a misnomer. If it's forced, it's not rehabilitation.

While these comments were representative of the majority, a few psychologists did point out that a genuine interest in treatment may occur after a prisoner is forced to participate. Here is one such comment: "Although 'forced' rehabilitation is usually not effective, sometimes real motivation can be created after the individual is required to participate."

In summary, psychologists in the criminal justice system strongly supported a right to refuse rehabilitation in prisons. Along with this support, they stressed the importance of adhering to the informed-consent doctrine, especially as it applies to providing prisoners with explicit information regarding the consequences of treatment refusal. While forced treatment was widely denounced, exceptional circumstances were noted in cases of mental incompetence, psychopathology, and/or prisoners dangerous to themselves or others. Moreover, psychologists also acknowledged that voluntariness and freedom of choice were variable notions and that strong pressure to accept treatment (in the form of longer incarceration for treatment refusal) does not necessarily deny a right to refuse treatment.

Confidentiality Dilemmas

While no question in this survey directly addressed the issue of confidentiality, the responses to most of the questions implicated confidentiality dilemmas as extremely troublesome, quite prevalent, and very much on the minds of psychologists in the criminal justice system. The central significance of confidentiality dilemmas was underscored by the fact that 75% of the psychologists identified them as one of the three major ethical dilemmas confronting the psychologist engaged in criminal justice system work. Furthermore, when asked to describe an actual dilemma that they personally encountered, 25% of those who responded to this item described a confidentiality dilemma.

This section focuses on an analysis of the difficulties enumerated by psychologists (in the personal dilemma data) in deciding whether or not to breach confidentiality. However, before exploring examples from the personal dilemma data, it seems necessary to set the stage with a brief discussion of current confidentiality debates.

An Overview of Current Confidentiality Debates

Current controversy surrounding confidentiality dilemmas focuses on the question "What exceptional circumstances, if any, should suggest a breach of confidentiality?" The issue hinges on a most difficult balancing of competing professional, institutional, and societal values. Principle 5a of APA's *Ethical Standards of Psychologists* (1979) reflects the nature of this balancing:

> Information received in confidence is revealed only after most careful deliberation and when there is a clear and imminent danger to an individual or to society, and then only to appropriate professional workers or public authorities. (p. 4)

Clearly this code implies that professional values reifying the privacy of client-clinician communications must be balanced against societal protection values. A constraint on the absoluteness of therapeutic confidentiality is thus recognized in those exceptional cases where "there is a clear and imminent danger to an individual or to society." However, given the primitive state of the art in predicting dangerousness, the determination of when "a clear and imminent danger" exists seems quite likely to be relegated to the realm of values.

Recent discussions have reflected both sides of the limits/no-limits debate on therapeutic confidentiality. Siegel (1977), for example, takes the position that *under no circumstances* should the psychologist breach the confidentiality of a client. He argues that progress in therapy is contingent upon complete trust in the privacy of client communications with "no strings attached." He also contends that the danger suggested by threats of violence or harm can almost always be removed without a breach of confidentiality. While he would not permit injury or death, he also would in no case breach confidentiality. In summary, Siegel (1977) states,

> I am taking the position that we seriously impair our ability in a helping profession such as ours when we attempt to arrogate unto ourselves powers we do not and should not have. When we agree to "exceptional circumstances" under which the confidentiality of information about individuals is waived, we not only violate the civil rights of children and adults, but we violate our essential role as psychologists. (p. 2)

Shah (1977), on the other hand, argues against the absoluteness of therapeutic confidentiality. While agreeing that the values associated with the maintenance of therapeutic confidentiality are important, he stresses that groups with special interests (e.g., psychotherapists) should not be allowed to be major

determiners of public policy. He points out that the self-interests of professions may not be consistent with the public interest. Moreover, Shah argues that psychologists as well as other professionals should concentrate on developing better knowledge and understanding of the social and legal guidelines under which they are supposed to function. Shah's (1977) concern that such guidelines may be ignored is reflected in the following statement:

> Some clinicians are utterly convinced that therapeutic confidentiality must remain an absolute and paramount value over all other societal interests. Such ethnocentric zeal seems to demand that the entire society should accept the values and ideologies of psychotherapists. In other words, what is good for psychotherapists is good for society. (p. 2)

Despite the apparent plethora of psychologists who support Siegel's "absolutist" position, a recent court ruling may endanger this stance. The California Supreme Court (*Tarasoff v. Regents of University of California*[8]) held that psychotherapists have a "duty to warn" potential victims of threats of violence made by their clients. The clinician in this case was held liable for not warning the potential victim of a murder threat made by a client during therapy. The case ensued because the client carried out his threat, and the parents of the victim sued for damages. The most controversial aspect of the court's decision stated,

> Once a therapist does in fact determine, or under applicable professional standards should have determined, that a patient poses a serious danger of violence to others, he bears a duty to exercise reasonable care to protect the foreseeable victim of that danger. (Shah, 1977, p. 2)

The clinician defended himself with two major arguments. First, he contended that it is

---

[8] Tarasoff v. Regents of University of California, 13 C.3d 177; 529 P.2d. 553; 118 Cal. Rptr. 129 (1974).

almost impossible to predict when violent threats will lead to violent actions, thus citing our inability to predict dangerousness as a major defense. Second, he argued that open communication permitting full disclosure—an essential to psychotherapeutic success—will be undermined by a duty to warn. While the court acknowledged these arguments, it remained unconvinced and asserted that these difficult decisions are like those typically made by mental health professionals. In a statement likely to haunt many psychotherapists for years to come, the court concluded,

> Public policy favoring protection of the confidential character of patient-psychotherapeutic communication must yield in instances in which disclosure is essential to avert danger to others. The protective privilege ends where the public peril begins. (Shah, 1977, p. 2)

While the *Tarasoff* decision has jurisdiction limited to California, its potential for affecting other rulings far and wide has been a major precipitant of the limits-of-confidentiality controversy. The controversy seems further complicated by our difficulties in predicting dangerousness and by the corresponding absence of guidelines for determining "where the public peril begins." Therefore, the nature of exceptional circumstances that may warrant a confidentiality breach remains quite nebulous.

Four Examples from the Personal Dilemma Data

The following four examples of confidentiality dilemmas were reported as "personal dilemmas" by psychologists in the criminal justice system. While the actual descriptions have been paraphrased, an attempt has been made to preserve the essential facts presented in each case. These particular examples were chosen primarily because they were rich in descriptive detail and representative of other cases reported in the data. Simply stated, the dilemma for the psychologist in each of the four cases is, "Under these specific circumstances, should the client's confidentiality be breached?"

The Case of Mr. E and the Group Therapy Session

The setting was a maximum-security correctional facility. The client, Mr. E, was an inmate serving time for a violent homicide. Mr. E had attended a number of group therapy sessions conducted by a correctional system psychologist. While it was apparent that Mr. E's initial motivation for treatment was to influence the parole board, the psychologist later became convinced that Mr. E genuinely "wanted" treatment, as he was actively involved in therapy and was making some positive short-term gains.

During a group therapy session, Mr. E's ostensibly growing trust in the psychologist culminated in a dilemma-engendering disclosure. Mr. E revealed that he had repeatedly stabbed another inmate who had antagonized him by perpetually seeking a sexual relationship. This disclosure was offered despite the fact that Mr. E had been warned regarding the limits of confidentiality imposed on the psychologist. Furthermore, Mr. E provided enough specific information to eliminate any doubts as to the veracity of the disclosure. The victim of the stabbing survived but refused to identify his assailant. Therefore, Mr. E was never charged with this near-fatal assault.

The psychologist reported a number of considerations in attempting to resolve this serious ethical dilemma. One consideration was the assessment of the consequences for the client's welfare if confidentiality were breached and the incident reported to prison officials. The psychologist stated that the consequences would have included prosecution for "assault with intent to murder," an immediate removal from all programs, and an indefinite assignment to the detention unit. Furthermore, breaching confidentiality would likely have destroyed the cohesiveness and trust of the other group members.

Another primary consideration focused on the prediction of Mr. E's dangerousness to others if confidentiality were not breached. In fact, the psychologist stated, "A lot of the problem centered around our inability to determine with any degree of certainty the actual threat to others posed by Mr. E." The psychologist also stated that while a strict consideration of Mr. E's past history of violence (which was relatively extensive) would suggest that he was a potentially dangerous person, his positive performance in therapy disallowed the conclusion that he currently constituted "a clear and imminent danger" to others.

In the last analysis, and despite a history of violence, the psychologist decided that Mr. E at the present time probably did not represent a serious threat to others. Therefore, based on this subjective assessment, the psychologist decided not to breach confidentiality.

The Case of the Confessing Juvenile

A psychologist employed by a family court was asked by the judge to evaluate a juvenile charged with car theft. The psychologist's evaluation of the potential dangerousness of this client was designed to help the judge decide whether or not to release him to go home prior to the trial date. During the interview with the psychologist, the juvenile revealed that he had stolen the car to escape from the scene where he had murdered someone. The murder, motive, and method of getting rid of the gun were all described in sufficient detail to substantiate the veracity of the confession.

Since the psychologist was an employee of the court and protector of society, he felt a responsibility to divulge the information. However, having entered into a confidential relationship with the juvenile, the psychologist also felt a loyalty to the juvenile and his per-

sonal welfare. In the final analysis, the psychologist chose not to breach confidentiality, although he did recommend that the juvenile not be released prior to the trial date.

The Case of the Adolescent and the Drug Transaction

During a therapy session, an adolescent revealed the time, date, and location of a sizeable drug transaction. Furthermore, it appeared to the psychologist that children or adolescents were the likely market for this possible merchandise. The conflict between the potential harm to society engendered by the drug market (if confidentiality was not breached) and the potential harm to the client (if confidentiality was breached) was the major focus of the psychologist's dilemma.

After weighing these competing concerns, the psychologist decided neither to breach confidentiality nor to pursue any kind of investigation. The fear that client welfare may have been jeopardized appeared to be the critical factor influencing this decision.

The Case of Client X and the Big Escape

Client X confessed his plans to escape during a therapy session. The escape plans were plausible and included the murder of two officers. Client X had an extensive history of violence and, in fact, had killed four other people unrelated to the current charge. Considering the plausibility of the plans and the client's previous violent history, the psychologist determined that there was a relatively high probability that the plans would be carried out.

Without breaching confidentiality, the psychologist decided to thwart these plans. He informed a trustworthy prison official of the impending incident. While names and descriptions were left out, sufficient information was provided to warn appropriate personnel to take additional security precautions. Client X did not escape and no one was injured, but the psychologist then feared that he would be in personal danger from this client's friends.

An Analysis of Confidentiality Personal Dilemmas: Two Common Denominators

While there are serious limits to any generalization from these cases, two common themes seem worthy of discussion. First, and not surprisingly, psychologists appeared strongly predisposed not to breach confidentiality—a predisposition that held up in the face of some rather "exceptional circumstances." For example, in almost all cases in our data, psychologists chose not to breach confidentiality when "victimless" crimes (e.g., sex offenses) were reported or threatened—even though these were clear violations of prison rules and/or state laws. Moreover, this tendency not to breach confidentiality was reflected even more dramatically in cases where violent crimes, for which the client had not been charged, were disclosed under confidentiality conditions. A felonious assault (in *The Case of Mr. E and the Group Therapy Session*) and a murder (in *The Case of the Confessing Juvenile*), for example, did not convince the psychologists involved that confidentiality should be breached. Their concern for the potential harm to their clients given a confidentiality breach appeared to overshadow any commitment to law enforcement, punishment, protection of society, or other institutional values. Psychologists also tended not to breach confidentiality when future harmful acts were explicitly threatened, including a drug transaction (*The Case of the Adolescent and the Drug Transaction*) and a double murder and escape attempt (*The Case of Client X and the Big Escape*). In the latter case it should be noted that the psychologist did find a way to prevent the murders and the escape.

The second common theme to emerge from the confidentiality cases was that the prediction of dangerousness seems to represent the most troublesome aspect of the decision-making process. In *The Case of Mr. E and the Group Therapy Session*, for example, the psychologist explicitly pointed out that a concern for the risk to others if confidentiality were not breached was the most difficult aspect of the decision. Moreover, if we extrapolate somewhat from *The Case of the Confessing Juvenile*, it again appears that a prediction of dangerousness may have been the primary concern. The psychologist's recommendation to the judge that the juvenile should be incarcerated prior to the trial date was precipitated by his concern for the protection of society. Once these protection-of-society concerns were "dispensed with," the psychologists chose not to breach confidentiality. Furthermore, the reporting of these previously committed violent crimes seemed to be of concern primarily to the extent that they reflected an increased probability of similar crimes being committed in the future. The fact that the acts themselves were egregious violations of the law did not seem to enter into the decisional calculus. Even more than past-crime cases, threats of future crimes highlighted the prediction of dangerousness as the critical concern. A client's threat to commit a violent crime, as in *The Case of Client X and the Big Escape*, set the stage for an extremely difficult (if not impossible) judgment—the judgment of the likelihood that a threat would be translated into action. These judgments, dramatically pitting "client welfare" against "societal protection," are perhaps the most troublesome aspect of the confidentiality dilemmas.

In summary, the personal dilemmas involving confidentiality suggest that the protection of society and the welfare of the client are the primary competing forces psychologists must struggle with in deciding whether or not to breach confidentiality. A more extensive (but certainly not exhaustive) list of important considerations derived from personal dilemma examples is presented in the boxed display on page 147.

Further Analysis and Implications of the Tarasoff Decision

Psychologists in the criminal justice system who report personal dilemmas involving confidentiality have indicated in almost all cases (encompassing a variety of circumstances) a refusal to breach confidentiality. Moreover, the tone of their solutions to these confidentiality dilemmas suggests that they support Siegel's (1977) position—that confidentiality should never be breached.

However, with the *Tarasoff* decision suggesting possible legal maladies that could stem from "absolutist" positions on therapeutic confidentiality, the strong tendency not to breach confidentiality may undergo some modification in the future. The fact that the psychologist may be held legally responsible not only for the client but also for potential victims of that client is likely to have some impact. The confidentiality debate, therefore, may move from the dichotomous limits/no-limits controversy to a more serious discussion of what the exceptional circumstances are under which confidentiality should be breached.

While the California Supreme Court affirmed a "duty to warn," it offered no guidelines for determining in the individual case "where the public peril begins." Furthermore, the current APA *Ethical Standards* suggesting that "a clear and imminent danger" must exist do not help psychologists in defining such clear and imminent danger. The psychologist is thus confronted with crucial decisions that may have implications for his or her own financial and professional welfare, the individual liberty and best interests of the client, and the protection of society against potential harm. Confronted with these crucial decisions, the psychologist is equipped with inadequate paradigms, a nebulous code of ethics, and an absence of specific guidelines from the courts.

Given this "crucial-decision/inadequate-tools" dilemma, it seems likely that decisions

---

Considerations in Confidentiality Dilemmas

1. **Assessment of Seriousness of Past or Planned Crimes**
   a. Where does crime fall on "seriousness" continuum?
   b. How much harm to society?

2. **Assessment of Risk to Society if Unreported**
   a. What is previous history of criminal behavior?
   b. What is best "prediction of dangerousness"?

3. **Assessment of Probable Consequences for Client if Reported**
   a. What individual liberties will be lost?
   b. What is effect on therapeutic relationship?

4. **Prognosis of Client Given Current or Potential Treatment Programs**
   a. What is probability of eventual return to society?
   b. What is probability of community adjustment given continuation of current treatment?
   c. What is estimated efficacy of existing treatment programs?

5. **Extent of "Informed Consent"**
   a. Prior to initiation of therapy relationship, to what extent did the client recognize the limits of confidentiality imposed on the psychologist?

6. **Consequences for Psychologist and for Therapy Relationship With Subject and With Others**
   a. What is the probability of various negative "personal consequences" associated with a confidentiality breach?
   b. What is the probability of various negative "personal consequences" associated with not breaching confidentiality?

---

will be based on a balancing of professional, personal, and societal values. It also seems likely that the tidal waves from *Tarasoff* (especially if reinforced by similar decisions elsewhere) will dent the tendency not to breach endorsed in the data and will result in increases in confidentiality breaches. Bersoff (1976) has pursued this argument and asserted the importance of disclosing to the client at the outset the limits of confidentiality suggested by the *Tarasoff* ruling. Bersoff contends that this "duty of disclosure to clients" is demanded under the auspices of informed consent.

When we consider the salience of societal protection concerns in psychologists' personal dilemmas and, furthermore, weigh the implications of *Tarasoff*, it seems likely that future confidentiality dilemmas will become even more troublesome to psychologists in the criminal justice system. Bersoff (1976) may have captured the essence of these future struggles:

> Therapists may find themselves in insolvable conflicts as they attempt to reconcile their own personal morality and training regarding confidentiality, the vague reminders of their professional codes of ethics that warn of the consequences of violating the moral and legal standards of the community, and the developing legal requirements that demand complex decision making and a balancing between client and public interests. (p. 272)

Three Sources of Ethical Dilemmas: Some Conclusions and Final Comments

In this concluding section we attempt to delineate the *sources* of ethical dilemmas confronting psychologists in the criminal justice system. Three major sources, or problem areas, represent the most salient concepts distilled from the data. While these problem areas are inextricably related, we have presented them separately for purposes of discussion: (a) the problem of inadequate tools for making crucial decisions, (b) the problem of role bastardiza-

tion, and (c) the problem of confounded intentions and the balancing of values.

The Problem of Inadequate Tools for Crucial Decisions

A plethora of responses extending across all survey questions suggested that psychologists are frequently forced to make decisions of client welfare versus societal welfare with inadequate decision-making instruments. Moreover, these decisions may have serious implications for the psychologist's own financial and professional welfare, the individual liberty and best interests of the client, and the protection of society against potential harm. For example, in response to the question on the accuracy of dangerousness predictions, many psychologists acknowledged the widespread tendency to overpredict dangerousness, with the concomitant deprivations of individual liberty for the false positives. However, even with the inadequacy of prediction tools empirically established, psychologists as alleged "experts" have continued to make predictions of dangerousness with full recognition of the potentially serious consequences of decision errors.

In response to the question of whether the indeterminate sentence should be maintained or abolished, the predominant themes of the qualifying comments focused on the potential for the abuse of indeterminate sentencing resulting from difficulties in determining when or if an offender has been rehabilitated. The absence of efficacious treatment programs, the invalidity of assessment paradigms, the inadequacy of evaluation strategies, and the difficulties in distinguishing true rehabilitation from "pseudorehabilitation" were all enumerated as problems mediating judgments of rehabilitation and thus undermining indeterminate sentencing procedures. Moreover, psychologists pointed out that the uncertainty of length of sentence engendered by inaccurate judgments and nebulous decision criteria caused considerable suffering for offenders. The difficulties for psychologists are obvious, since their primary roles are treating offenders, evaluating their progress, and making significant contributions to rehabilitation judgments.

In descriptions of personally experienced confidentiality dilemmas, the majority of psychologists implicated their inability to predict dangerousness as the most troublesome aspect of the decision to breach or not to breach confidentiality. The determination of whether a threat to carry out a violent act (reported in confidence) will be translated into action is an exceedingly difficult, if not impossible, judgment, with potentially serious consequences for the client, society, and the psychologist. Moreover, if the *Tarasoff* decision is reaffirmed in other courts, confidentiality dilemmas will become even more troubling if psychologists acquire a legally enforceable "duty to warn" potential victims. It is doubtful, however, that future guidelines from the courts on professional codes of ethics will offer easy solutions to the complexities of specific cases. Instead, psychologists will be bombarded with these crucial decisions but continue to be equipped with an arsenal of inadequate prediction methods and nebulous professional and legal guidelines.

The qualifying comments in answer to the questions on right to rehabilitation and use of behavior modification also implicated the crucial-decisions/inadequate-tools problem as a primary source of ethical dilemmas. A number of psychologists, for example, pointed out that the determination of treatment goals for behavior modification (and the assurance that these goals facilitate "client growth" rather than "institutional control") is complicated by the paucity of research showing generalization of treatment gains beyond the prison environment. Furthermore, many of psychologists' concerns about right-to-rehabilitation issues focused on the inadequacy of treatment approaches and the inability to define and evaluate rehabilitation.

The Problem of Role Bastardization

The majority of psychologists who responded to this survey provided psychological assessment and treatment services to offenders in correctional settings. Moreover, most had been inculcated in their professional training with the importance of "help-the-individual" values and the relevance of assessment-treatment functions in supporting these values. With this in mind, it is perhaps not surprising that one of the most often mentioned response themes focused on the vitiating influences of conflicting organizational goals on the performance of assessment-treatment duties. While several responses indicated direct and flagrant encroachments on these roles, by far the most frequent and ostensibly bothersome role distortions stemmed from the subtle linking of conflicting treatment, punishment, and custody goals.

The linkage of treatment participation (and judgments of progress) with reduction of sentence appeared to engender the most aggravating distortions of psychologists' assessment-treatment roles. The offender's perception that participation in treatment and evidence of progress may result in a reduction of sentence sets the stage for offenders who "volunteer" for treatment with the primary motivation of influencing the parole board decision. This contamination of psychologist-client relationships creates major problems for the psychologist in establishing a genuine client interest in treatment and in differentiating true motivation from "pseudomotivation" and true rehabilitation from good acting.

The motivational problem stemming from treatment-punishment linkages was also acknowledged quite frequently in psychologists' responses to the right-to-rehabilitation questions. Psychologists pointed out the positive relationship between prisoner motivation and the success of treatment but accentuated the difficulty of determining the existence of genuine motivation in any given client. Furthermore, while most psychologists were in favor of informed consent and the right to refuse treatment, a substantial number also appeared to acknowledge the right of society to protect itself and, with potentially dangerous persons, to impose longer sentences for treatment refusal. Ironically, psychologists' general support for the imposition of penalties for treatment refusal is also inadvertent support for the negative reinforcement mechanism (participation in treatment avoids more punishment) that ensures the proliferation of "pseudomotivation" and game-playing dilemmas.

The treatment-punishment linkage also contaminates client-trust issues in psychologist-client relationships. Since psychologists in the criminal justice system function simultaneously in the conflicting roles of *evaluator* (for purposes of punishment and custody) and *confidant-diagnostician* (for purposes of treatment), the establishment of positive psychologist-client relationships is often complicated by the client's perception of the psychologist as a cog in the punishment-control system. This perception is reinforced by the ubiquity of the prediction of dangerousness as a major task for psychologists in the criminal justice system. As pointed out in a number of comments, assessment in dangerousness predictions is not for the purpose of prescribing psychological treatment but rather to facilitate administrative-judicial decision making regarding who is detained and for how long. It is thus no surprise that psychologists in criminal justice—often cast in "evaluation for punishment" roles—encounter major difficulties in attempting to establish treatment relationships in which full and honest self-disclosures prevail.

Finally, psychologists in the criminal justice system have not only acknowledged these role encroachments but have communicated a tone of helplessness (and concomitant frustration) in the face of trying to effect changes in either their own roles or organizational policies. A number of psychologists' comments, for example, reflected considerable frustration stemming from unsuccessful attempts to correct

flagrant abuses of offenders' rights. Still other psychologists enumerated the frustration stemming from limitations of treatment resources. The shortage of psychologists to coordinate treatment programs, the overall lack of trained staff to carry out such programs, and the general lack of accountability all seem to have contributed to this sense of helplessness. In summary, psychologists' comments throughout this survey reflect both a dissatisfaction with distortions of their assessment-treatment roles and a sense of helplessness in trying to change the organizational policies that contribute to such distortions.

The Problem of Confounded Intentions and the Balancing of Values

The daily ethical dilemmas of psychologists in the criminal justice system appear to be more often resolved by a delicate balancing of professional, institutional, and societal values than by any systematic application of expertise. With competing interests frequently at work, psychologists must determine their own value priorities and, consequently, whether their loyalties lies with professional, institutional, or societal interests. Even though psychologists' training emphasizes individual client welfare, it seems likely that those psychologists who remain employed by the criminal justice system (Brodsky's "system professionals") necessarily acquire skills in balancing values and resolving dilemmas by compromise. However, the difficulty of balancing values is complicated further by the "confounding-of-intentions" problem. This problem arises from difficulties in distinguishing between treatment and punishment that is called treatment. The central issue can be reduced to the question "When do the explicit functions of psychologists' role activities (e.g., assessment-treatment) differ from the de facto functions these activities accomplish (custody-punishment)?"

The confounding-of-intentions problem emerged most lucidly from responses to the question on the use of behavior modification. In fact, the major qualifications to employing behavior modification in prisons focused on the potential abuses of client rights that could result from the obfuscation of values governing its use. Many psychologists acknowledged that behavior modification techniques could effectively serve either treatment or institutional control. Furthermore, while they supported behavior modification only for treatment purposes, a number of psychologists pointed out sources of difficulty in determining which values were really operative. One difficulty appeared to be the lack of evidence revealing that even ostensibly appropriate treatment goals have more than dubious long-range or real-world relevance. Another difficulty inhered in the cosmetic "treatment" language common to the criminal justice system and for which behavior modification terminology is ideally suited. For example, several psychologists suggested that the language of behavior modification served to disguise the actual goals of such techniques, that is, more efficient institutional control.

Confounding of intentions was far more pervasive, however, than reservations regarding the use of behavior modification. Indeed, psychologists' concerns about the values governing behavior modification appeared symptomatic of larger concerns, including the following: (a) What are the real values governing psychological assessment and treatment in the criminal justice system? and, following directly, (b) What are the real values governing the role of psychologists? Of course, these concerns are inextricably related to the already mentioned issue of role bastardization. The confusion over the values governing psychologists' roles is reinforced both by continued exposure to contaminated treatment relationships, where more treatment may mean more punishment, and to contaminated assessment, where psychological evaluations may contribute more to custody decisions than to treatment prescriptions. Psychologists in the criminal justice system recognize that what they do in the name of treatment may actually accomplish nontreatment functions. Therefore, given psychologists' general adherence to the "help-the-individual" ethos, it appears dilemma-engendering for them to be grappling with the questions "When am I helping individuals as clients?" and "When am I helping the system to the detriment of these individuals?" This confusion goes beyond the issues of "Who is the client?" and "custody versus treatment," which have also demanded a balancing of values and loyalties. In fact, the problem continues *after* the psychologist has made the choice of clients and of values, since the question still remains: "In the performance of my role activities, am I accomplishing unintended goals for unintended clients?"

Final Comments

In conclusion, in this chapter we have attempted neither to formulate guidelines nor to offer solutions. Instead, our efforts have been directed toward elucidating the critical issues and providing further insight into the ethical imbroglios of psychologists in the criminal justice system. While this chapter will have served its purpose if it enhances an appreciation of these ethical dilemmas, it seems likely that even a cognitive understanding of them will not adequately convey the totality of their impact. Perhaps, taking a phenomenological perspective, only actual experience wrestling with these dilemmas (as a psychologist in the criminal justice system) can fully communicate their complexity.

Questionnaire Used by the APA Task Force on the Role of Psychologists in the Criminal Justice System

Task Force on the Role of Psychology in the Criminal Justice System, Board of Social & Ethical Responsibility for Psychology, American Psychological Association April, 1976

Please return to: John Monahan

I. Background Information: Please do not put your name on this form. We would appreciate it, however, if you would supply us with some information about yourself.

1. Highest Degree: Bachelor's____; Master's____;
   Doctorate____; Other____.
2. Years since final degree: _____.
3. Sex: M_____ F_____
4. Ethnicity: _____.

II. Criminal Justice Involvement: What is the nature of your involvement with the criminal justice system? (Can check more than one.)

5. Offering direct or indirect *psychological services* to:
   (a) police agencies _____
   (b) courts _____
   (c) probation departments _____
   (d) correctional institutions _____
   (e) community correctional agencies
       (e.g., half-way house) _____
   (f) parole agencies _____
   (g) other criminal justice agencies (Please specify:
       _____.)

6. Performing *psychological research* or program evaluation in the area of:
   (a) police behavior _____
   (b) courts/juries/witnesses _____
   (c) criminal behavior _____
   (d) crime victims _____
   (e) criminal law _____
   (f) legal socialization _____
   (g) rehabilitation programs _____
   (h) diversion from justice system _____
   (i) correctional institutions _____
   (j) other (Please specify: _____
       _____.)

7. *Teaching courses* concerned with psychology and criminal justice in:
   (a) colleges & universities (undergraduate level) _____
   (b) colleges & universities (graduate level) _____
   (c) law schools _____
   (d) police academies/departments _____
   (e) other (Please specify:
       _____.)

8. About what percentage of your total professional activities are criminal justice related (either service, research, or teaching)? _____ %

9. About what percentage of your criminal justice related professional activities are concerned with juveniles and what percentage with adults?
   Juveniles _____%
   Adults _____%

10. If you are offering direct or indirect psychological services to the criminal justice system (i.e., if you checked a response to question 5), what kinds of services are they?
    (a) psychological screening of applicants for criminal justice work (police, correctional officers, etc.) _____
    (b) training of criminal justice personnel _____
    (c) consultation with criminal justice administrators _____
    (d) psychological assessment of offenders _____
    (e) psychological treatment of offenders _____
    (f) other (Please specify: _____
        _____.)

III. Ethical Issues: The Task Force is specifically charged with addressing issues of social and ethical responsibility which arise when psychologists interact with the criminal justice system. To that end, we would appreciate your opinions on the following general question, and on several specific issues which have been raised in recent writings and discussions on psychology and criminal justice.

11. What do you see as the *three major ethical issues* currently confronting the psychologist engaged in criminal justice work?
    (a) _____
    (b) _____
    (c) _____

12. Should a "right to rehabilitation" exist in prison? (That is, should every prisoner have a legal right to have rehabilitation services, including the services of a psychologist, provided for him or her while in prison?) (Circle one)

| Definitely no | Qualified no | No opinion | Qualified yes | Definitely yes |

Comment: _____

13. Should a "right to refuse rehabilitation" exist in prison? (That is, should every prisoner have a legal right to refuse to participate in rehabilitation services, including psychological services, while in prison?) (Circle one)

| Definitely no | Qualified no | No opinion | Qualified yes | Definitely yes |

Comment: _____

14. The indeterminate sentence, as it exists in many states, provides for the judge to sentence an offender to a vaguely specified period of time in prison (e.g., 1 to 10 years), with the exact release date determined

by prison authorities often partly on the basis of reports from psychologists. The ethical validity of indeterminate sentencing has recently come under challenge. Do you believe that the indeterminate sentence should be maintained or abolished? (Circle one)

| Maintain as is | Maintain but modify | No opinion | Drastically modify | Abolish |

Comment: (If it should be abolished, what should take its place?) _____

15. Several persons have recently claimed that psychological treatment fails to rehabilitate offenders (i.e., that the recidivism rate for offenders given treatment is no lower than for those not given treatment). Do you believe that attempting to rehabilitate offenders by means of psychological treatment is effective? (Circle one)

| Very effective | Somewhat effective | Don't know | Little effect | No effect |

Comment: _____

16. Other persons have claimed that psychologists and psychiatrists are very inaccurate predictors of dangerous or violent behavior, and that as a result their predictions should not play a major role in the criminal justice system. How accurate do you believe psychologists and psychiatrists are in predicting whether an offender will be dangerous? (Circle one)

| Very accurate | Fairly accurate | Don't know | Fairly inaccurate | Very inaccurate |

Comment: _____

17. Probably the most controversial issue in the psychology/criminal justice area today concerns the ethics of rehabilitation programs based on principles of behavior modification. What is your view of the use of behavior modification in corrections?

| Very much opposed | Opposed with qualification | No opinion | In favor, with qualification | Very much in favor |

Comment: (If you have a qualification, what is it?)

_____

18. The question of what role psychology should play in the criminal justice system has evoked a wide range of answers. Some claim that psychologists should play no role, and others would have psychologists run the system. Where do you fall on this continuum?

| No role for psychologists | | Very limited role | No opinion |
| Substantial role | | Controlling role | |

Comment: (Ideally, what *should* the role(s) of the psychologist in the criminal justice system be?)

_____

19. Finally, we are most interested in adding to the APA's *Casebook on Ethical Standards* incidents which are directly relevant to the criminal justice system. Could you please describe an *actual ethical problem* which you have encountered in your criminal justice work? Please describe the problem in sufficient detail so that a person not familiar with your particular situation will be able to understand the ethical issue involved. If you choose, also indicate how you dealt with the issue. These cases will not be identified with you or with any particular institution. Please use additional sheets if necessary, or attach any material you see fit.

(Check here if you have not personally encountered an ethical problem in criminal justice work: _____ .)

Thank you very much for your help.

7

Bibliography

Chapter 1: Report of the Task Force on the Role of Psychology in the Criminal Justice System

Reference Notes

1. Levinson, R. *Changing correctional systems: Influencing change from the "inside."* Paper presented at the Alabama Symposium on Justice and the Behavior Sciences, Center for Correctional Psychology, University of Alabama, 1973.
2. Federal Bureau of Prisons. *Task force and executive staff report on the role of psychologists in federal prisons.* Washington, D.C.: Federal Bureau of Prisons, 1977.

References

American Friends Service Committee. *Struggle for justice.* New York: Hill & Wang, 1971.

American Psychiatric Association. *Clinical aspects of the violent individual.* Washington, D.C.: American Psychiatric Association, 1974.

Bard, M. Extending psychology's impact through existing community institutions. *American Psychologist,* 1969, *24,* 610–612.

Bazelon, D. Psychologists in corrections—Are they doing good for the offender or well for themselves? In S. Brodsky, *Psychologists in the criminal justice system.* Urbana, Ill.: University of Illinois Press, 1973.

Bermant, G., Kelman, H., & Warwick, D. (Eds.). *The ethics of social intervention.* New York: Halsted Press, 1978.

Bittner, E. *The functions of police in modern society.* Washington, D.C.: U.S. Government Printing Office, 1970.

Bloomberg, S., & Wilkins, L. Ethics of research involving human subjects in criminal justice. *Crime and Delinquency,* October 1977, 435–444.

Brodsky, S. *Psychologists in the criminal justice system.* Urbana: University of Illinois Press, 1973.

Cederblom, J., & Blizek, W. (Eds.). *Justice and punishment.* Cambridge, Mass.: Ballinger, 1977.

Clark, R. *Crime in America.* New York: Simon & Schuster, 1970.

Corsini, R. Two therapeutic groups that failed. *The Journal of Correctional Psychology,* 1956, *1,* 16–22.

Driscoll, J., Meyer, R., & Schanie, C. Training police in family crisis intervention. *Journal of Applied Behavioral Science,* 1973, *9,* 62–82.

Ethical standards of psychologists. Washington, D.C.: American Psychological Association, 1963. (Reprinted and edited from the *American Psychologist,* January 1963).

Ethical standards of psychologists. Washington, D.C.: American Psychological Association, 1979.

Fogel, D. *We are the living proof: The justice model for corrections.* Cincinnati: W. H. Anderson, 1975.

Gottfredson, D., Wilkins, L., & Hoffman, P. *Guidelines for parole and sentencing.* Lexington, Mass.: Lexington Books, 1978.

Greenberg, D. The correctional effects of corrections: A survey of evaluations. In D. Greenberg (Ed.), *Corrections and punishment.* Beverly Hills, Calif.: Sage, 1977.

Halleck, S., & Witte, A. Is rehabilitation dead? *Crime and Delinquency,* October 1977, 372–380.

Kassebaum, G., Ward, D., & Wilner, D. *Prison treatment and parole survival: An empirical assessment.* New York: Wiley, 1971.

Konečni, V., & Ebbesen, E. (Eds.). *Social psychological analysis of legal processes.* San Francisco: W. H. Freeman, in press.

Lipsitt, P., & Sales, B. (Eds.). *New directions in psycholegal research.* New York: Van Nostrand Reinhold, 1980.

Martinson, R. What works?—Questions and answers about prison reform. *The Public Interest,* 1974, *35,* 22–54.

McGarry, L., et al. *Competency to stand trial and mental illness* (HSM 73-9105). Washington, D.C.: U.S. Government Printing Office, 1973.

Meehl, P. Psychology and the criminal law. *University of Richmond Law Review,* 1970, *5,* 1–30.

Mitford, J. *Kind and usual punishment: The prison business.* New York: Random House, 1973.

Monahan, J. (Ed.). *Community mental health*

and the criminal justice system. New York: Pergamon, 1976.

Monahan, J. The prediction of violent criminal behavior: A methodological critique and prospectus. In A. Blumstein, J. Cohen, and D. Nagin (Eds.), *Deterrence and incapacitation: Estimating the effects of criminal sanctions on crime rates*. Washington, D.C.: National Academy of Sciences, 1978.

Morris, N. *The future of imprisonment*. Chicago: University of Chicago Press, 1974.

Morris, N., & Hawkins, G. *Letter to the President on crime control*. Chicago: University of Chicago Press, 1977.

Morse, S. Crazy behavior, morals and science: An analysis of mental health law. *Southern California Law Review*, 1978, *51*, 527–654.

National Commission for the Protection of Human Subjects of Biomedical and Behavioral Research. Research involving prisoners—Report and recommendations. *Federal Register*, 1977, *42*, 3075–3091.

Novaco, R. A stress inoculation approach to anger management in the training of law enforcement officers. *American Journal of Community Psychology*, 1977, *5*, 327–346.

Palmer, T. Martinson revisited. *Journal of Research in Crime and Delinquency*, July 1975, 113–152.

Quay, H. The three faces of evaluation: What can be expected to work. *Criminal Justice and Behavior*, 1977, *3*, 341–354.

Reiser, M. *The police department psychologist*. Springfield, Ill.: Charles C Thomas, 1972.

Ryan, W. *Blaming the victim*. New York: Vintage, 1971.

Sales, B. (Ed.). *Perspectives in law and psychology: The criminal justice system*. New York: Plenum, 1977. (a)

Sales, B. (Ed.). *Psychology in the legal process*. New York: Spectrum, 1977. (b)

Sarbin, T. (Ed.). *Challenges to the criminal justice system*. New York: Human Sciences Press, 1979.

Shah, S. Foreword. In A. Stone, *Mental health and the law: A system in transition*. Washington, D.C.: U.S. Government Printing Office, 1975.

Shah, S. Editorial. *APA Monitor*, February 1977, p. 2.

Shah, S. Dangerousness: A paradigm for exploring some issues in law and psychology. *American Psychologist*, 1978, *33*, 224–238.

Siegel, M. Editorial. *APA Monitor*, February 1977, p. 5.

Tannenbaum, A., & Cooke, R. Research in prisons: A preliminary report. In National Commission for the Protection of Human Subjects of Biomedical and Behavioral Research, *Research involving prisoners: Appendix to report and recommendations* (Publication OS-76-132). Washington, D.C.: U.S. Department of Health, Education and Welfare, 1976.

Tapp, J. Psychology and the law: An overture. *Annual Review of Psychology*, 1976, *27*, 359–404.

Tapp, J., Kelman, H., Triandis, H., Wrightsman, L., & Coelho, G. Continuing concerns in cross-cultural ethics: A report. *International Journal of Psychology*, 1974, *9*, 231–249.

Tapp, J., & Levine, F. (Eds.). *Law, justice, and the individual in society: Psychological and legal issues*. New York: Holt, Rinehart & Winston, 1977.

Toch, H. *The psychology of crime and criminal justice*. New York: Holt, Rinehart & Winston, 1979.

Twentieth Century Fund. *Fair and certain punishment*. New York: McGraw-Hill, 1976.

von Hirsch, A. *Doing justice: The choice of punishments*. New York: Hill & Wang, 1976.

von Hirsch, A., & Hanrahan, K. *Abolish parole?* Cambridge, Mass.: Ballinger, 1979.

Wasserstrom, R. The obligation to obey the law. *UCLA Law Review*, 1963, *10*, 780.

Watzlawick, P., Weakland, J., & Fisch, R. *Change: Principles of problem formation and problem resolution*. New York: Norton, 1974.

Wilkins, L. Comment. In A. von Hirsch, *Doing Justice: The choice of punishments*. New York: Hill & Wang, 1976.

Chapter 2: Ethical Issues for Psychologists in Police Agencies

Reference Notes

1. Shellow, R. *Active participation in police decision making*. Paper presented at the annual meeting of the American Psychological Association, Washington, D.C., September, 1971.

2. Lambert, N. *Variants of consultation service to schools and implications for training*. Washington, D.C.: American Psychological Association, 1963.

3. Sacon, S. *An intensive training program for a police department*. Paper presented at the annual meeting of the American Psychological Association, Washington, D.C., September, 1971.

4. Bard, M., Zacker, J., & Rutter, E. *Police family crisis intervention and conflict management: An action research analysis*. Report prepared for the U.S. Department of Justice, Law Enforcement Assistance Administration, 1972.

5. Bailey, W. D. *Family disturbances*. Unpublished manuscript, Criminal Justice Project, University of Texas School of Law, Austin, Texas, 1970.

6. Wright, R., Heilrveil, M., Pelletier, P., & Dickinson, K. *The impact of street lighting on street crime*. Unpublished manuscript, University of Michigan, Ann Arbor, 1974.

References

Angell, R. C. The ethical problems of applied sociology. In P. F. Lazarsfeld, W. H. Sewell, & H. L. Wilensky (Eds.), *The uses of sociology.* New York: Basic Books, 1967.

Argyris, C. Theories of action that inhibit individual learning. *American Psychologist*, 1976, *31*, 638–654.

Azen, S. P., Snibbe, H. M., & Montgomery, H. R. A longitudinal predictive study of success and performance of law enforcement officers. *Journal of Applied Psychology*, 1973, *57*, 190–192.

Azen, S. P., Snibbe, H. M., Montgomery, H. R., Fabricatore, J., & Earle, H. H. Predictors of resignation and performance of law enforcement officers. *American Journal of Community Psychology*, 1974, *2*, 79–86.

Baehr, M. E., Furcon, J. E., & Froemel, E. C. *Psychological assessment of patrolman qualifications in relation to field performance* (Law Enforcement Assistance Administration, U.S. Department of Justice). Washington, D.C.: U.S. Government Printing Office, 1969.

Bard, M. *Training police as specialists in family crisis intervention* (U.S. Department of Justice). Washington, D.C.: U.S. Government Printing Office, 1970.

Bard, M., & Berkowitz, B. Training police as specialists in family crisis intervention: A community psychology action project. *Community Mental Health Journal*, 1967, *3*, 315–317.

Bard, M., & Shellow, R. (Eds.). *Issues in law enforcement: Essays and case studies.* Reston, Va.: Reston Publishing Co., 1976. (a)

Bard, M., & Shellow, R. Neighborhood police teams. In M. Bard & R. Shellow (Eds.), *Issues in law enforcement: Essays and case studies.* Reston, Va.: Reston Publishing Co., 1976. (b)

Bennis, W. G. Changing organizations. *Journal of Applied Behavioral Science*, 1966, *2*, 247–263.

Bittner, E. *The functions of the police in modern society.* Washington, D.C.: U.S. Government Printing Office, 1970.

Block, P. B., & Specht, D. *Neighborhood team policing* (Law Enforcement Assistance Administration, U.S. Department of Justice). Washington, D.C.: U.S. Government Printing Office, 1973.

Blum, R. H. *Police selection.* Springfield, Ill.: Charles C Thomas, 1964.

Brown, W. P. Police-victim relationships in sex crime investigations. *Police Chief*, 1970, *37*(1), 20–24.

Campbell, D. T., & Stanley, J. C. *Experimental and quasi-experimental designs for research.* Chicago: Rand-McNally, 1966.

Caplan, G. *The theory and practice of mental health consultation.* New York: Basic Books, 1970.

Cumming, E., Cumming, I., & Edell, L. Policeman as philosopher, guide, and friend. *Social Problems*, 1965, *12*, 276–286.

Driscoll, J. M., Meyer, R. G., & Schanie, C. F. Training police in family crisis intervention. *Journal of Applied Behavioral Science*, 1973, *9*, 62–82.

Ellinson, K., Investigation of forcible rape. In M. Bard & R. Shellow (Eds.), *Issues in law enforcement: Essays and case studies.* Reston, Va.: Reston Publishing Co., 1976.

Eron, C. The rape crisis center. *The Washington Post*, July 15, 1973, pp. 10–11; 22–23; 27.

Ethical standards of psychologists. Washington, D.C.: American Psychological Association, 1953.

Ethical standards of psychologists. Washington, D.C.: American Psychological Association, 1963. (Reprinted and edited from the *American Psychologist*, January 1963).

Ethical standards of psychologists. Washington, D.C.: American Psychological Association, 1977. (Reprinted from the APA *Monitor*, March 1977).

Ethical standards of psychologists. Washington, D.C.: American Psychological Association, 1979.

Fox, S. S., & Scherl, D. J. Crisis intervention with victims of rape. *Social Work*, 1972, *17*(1), 37–42.

Golann, S. E. Emerging areas of ethical concern. *American Psychologist*, 1969, *24*, 454–459.

Green, E. J. *Psychology for law enforcement.* New York: Wiley, 1976.

Gustin, A. C. A police officer reacts. *Journal of Social Issues*, 1975, *31*(1), 211–216.

Hillgren, J., & Jacobs, P. The consulting psychologist's emerging role in law enforcement, *Professional Psychology*, 1976, *7*, 256–266.

Hollingshead, A. B., & Redlich, F. C. *Social class and mental illness.* New York: Wiley, 1958.

Hornstein, H. A., Bunker, B. B., Burke, W. W., Gindes, M., & Lewicki, R. J. (Eds.). *Social intervention: A behavioral science approach.* New York: Free Press, 1971.

Kelling, G. L., Pate, T., Dieckman, D., & Brown, C. E. *The Kansas City Preventive Patrol Experiment.* Washington, D.C.: The Police Foundation, 1974.

Kelly, R. M. On improving police-community relations: Generalizations from an OEO experiment in Washington, D.C. *Journal of Social Issues*, 1975, *31*(1), 57–86.

Lalley, T. L. Pilot district project. In M. Bard & R. Shellow (Eds.), *Issues in law enforcement: Essays and case studies.* Reston, Va.: Reston Publishing Co., 1976.

Lefkowitz, J. Psychological attributes of policemen: A review of research and opinion. *Journal of Social Issues*, 1975, *31*(1), 3–26.

Liberman, R. Police as a community mental health resource. *Community Mental Health Journal*, 1969, *5*, 111–120.

Lipsitt, P. D., & Steinbruner, M. An experiment in police-community relations: A small group approach. *Community Mental Health Journal*, 1969, *5*, 172–179.

Mann, P. A. Police responses to a course in psychology. *Crime and Delinquency*, 1970, *16*, 403–408.

Mann, P. A. Establishing a mental health consultation program with a police department. *Community Mental Health Journal*, 1971, *7*, 118–126.

Mann, P. A. *Psychological consultation with a police department: A demonstration of cooperative training in mental health.* Springfield, Ill.: Charles C Thomas, 1973.

Mann, P. A. Psychology of police organization: Reward structures and group dynamics. In T. R. Armstrong & K. M. Cinnamon (Eds.), *Power and authority in law enforcement.* Springfield, Ill.: Charles C Thomas, 1976.

Mann, P. A., & Iscoe, I. Mass behavior and community organization: Reflections on a peaceful demonstration. *American Psychologist*, 1971, *26*, 108–113.

Matthews, R. A., & Rowland, L. W. *How to recognize and handle abnormal people.* New York: National Association for Mental Health, 1974.

McDonough, L. B., & Monahan, J. The quality control of community caretakers: A study of mental health screening in a sheriff's department. *Community Mental Health Journal*, 1975, *11*, 33–43.

Monahan, J., The prediction of violence, In D. Chappell & J. Monahan (Eds.), *Violence and criminal justice.* Lexington, Mass.: Lexington Books, 1975.

Monahan, J. The prevention of violence. In J. Monahan (Ed.), *Community mental health and the criminal justice system.* New York: Pergamon Press, 1976.

Monahan, J., & Catalano, R. Toward the safe society: Police agencies and environmental planning. *Journal of Criminal Justice*, 1976, *4*, 1–7.

Murphy, J. J. Current practices in the use of psychological testing by police agencies. *Journal of Criminal Law, Criminology, and Police Science*, 1972, *63*, 570–576.

Narrol, H. G., & Levitt, E. E. Formal assessment procedures in police selection. *Psychological Reports*, 1963, *12*, 691–693.

Niederhoffer, A. *Behind the shield: The police in urban society.* Garden City, N.Y.: Doubleday, 1967.

Pfister, G. Outcomes of laboratory training for police officers. *Journal of Social Issues*, 1975, *31*(1), 115–122.

President's Commission on Law Enforcement and Administration of Justice. *Task force report: The police.* Washington, D.C.: U.S. Government Printing Office, 1967.

Rapoport, L. The state of crisis: Some theoretical considerations. *The Social Science Review*, 1962, *36*, 22–31.

Reddy, W. B., & Lansky, L. M. Nothing but the facts—and some observations on norms and values: The history of a consultation with a Metropolitan Police Division. *Journal of Social Issues*, 1975, *31*(1), 123–138.

Reiff, R. Community psychology and public policy. In Division 27 of the American Psychological Association, *Issues in community psychology and preventive mental health.* New York: Behavioral Publications, 1971.

Rein, M. Choice and change in the American welfare system. *Annals of the American Academy of Political and Social Science*, 1969, *385*(5), 89–109.

Reiser, M. The police psychologist as consultant. *Police*, 1971, *16*(1), 58–60.

Reiser, M. *The police department psychologist.* Springfield, Ill.: Charles C Thomas, 1972.

Reiser, M. Stress, distress, and adaptation in police work. *The Police Chief*, 1976, *43*(1), 24; 26–27.

Rhead, C., Abrams, A., Trossman, H., & Margolis, P. The psychological assessment of police candidates. *American Journal of Psychiatry*, 1968, *124*, 1575–1580.

Rhodes, W. C. Regulation of community behavior: Dynamics and structure. In S. E. Golann & C. Eisdorfer (Eds.), *Handbook of community mental health.* New York: Appleton-Century-Crofts, 1972.

Sarason, S. B. Community psychology, networks, and Mr. Everyman. *American Psychologist*, 1976, *31*, 317–328.

Sata, L. S. Laboratory training for police officers. *Journal of Social Issues*, 1975, *31*(1), 107–114.

Shellow, R. Evaluating an evaluation. *Journal of Social Issues*, 1975, *31*(1), 87–94.

Shellow, R. Block party: A step towards police professionalism. In M. Bard & R. Shellow (Eds.), *Issues in law enforcement: Essays and case studies.* Reston, Va.: Reston Publishing Co., 1976.

Shellow, R., & Roemer, D. No heaven for Hell's Angels. *Transaction*, 1966, *3*, 12–19.

Sikes, M., & Cleveland, S. Human relations training for police and community. *American Psychologist*, 1968, *23*, 766–769.

Snibbe, H. M., Fabricatore, J., Azen, S. P., & Snibbe, J. Race differences in police patrolmen: A failure to replicate the Chicago study. *American Journal of Community Psychology*, 1976, *4*, 155–160.

Sterling, J., & Watson, N. S. Changes in role concepts of police officers. *Mental Health Program Reports*, No. 4. Bethesda, Md.: National Institute of Mental Health, 1970. (Publication No. 5026)

Teahan, J. E. A longitudinal study of attitude shifts among black and white police officers. *Journal of Social Issues*, 1975, *31*(1), 47–56.

Toch, H., Grant, J. D., & Galvin, R. T. *Agents of*

change: A study in police reform. Cambridge, Mass.: Schenkman, 1975.

Twain, D., McGee, R., & Bennett, L. A. Functional areas of psychological activity. In S. L. Brodsky (Ed.), *Psychologists in the criminal justice system.* Urbana: University of Illinois Press, 1973.

Westley, W. A. *Violence and the police: A sociological study of law, custom, and morality.* Cambridge, Mass.: MIT Press, 1970.

Chapter 3: Ethical Issues for Psychologists in Court Settings

Reference Notes

1. Commonwealth of Massachusetts, Committee on Criminal Justice. *1976 Comprehensive Criminal Justice Plan.* Boston: Commonwealth of Massachusetts, 1976.
2. Boyer, E., Fersch, E., & Rolde, E. *A study of persons committed to the Massachusetts Mental Health Center for determination of competency to stand trial.* Unpublished paper, 1974.

References

American Friends Service Committee. *Struggle for justice.* New York: Hill & Wang, 1971.

Annas, G. *The rights of hospital patients.* New York: Avon, 1975.

Bayh, B. New directions for juvenile justice. *Trial,* 1977, *13*(2), 20–23.

Bazelon, D. The morality of the criminal law. *Southern California Law Review,* 1976, *49,* 385–405.

Bendt, R., & Balcanoff, E. Psychiatric examination of alleged offenders: A proposed protocol. *American Bar Association Journal,* 1972, *58,* 371–373.

Bennett, J., & Matthews, A. The dilemma of mental disability and the criminal law. *American Bar Association Journal,* 1968, *54,* 467–471.

Brakel, S., & Rock, R. *The mentally disabled and the law* (rev. ed.). Chicago: University of Chicago Press, 1971.

Brodsky, S. *Psychologists in the criminal justice system.* Urbana: University of Illinois Press, 1973.

Buckhout, R. Eyewitness testimony. *Scientific American,* 1974, *321*(6), 23–31.

Buckhout, R. Nobody likes a smartass: Expert testimony by psychologists. *Social Action and the Law,* 1976, *3*(4), 41–53.

Casebook on ethical standards of psychologists. Washington, D.C.: American Psychological Association, 1967.

Cohen, F. Juvenile justice: New York's act is hard to follow. *Trial,* 1977, *13*(2), 28–35.

Corbett, R., & Fersch, E. Punishing young criminals. In E. Fersch, *Law, psychology, and the courts: Rethinking treatment of the young and the disturbed.* Springfield, Ill.: Charles C Thomas, 1979.

Cryan, T. McLean is at Bridgewater. *McLean Review,* 1977, *7*(2), 1–11.

Curran, W. Law-medicine notes: Confidentiality and the prediction of dangerousness in psychiatry. *New England Journal of Medicine,* 1975, *293*(6), 285–286.

Davison, G., & Stuart, R. Behavior therapy and civil liberties. *American Psychologist,* 1975, *30,* 755–763.

Dershowitz, A. The psychiatrist's power in civil commitment. *Psychology Today,* February 1969, pp. 43–47.

Dershowitz, A., Indeterminate confinement: Letting the therapy fit the harm. *University of Pennsylvania Law Review,* 1974, *123,* 297–339.

Dershowitz, A. Let the punishment fit the crime. *New York Times Magazine,* December 28, 1975, pp. 7–8; 26–27.

Dix, G. Psychological abnormality as a factor in grading criminal liability: Diminished capacity, diminished responsibility and the like. *Journal of Criminal Law, Criminology and Police Science,* 1971, *72,* 313–335.

Dix, G. Determining the continued dangerousness of psychologically abnormal sex offenders, *Journal of Psychiatry and Law,* 1975, *3*(3).

Donaldson, K. *Insanity inside out.* New York: Crown, 1976.

Donnelly, R., Goldstein, J., & Schwartz, R. *Criminal law: Problems for decision in the promulgation, invocation, and administration of a law of crimes.* New York: Free Press, 1962.

Elwork, A., & Sales, B. Psycholegal research on the jury and trial processes. In C. Petty, W. Curran & A. McGarry, *Modern legal medicine and forensic science.* Philadelphia: Davis, 1977.

Ennis, B., & Litwack, T. Psychiatry and the presumption of expertise: Flipping coins in the courtroom. *California Law Review,* 1974, *62.*

Ennis, B., & Siegel, L. *The rights of mental patients.* New York: Avon, 1973.

Ethical standards of psychologists. Washington, D.C.: American Psychological Association, 1953.

Ethical standards of psychologists. Washington, D.C.: American Psychological Association, 1963. (Reprinted and edited from the *American Psychologist,* January 1963)

Ethical standards of psychologists. Washington, D.C.: American Psychological Association, 1977. (Reprinted from the APA *Monitor,* March 1977)

Ethical standards of psychologists. Washington,

D.C.: American Psychological Association, 1979.

Faust, F., & Brantingham, P. *Juvenile justice philosophy: Readings, cases and comments* (2nd ed.). St. Paul, Minn.: West, 1979.

Fersch, E. Court clinic treatment in Massachusetts: Civil liberties v. mental health care. *International Journal of Offender Therapy and Comparative Criminology*, 1974, *18*(3), 275–282.

Fersch, E. When to punish, when to rehabilitate. *American Bar Association Journal*, 1975, *61*, 1235–1237.

Fersch, E. *Law, psychology, and the courts: Rethinking treatment of the young and the disturbed.* Springfield, Ill.: Charles C Thomas, 1979.

Fersch, E. *Psychology and psychiatry in courts and corrections: Controversy and change.* New York: Wiley, 1980.

Fingarette, H. *The meaning of criminal insanity.* Berkeley: University of California, 1972.

Flaschner, R. The new Massachusetts Mental Health Code. *Massachusetts Law Quarterly*, 1971, *56*(1), 49–63.

Fox, S. Juvenile justice reform: An historical perspective. *Stanford Law Review*, 1970, *22*(6), 1187–1239.

Fox, S. Abolishing the juvenile court. *Harvard Law School Bulletin*, 1977, *28*(3), 22–27.

Frankel, M. *Criminal sentences: Law without order.* New York: Hill & Wang, 1973.

Freedman, M. *Lawyers' ethics in an adversary system.* Indianapolis: Bobbs-Merrill, 1975.

Goldstein, A. *The insanity defense.* New Haven: Yale, 1967.

Gorelick, J. Pretrial diversion: The threat of expanding social control. *Harvard Civil Rights–Civil Liberties Law Review*, 1975, *10*(1), 180–214.

Joost, R., & McGarry, A. Massachusetts Mental Health Code: Promise and performance. *American Bar Association Journal*, 1974, *60*, 95–98.

Kennedy, E. Mandatory sentencing. *Boston Sunday Globe*, February 8, 1976, p. A7.

Kittrie, N. *The right to be different: Deviance and enforced therapy.* Baltimore: Johns Hopkins University Press, 1971.

Laboratory of Community Psychiatry, Harvard Medical School. *Competency to stand trial and mental illness.* Washington, D.C.: U.S. Government Printing Office, 1973.

Laves, R. The prediction of dangerousness as a criterion for involuntary committment: Constitutional considerations. *Journal of Psychiatry and Law*, 1975, *3*(3), 291–326.

Leifer, R. The competence of the psychiatrist to assist in the determination of incompetency: A skeptical inquiry into the courtroom functions of psychiatrists. *Syracuse Law Review*, 1962–1963, *14*, 564–575.

Levine, F., & Tapp, J. The psychology of criminal identification: The gap from *Wade* to *Kirby*.

University of Pennsylvania Law Review, 1973, *121*(5), 1079–1131.

Lipsitt, P., Lelos, D., & McGarry, A. Competency for trial: A screening instrument. *American Journal of Psychiatry*, 1971, *128*, p. 105.

Loftus, E. *Eyewitness testimony.* Cambridge, Mass.: Harvard University Press, 1979.

Marino, R., New York's juvenile criminals: A call for trial by adult courts. *Trial*, 1977, *13*(2), 24–27.

Martinson, R. What works? Questions and answers about prison reform. *The Public Interest*, 1974, *35*, 22–54.

Monahan, J. Abolish the insanity defense? Not yet. *Rutgers Law Review*, 1973, *26*(4), 719–740.

Monahan, J. (Ed.). *Community mental health and the criminal justice system.* New York: Pergamon, 1975.

Monahan, J. Social accountability: Preface to an integrated theory of criminal and mental health sanctions. In B. Sales (Ed.), *Perspectives in law and psychology: The criminal justice system.* New York: Plenum, 1976.

Monahan, J. The prediction of violent criminal behavior: A methodological critique and prospectus. In A. Blumstein, J. Cohen, & D. Nagin (Eds.), *Deterrence and incapacitation: Estimating the effects of criminal sanctions on crime rates.* Washington, D.C.: National Academy of Sciences, 1978.

Monahan, J., & Hood, G. Psychologically disordered and criminal offenders: Perception of their volition and responsibility. *Criminal Justice and Behavior*, 1976, *3*(2), 123–134.

Morse, S. The twilight of welfare criminology: A reply to Judge Bazelon. *Southern California Law Review*, 1976, *49*(6), 1247–1268.

Morse, S. Law and mental health professionals: The limits of expertise. *Professional Psychology*, 1978, *9*(3), 389–399.

Oran, D. Judges and psychiatrists lock up too many people. *Psychology Today*, August 1973, pp. 20–22; 27–28; 93.

Platt, A. *The child savers: The invention of delinquency* (2nd ed.). Chicago: University of Chicago Press, 1977.

Powers, E. *The basic structure of the administration of criminal justice in Massachusetts.* Boston: Massachusetts Correctional Association, 1973.

President's Commission on Law Enforcement and Administration of Justice. *The challenge of crime in a free society.* Washington, D.C.: U.S. Government Printing Office, 1967.

Roesch, R., & Golding, S. *A systems analysis of competency to stand trial procedures: Implications for forensic services in North Carolina.* Washington, D.C.: National Clearinghouse for Criminal Justice Planning and Architecture, 1977.

Rosenhan, D. On being sane in insane places. *Science*, 1973, *179*, 250–258.

Saks, M. The limits of scientific jury selection: Ethical and empirical. *Jurimetrics Journal*, 1976, *17*(1), 3–22.

Saks, M. *Jury verdicts*. Lexington, Mass.: Lexington Books, 1977.

Saks, M., & Hastie, R. *Social psychology in court*. New York: Van Nostrand Reinhold, 1978.

Sales, B., Elwork, A., & Alfini, J. Improving comprehension for jury instructions. In B. Sales (Ed.), *Perspectives in law and psychology*. New York: Plenum, 1976.

Schur, E., & Bedau, H. *Victimless crimes*. Englewood Cliffs, N.J.: Prentice-Hall, 1974.

Shah, S. Dangerousness: Some definitional, conceptual, and public policy issues. In B. Sales (Ed.), *Perspectives in law and psychology*. New York: Plenum, 1976.

Shah, S. Dangerousness: A paradigm for exploring some issues in law and psychology. *American Psychologist*, 1978, *33*(3), 224–238.

Silber, D., Controversies concerning the criminal justice system and its implications for the role of mental health workers. *American Psychologist*, 1974, *29*, 239–244.

Stone, A. *Mental health and law: A system in transition*. Washington, D.C.: U.S. Government Printing Office, 1975.

Szasz, T. *The myth of mental illness*. New York: Harper, 1961.

Szasz, T. *Law, liberty, and psychiatry*. New York: Macmillan, 1963.

Szasz, T. *Psychiatric justice*. New York: Macmillan, 1965.

Szasz, T. *Psychiatric slavery*. New York: Free Press, 1977.

Szasz, T. Dreyfus redux in reverse. *New York Times*, August 4, 1979, p. 19.

Tapp, J. L. Psychology and the law: An overture. *Annual Review of Psychology*, 1976, *27*, 359–404.

Tullock, G. Does punishment deter crime? *The Public Interest*, 1974, *36*, 103–111.

Wilson, J. *Thinking about crime*. New York: Basic Books, 1975.

Wolitzky, D. Insane versus feigned insane: A reply to Dr. D. L. Rosenhan. *Journal of Psychiatry and Law*, 1973, *1*, 463–473.

Ziskin, J. *Coping with psychiatric and psychological testimony* (2nd ed.). Beverly Hills, Calif.: Law and Psychology Press, 1975. (With Pocket Supplement, 1977).

Chapter 4: Ethical Issues for Psychologists in Corrections

Reference Notes

1. Fowler, R. D., Jr. *The use of computer-produced MMPI reports with a prison population.* Unpublished manuscript, University of Alabama, 1974.

2. Megargee, E. I. Discussant's comments at the symposium *Ethical dilemmas of psychologists in the criminal justice system* presented at the meeting of the Southeastern Psychological Association, Hollywood, Florida, May 1977.

3. Kaplan, M. F., & ScherHching, C. *Juridical judgement viewed as information integration: Concepts and applications.* Paper presented at the Third National Conference of the American Psychology-Law Society, Snowmass, Colorado, June 28, 1977.

4. Brodsky, S. L. *Legal and ethical issues in behavior change: The scriptures according to Goldilocks.* Paper presented at the Seventh Behavior Modification Institute, Tuscaloosa, Alabama, September 1974.

5. Grisso, J. T., Manoogian, S., & Kissling, E. *Can juveniles understand Miranda warnings?* Paper presented at the Third National Conference of the American Psychology-Law Society, Snowmass, Colorado, June 27, 1977.

6. West, S. G., & Gunn, S. P. Some issues of ethics and social psychology. In B. Latané (Chair), *Ethical issues in social psychological research: Some current thoughts*. Symposium presented at the meeting of the American Psychological Association, Washington, D.C., September 1976.

References

Abel, G. G., Blanchard, E. B., & Becker, J. V. Psychological treatment of rapists. In M. J. Walker & S. L. Brodsky (Eds.), *Sexual assault: The victim and the rapist*. Lexington, Mass.: Lexington Books, 1976.

American Correctional Association Parole-Corrections Project. *The Mutual Agreement Program: A planned change in correctional service delivery*. College Park, Md.: American Correctional Association, 1973.

American Correctional Association. The use of prisoners and detainees as subjects of human experimentation: Position statement officially adopted. *American Journal of Correction*, 1976, *38*(3), 14.

American Friends Service Committee. *Struggle for justice*. New York: Hill & Wang, 1971.

Ayllon, T. Behavior modification in institutional settings. *Arizona Law Review*, 1975, *17*(1), 3–19.

Aynes, R. L. Behavior modification: Winners in the game of life? *Cleveland State Law Review*, 1975, *24*, 422–462.

Bazelon, D. Psychologists in corrections—Are they doing good for the offender or well for themselves? In S. L. Brodsky, *Psychologists in the criminal justice system*. Urbana: University of Illinois Press, 1973.

Bierce, A. *The devil's dictionary*. New York: Neale, 1911.

Branson, R. Philosophical perspectives on experimentation with prisoners. In National Commission for the Protection of Human Subjects of Biomedical and Behavioral Research, *Research involving prisoners: Appendix to report and recommendations* (DHEW Publication No. (OS) 76-132). Washington, D.C.: U.S. Department of Health, Education and Welfare, 1976.

Braukmann, C., Fixsen, D. L., Phillips, E. L., & Wolf, M. M. Behavioral approaches to treatment in the crime and delinquency field. *Criminology*, 1975, *13*, 299-323.

Brodsky, A. M. Accountability in testing and theory, Part I. *POCA Press*, 1976, *10*(2), 14-15.

Brodsky, S. L. Shared results and open files with the client. *Professional Psychology*, 1972, *4*, 362-364.

Brodsky, S. L. *Psychologists in the criminal justice system*. Urbana: University of Illinois Press, 1973.

Brodsky, S. L. Go away; I'm looking for the truth: Research utilization in corrections. *Criminal Justice and Behavior*, 1977, *4*, 1-9.

Brodsky, S. L., & Buchanan, R. A. The search for psychological health in offenders. *Corrections Quarterly*, 1971, *1*, 5-11.

Brodsky, S. L., & Eggleston, N. (Eds.). *The military prison: Theory, research, and programs*. Carbondale: Southern Illinois University Press, 1970.

Brodsky, S. L., & Horn, C. L. The politics of correctional treatment. In A. A. Roberts (Ed.), *Correctional treatment of the offender*. Springfield, Ill.: Charles C Thomas, 1973.

Brodsky, S. L., & Hobart, S. Blame models and assailant research. *Criminal Justice and Behavior*, 1978, *5*, 379-388.

Burgess, A. *Clockwork orange*. New York: Norton, 1963.

Burns, H. A miniature totalitarian state: Maximum security prison. *Canadian Journal of Corrections*, 1969, *11*, 153-164.

Bush, M., Wittner, J., & Gordon, A. *The university in the community: Problems and opportunities*. Evanston, Ill.: Northwestern University, Center for Urban Affairs, 1976.

Camus, A. *The fall*. New York: Knopf, 1957.

Castaneda, C. *A separate reality: Further conversations with Don Juan*. New York: Pocket Books, 1971.

Chekhov, A. *The lady with the dog and other stories*. New York: MacMillan, 1928.

The CIA. Mind-bending disclosures: The agency's search for the secret of brainwashing. *Time*, August 15, 1977, p. 9.

Clements, C. B., & McKee, J. F. Programmed instruction for institutionalized offenders: Contingency management and performance contracts. *Psychological Reports*, 1968, *22*, 957-964.

Clemons, R. Proposed legal regulation of applied behavior analysis in prisons: Consumer issues and concerns. *Arizona Law Review*, 1975, *17*(1), 127-131.

Corsini, R. J. Two therapeutic groups that failed. *Journal of Correctional Psychology*, 1956, *1*(1), 16-22.

Corsini, R. J. Intelligence in prisons. *Journal of Correctional Psychology*, 1959, *4*(2), 1-9.

Cunningham, C. Korean War studies in forensic psychology. *Bulletin of the British Psychological Society*, 1970, *23*, 309-311.

Dohrenwend, B. P., & Dohrenwend, B. S. The problem of validity in field studies of psychological disorder. *Journal of Abnormal Psychology*, 1965, *70*, 52-69.

Ethical principles in the conduct of research with human participants. Washington, D.C.: American Psychological Association, 1973.

Ethical standards of psychologists. Washington, D.C.: American Psychological Association, 1979.

Fischer, C. T., & Brodsky, S. L. *Client participation in human services: The Prometheus principle*. New Brunswick, N.J.: Transaction Books, 1978.

Foster, H. H., Jr. The conflict and reconciliation of the ethical interests of therapist and patient. *Journal of Psychiatry and Law*, 1975, *3*, 39-62.

Friedman, P. R. Legal regulation of applied behavior analysis in mental hospitals and prisons. *Arizona Law Review*, 1975, *17*(1), 39-104.

Glad, D. *Operational values in psychotherapy*. New York: Oxford, 1959.

Geis, G. Ethical and legal issues in experimentation with offender populations. In R. M. Carter, D. Glaser, & L. T. Wilkins (Eds.), *Correctional institutions*. Philadelphia, Pa.: Lippincott, 1972.

Geller, E. S., Johnson, D. F., Hamlin, P. H., & Kennedy, T. D. Behavior modification in a prison: Issues, problems and compromises. *Criminal Justice and Behavior*, 1977, *1*, 11-44.

Goldiamond, I. Toward a constructional approach to social problems: Ethical and constitutional issues raised by applied behavior analysis. *Behaviorism*, 1974, *2*, 1-84.

Goldstein, E. Compulsory treatment in Soviet psychiatric hospitals: A view from the inside. *Psychiatric Opinion*, 1975, *12*(7), 14-20.

Halleck, S. L. Legal and ethical aspects of behavior control. *American Journal of Psychiatry*, 1974, *131*, 381-385.

Hawkins, G. *The prison: Policy and practice*. Chicago: University of Chicago Press, 1976.

Hindelang, M. J., Gottfredson, M. R., Dunn, C. S., & Parisi, N. *Sourcebook of criminal justice statistics—1976* (U.S. Department of Justice). Washington, D.C.: U.S. Government Printing Office, 1977.

Ingram, G. Graduate training in correctional psychology. *Criminal Justice and Behavior*, 1974, *1*, 162-169.

Irwin, J. An acceptable context for biomedical research. In National Commission for the Protection of Human Subjects of Biomedical and Behavioral Research, *Research involving prisoners: Appendix to report and recommendations* (DHEW Publication No. (OS) 76-132). Washington: D.C.: U.S. Department of Health, Education, and Welfare, 1976.

Jessness, C. F. *The Jessness Inventory: Manual.* Palo Alto, Calif.: Consulting Psychologists Press, 1966.

Jourard, S. M. *Disclosing man to himself.* Princeton, N.J.: Van Nostrand, 1968.

Jourard, S. M. *Self disclosure: A compendium of research.* New York: Wiley, 1971.

Kassebaum, G., Ward, D., & Wilner, D. *Prison treatment and parole survival: An empirical assessment.* New York: Wiley, 1971.

Kaufman, E. Can comprehensive mental health care be provided in an overcrowed prison system? *Journal of Psychiatry and Law,* 1973, *1,* 243–262.

Kirkpatrick, A. M. Confidentiality in the correctional services. *Canadian Journal of Corrections,* 1963, *5*(2), 1–15.

Kittrie, N. *The right to be different: Deviance and enforced therapy.* Baltimore, Md.: Johns Hopkins Press, 1971.

Koran, L. M., & Brown, B. S. Psychologists in corrections and justice: Another view. In S. L. Brodsky, *Psychologists in the criminal justice system.* Urbana: University of Illinois Press, 1973.

LaFrance, M., & Mayo, C. *Moving bodies: Nonverbal communication in social relationships.* Monterey, Calif.: Brooks/Cole, 1978.

Loomer, A. Whatsoever cataclysm shall reign, psychotherapy goes on forever. *Voices,* 1977, *13,* 4–6.

Lourens, P. J. D. Skinner versus freedom: Concurrence and dissent. *Cumberland-Sanford Law Review,* 1973-1974, *4*(3), 425–439.

McConnell, J. V. Criminals can be brainwashed now. *Psychology Today,* November 1970, pp. 14–18; 74.

Megargee, E. I. The prediction of dangerousness. *Criminal Justice and Behavior,* 1976, *3,* 1–21.

Megargee, E. I. (Ed.). A new classification system for criminal offenders. *Criminal Justice and Behavior,* 1977, *4,* 107–216.

Milan, M. A., Wood, L. F., Williams, R. C., Rogers, J. G., Hampton, L. R., & McKee, J. M. *Applied behavior analysis and the imprisoned adult felon. Project I: The cellblock token economy.* Montgomery, Ala.: Rehabilitation Research Foundation, 1974.

Milgrams, S. Issues in the study of obedience: A reply to Baumrind. *American Psychologist,* 1964, *19,* 848–852.

Mills, M., & Morris, N. Prisoners as laboratory animals. *Transaction: Social Science and Modern Society,* 1974, *11*(5), 60–69.

Mitford, J. *Kind and usual punishment.* New York: Random House, 1973.

Monahan, J. The prevention of violence. In J. Monahan (Ed.), *Community mental health and the criminal justice system.* New York: Pergamon, 1976.

National Advisory Commission on Criminal Justice Standards and Goals. *Corrections.* Washington, D.C.: U.S. Government Printing Office. 1973.

National Minority Conference on Human Experimentation. Summary of the plenary and workshop sessions. In National Commission for the Protection of Human Subjects of Biomedical and Behavioral Research, *Research involving prisoners: Appendix to report and recommendations.* (DHEW Publication No. (OS) 76-132). Washington, D.C.: U.S. Government Printing Office, 1976.

National Commission for the Protection of Human Subjects of Biomedical and Behavioral Research, Department of Health, Education and Welfare. Protection of human subjects: Research involving prisoners—report and recommendations (DHEW Publication No. (OS) 76–131). *Federal Register,* January 14, 1977, *42*(10), 3075–3091.

Opton, E. M., Jr. Institutional behavioral modification as a fraud and sham. *Arizona Law Review,* 1975, *17*(1), 20–27.

Paulus, P., McCain, G., & Cox, V. A note on the use of prisons as enviroments for investigation of crowding. *Bulletin of the Psychonomic Society,* 1973, *1,* 427–428.

Peizer, S. R. Rebuttal to Armageddon. *The Journal of Correctional Psychology,* 1957, *2*(1), 10–16.

President's Commission on Law Enforcement and Administration of Justice. *Task force report: Corrections.* Washington, D.C.: U.S. Government Printing Office, 1967.

Quay, H. C., & Parsons, L. B. *The differential behavior classification of the juvenile offender.* Morgantown, W.Va.: Robert F. Kennedy Youth Center, 1970.

Redmountain, A. Two postulates, two memories, and a brief comment on the ubiquity of evil. *Voices,* 1977, *13,* 38–40.

Roth, L. H. Correctional psychiatry. In W. J. Curran, C. S. Petty, & A. L. McGarry (Eds.), *Modern legal medicine, psychiatry, and forensic science.* Philadelphia, Pa.: F. A. Davis, 1980.

Ryan, W. *Blaming the victim.* New York: Vintage, 1970.

Shah, S. A. Privileged communications. *Professional Psychology,* 1969, *1,* 56–69.

Shah, S. A. *Tarasoff* and its implications: A broader perspective. *APA Monitor,* February 1977, p. 2.

Shah, S. A. Dangerousness: A paradigm for exploring some issues in law and psychology. *American Psychologist,* 1978, *33,* 224–238.

Siegel, M. Confidentiality. *The Clincal Psychologist,* 1976, *30,* 1–23.

Slovenko, R. *Psychiatry and law.* Boston, Mass.: Little, Brown, 1973.

Sternberg, D. Legal frontiers in prison group psychotherapy. *Journal of Criminal Law, Criminology, and Police Science,* 1965, *56,* 446–449.

Stone, A. A. Recent mental health litigation: A critical perspective. *American Journal of Psychiatry,* 1977, *134,* 273–279.

Susman, J. Two images of the prison influence structure and their meaning for prisoner participation in biomedical and behavioral research. In National Commission for the Protection of Human Subjects of Biomedical and Behavioral Research, *Research involving prisoners: Appendix to report and recommendations* (DHEW Publication No. (OS) 76-132). Washington, D.C.: U.S. Department of Health, Education, and Welfare, 1976.

Suzuki, S. *Zen mind, beginner's mind.* New York: Weatherhill, 1970.

Swan, L. A. Ethical issues in research and experimentation in prisons. In National Commission for the Protection of Human Subjects of Biomedical and Behavioral Research, *Research involving prisoners: Appendix to report and recommendations* (DHEW Publication No. (OS) 76-132). Washington, D.C.: U.S. Department of Health, Education, and Welfare, 1976.

Tannenbaum. A. S., & Cooke, R. A. Research in prisons: A preliminary report. In National Commission for the Protection of Human Subjects of Biomedical and Behavioral Research, *Research involving prisoners: Appendix to report and recommendations* (DHEW Publication No. (OS) 76-132). Washington, D.C.: U.S. Department of Health Education, and Welfare, 1976.

Thorne, R. C. Community psychology and correctional reform. *Journal of Community Psychology,* 1975, *3,* 163–165.

Warren, M. Q. Classification of offenders as an aid to efficient management and effective treatment. *Journal of Criminal Law, Criminology, and Police Science,* 1971, *62,* 239–258.

West, C. Philosophical perspective on the participation of prisoners in experimental research. In National Commission for the Protection of Human Subjects of Biomedical and Behavioral Research, *Research involving prisoners: Appendix to report and recommendations* (DHEW Publication No (OS) 76-132). Washington, D.C.: U.S. Department of Health, Education, and Welfare, 1976.

Wexler, D. B. Token and taboo: Behavior modification, token economies, and the law. *California Law Review,* 1973, *61,* 81–109.

Wexler, D. B. Reflections on the legal regulation of behavior modification in an institutional setting. *Arizona Law Review,* 1975, *17*(1), 132–143.

Wicks, R. *Correctional psychology.* San Francisco: Canfield, 1974.

Wilson, D. P. *My six convicts.* New York: Rinehart, 1951.

Wilson, D. W., & Donnerstein, E. Legal and ethical aspects of nonreactive social psychological research. *American Psychologist,* 1976, *31,* 765–773.

Chapter 5: Ethical Issues for Psychologists in the Juvenile Justice System—Know and Tell

Reference Notes

1. Davidson, W. S. *The diversion of juvenile delinquents: An examination of the processes and relative efficacy of child advocacy and behavioral contracting.* Unpublished doctoral dissertation, University of Illinois at Urbana-Champaign, 1975.

2. Monahan, J. *The prediction of violent behavior in juveniles.* Paper presented at the National Symposium on the Serious Juvenile Offender, Minneapolis, Minnesota, September 19–20, 1977.

3. Robison, J. & Takagi, P. *Case decisions in a state parole system* (Administrative Abstract Research Report 31). Sacramento: Research Division, California Department of Corrections, 1968.

4. Lamiell, J. T. *Human judgment and adolescent deviance in the community.* Unpublished doctoral dissertation, Kansas State University, 1976.

References

Alinsky, S. D. *Rules for radicals.* New York: Random House, 1971.

Alexander, J. F. Defensive and supportive communications in normal and deviant families. *Journal of Consulting and Clinical Psychology,* 1973, *40,* 223–231.

Ariessohn, R. M. Offense vs. offender in juvenile court. *Juvenile Justice,* August 1972. pp. 17–22.

Bard, M. *Training police as specialists in family crisis intervention* (National Institute of Law Enforcement and Criminal Justice). Washington, D.C.: U.S. Government Printing Office, 1970.

Baron, R., & Feeney, F. *Juvenile diversion through family counseling.* Washington, D.C.: National Institute of Law Enforcement and Criminal Justice, Law Enforcement Assistance Administration, 1976.

Baron, R., Feeney, F., & Thornton, W. Preventing delinquency through diversion: The Sacramento County 601 diversion project. *Federal Probation,* 1973, *37,* 13–18.

Barton, W. H. Discretionary decision-making in juvenile justice. *Crime and Delinquency*, 1976, *22*, 470–480.

Bixenstine, V. E., & Buterbaugh, R. L. Integrative behavior in adolescent boys as a function of delinquency and race. *Journal of Consulting Psychology*, 1967, *31*, 471–476.

Brodsky, S. L. *Psychologists in the criminal justice system*. Urbana: University of Illinois Press, 1973.

Camp, B. W. Verbal mediation in young aggressive boys. *Journal of Abnormal Psychology*, 1977, *86*, 145–153.

Cantor, P. C. Personality characteristics found among youthful female suicide attempters. *Journal of Abnormal Psychology*, 1976, *85*, 324–329.

Caplan, N., & Nelson, S. D. On being useful: The nature and consequences of psychological research on social problems. *American Psychologist*, 1973, *28*, 199–211.

Churchman, C. W. *The design of inquiring systems*. New York: Basic Books, 1971.

Cronbach, L. J. Beyond the two disciplines of scientific psychology. *American Psychologist*, 1975, *30*, 116–127.

Davidson, W. S., & Rapp, C. Child advocacy in the justice system. *Social Work*, 1976, *21*, 225–232.

Davidson, W. S., & Rappaport, J. Toward a model for advocacy: Values, roles and conceptions from community psychology. In G. H. Weber & G. J. McCall, (Eds.), *Social scientists as advocates: Views from the applied disciplines*. Beverly Hills, Calif.: Sage, 1978.

Davidson, W. S., Rappaport, J., Seidman, E., Berck, P., Rapp, C., Rhodes, W., & Herring, J. A diversion program for juvenile offenders. *Social Work Research and Abstracts*, 1977, *1*, 47–56.

Davidson, W. S., & Seidman, E. Studies of behavior modification and juvenile delinquency: A review, methodological critique and social perspective. *Psychological Bulletin*, 1974, *81*, 998–1011.

Dean, C. W., & Reppucci, N. D. Juvenile correctional institutions. In D. Glaser (Ed.), *Handbook of criminology*. New York: Rand McNally, 1974.

DeMyer-Gapin, S., & Scott, T. J. Effect of stimulus novelty on stimulation seeking in antisocial and neurotic children. *Journal of Abnormal Psychology*, 1977, *86*, 96–98.

Doleschal, E., & Klapmuts, N. *Toward a new criminology*. Hackensack, N.J.: National Council on Crime and Delinquency, 1973.

Douglas, J. D. *American social order: Social rules in a pluralistic society*. Glencoe, Ill.: Free Press, 1971.

Edelman, P. B. The Massachusetts task force reports: Advocacy for children. *Harvard Educational Review*, 1973, *43*, 639–652.

Ethical standards of psychologists. Washington, D.C.: American Psychological Association, 1979.

Fairweather, G. W., Sanders, D. H., & Tornatzky, L. G. *Creating change in mental health organizations*. New York: Permagon, 1974.

Fo, W. S. O., & O'Donnell, C. R. The buddy system: Effect of community intervention on delinquent offenses. *Behavior Therapy*, 1975, *6*, 522–524.

Fox, S. J. Abolishing the juvenile court. *Harvard Law School Bulletin*, 1977, *28*, 22–27.

Frank, S., & Quinlan, D. M. Ego development and female delinquency: A cognitive-developmental approach. *Journal of Abnormal Psychology*, 1976, *85*, 505–510.

Galliher, J. F., & McCartney, J. L. The influence of funding agencies on juvenile delinquency research. *Social Problems*, 1973, *21*, 77–90.

Ganzer, V. J., & Sarason, I. G. Variables associated with recidivism among juvenile delinquents. *Journal of Consulting and Clinical Psychology*, 1973, *40*, 1–5.

Gergen, K. J. Social psychology as history. *Journal of Personality and Social Psychology*, 1973, *26*, 309–320.

Glueck, S., & Glueck, E. *Unraveling juvenile delinquency*. Cambridge, Mass.: Harvard University Press, 1951.

Glueck, S., & Glueck, E. *Towards a typology of juvenile offenders*. New York: Grunne & Stratton, 1971.

Goldenberg, I. I. *Build me a mountain: Youth, poverty and the creation of new settings*. Cambridge, Mass.: MIT Press, 1971

Green, P. The obligations of American social scientists. *The Annals* (The American Academy of Political and Social Science), 1971, *394*, 13–27.

Heisler, G. Ways to deter law violators: Effects of levels of threat and vicarious punishment on cheating. *Journal of Consulting and Clinical Psychology*, 1974, *42*, 577–582.

Hetherington, E. M., Stouwie, R. J., & Ridberg, E. H. Pattern of family interaction and child-rearing attitudes related to three dimensions of juvenile delinquency. *Journal of Abnormal Psychology*, 1971, *78*, 160–176.

Hoefler, S. A., & Bornstein, P. H. Achievement place: An evaluative review. *Criminal Justice and Behavior*, 1975, *2*, 146–168.

Institute of Judicial Administration–American Bar Association Joint Commission on Juvenile Justice Standards. *Standards relating to juvenile delinquency and sanctions* (Juvenile Justice Standards Project Series, tentative draft). Cambridge, Mass.: Ballinger, 1976.

Johnson, R. W. Research objectives for policy analysis. In K. M. Dolbeare (Ed.), *Public policy evaluation*. Beverly Hills, Calif.: Sage Publications, 1975.

Jurkovic, G. J., & Prentice, N. M. Dimensions of moral interaction and moral judgment in delinquent and nondelinquent families. *Journal of Consulting and Clinical Psychology*, 1974, *42*, 256–262.

Kantor, J. E., Walker, C. E., & Hays, L. A study of the usefulness of Lanyon's psychological screening inventory with adolescents. *Journal of Consulting and Clinical Psychology*, 1976, *44*, 313–316.

Kassebaum, G. *Delinquency and social policy*. Englewood Cliffs, N.J.: Prentice-Hall, 1974.

Kelman, H. *A time to speak: On human values and social research*. San Francisco: Jossey-Bass, 1968.

Kirkegaard-Sorensen, L., & Mednick, S. A. Registered criminality in families with children at high risk for schizophrenia. *Journal of Abnormal Psychology*, 1975, *84*, 197–204.

Klapmuts, N. Community alternatives to prison. *Crime & Delinquency*, 1973, *5*, 305–337.

Klein, M. W., & Teilman, K. S. *Pivotal ingredients of police juvenile diversion programs*. Washington, D.C.: National Institute for Juvenile Justice and Delinquency Prevention, Law Enforcement Assistance Administration, 1976.

Klein, N. C., Alexander, J. F., & Parsons, B. V. Impact of family systems intervention on recidivism and sibling delinquency: A model of primary prevention and program evaluation. *Journal of Consulting and Clinical Psychology*, 1977, *45*, 469–474.

Kulik, J. A., Stein, K. B., & Sarbin, T. R. Dimensions and patterns of adolescent antisocial behavior. *Journal of Consulting and Clincial Psychology*, 1968, *32*, 375–382.

Lemmert, E. M. *Instead of court: Diversion in juvenile justice* (DHEW Publication No. (ADM) 74–59). Rockville, Md.: National Institute of Mental Health, 1974.

Levenson, M., & Neuringer, C. Problem-soving behavior in suicidal adolescents. *Journal of Consulting and Clinical Psychology*, 1971, *31*, 433–436.

Livermore, J. M., Malmquist, C. P., & Meehl, P. E. On the justification for civil commitment. *University of Pennsylvania Law Review*, 1968, *117*, 75–96.

Lyons, G. M. (Ed.). Social science and the federal government. *The Annals* (The American Academy of Political & Social Science), 1971, *394*, 1–120.

Martinson, R. What works?—Questions and answers about prison reform. *The Public Interest*, 1974, *35*, 22–54.

Maruyama, M. Monopolarization, family, and individuality. *Psychiatric Quarterly*, 1966, *40*, 133–149.

Maruyama, M. Cultural, social and psychological considerations in the planning of public works. *Technological Forecasting and Social Change*, 1973, *5*, 135–143.

Maruyama, M. Paradigms and communication. *Technological Forecasting & Social Change*, 1974, *6*, 3–32.

Massachusetts Advocacy Center. *Second annual report*. Boston, Mass.: Author, 1975.

McCarthy, F. B. Should juvenile delinquency be abolished? *Crime and Delinquency*, 1977, *23*, 196–203.

McGee, R. K. *Crisis intervention in the community*. Baltimore, Md.: University Park Press, 1974.

Megargee, E. I. The prediction of dangerous behavior. *Criminal Justice and Behavior*, 1976, *3*, 3–22.

Mitroff, I. *The subjective side of science: A philosophical inquiry into the psychology of the Apollo moon scientists*. New York: American Elsevier Publishing, 1974.

Mitroff, I. I., & Blankenship, L. V. On the methodology of the holistic experiment: An approach to the conceptualization of large-scale experiments. *Technological Forecasting and Social Change*, 1973, *4*, 339–353.

Mitroff, I. I., & Turoff, M. Technological forecasting and assessment: Science and/or mythology. *Technical Forecasting and Social Change*, 1973, *5*, 113–134.

Mitroff, I. I., & Turoff, M. On measuring the conceptual errors in large scale social experiments: The future as decision. *Technological Forecasting and Social Change*, 1974, *6*, 389–402.

Monahan, J. The psychiatrization of criminal behavior. *Hospital and Community Psychiatry*, 1973, *24*, 105–107.

Monahan, J. The prevention of violence. In J. Monahan (Ed.), *Community mental health and the criminal justice system*. New York: Pergamon, 1976.

Monahan, J. & Cummings, L. Social policy implications of the inability to predict violence. *Journal of Social Issues*, 1975, *31*, 153-164.

Moore, T., & Nay, W. R. Control of freedom in social research. Unpublished manuscript, University of Illinois, 1977.

Morris, N. *The future of imprisonment: Studies in crime and justice*. Chicago: University of Chicago Press, 1974.

Mullen, J. *Pre-trial services: An evaluation of policy related research*. Cambridge, Mass.: ABT Associates, 1974.

National Council on Crime and Delinquency. The nondangerous offender should not be imprisoned. *Crime & Delinquency*, 1973, *21*, 315–322.

Newman, R. C., II, & Pollack, D. Proxemics in deviant adolescents. *Journal of Consulting and Clinical Psychology*, 1973, *40*, 6–8.

O'Brien, K. E., & Marcus, M. *Juvenile diversion: A selected bibliography*. Washington, D.C.: National Criminal Justice Reference Service, Law Enforcement Assistance Administration, 1976.

Olmstead, B. The great mail robbery. *Chicago Sun-Times*, March 4, 1977.

O. M. Collective. *The organizer's manual*. New York: Bantam, 1971.

Palmer, T. B. California's treatment program for delinquent adolescents. *Journal of Research in Crime and Delinquency*, 1971, *8*, 74–92.

Palmer, T. B. The youth authority's community treatment project. *Federal Probation*, 1974, *38*, 3-14.

Platt, A. *The child savers*. Chicago: University of Chicago Press, 1969.

Rappaport, J. *Community psychology: Values, research, and action*. New York: Holt, Rinehart & Winston, 1977. (a)

Rappaport, J. From Noah to Babel: Relationships between conceptions, values, analysis levels and social intervention strategies. In I. Iscoe, B. Bloom, & C. D. Spielberger (Eds.), *Community Psychology in transition*. New York: Hemisphere Press, 1977. (b)

Rappaport, J., Seidman, E., & Davidson, W. S. Demonstration research and manifest versus true adoption. In R. F. Muñoz, L. R. Snowden, & J. G. Kelly (Eds.), *Social and psychological research in community settings*. San Francisco: Jossey-Bass, 1979.

Riegel, K. F. Influence of economic and political ideologies on the development of developmental psychology. *Psychological Bulletin*, 1972, *78*, 129–141.

Roberts, A. H., Erikson, R. V., Riddle, M., & Bacon, J. G. Demographic variables, base rates, and personality characteristics associated with recidivism in male delinquents. *Journal of Consulting and Clinical Psychology*, 1974, *42*, 833–841.

Rothman, J. *Planning and organizing for social change: Action principles from social science research*. New York: Columbia University Press, 1974.

Rubin, H. T. The juvenile court's search for identity and responsibility. *Crime and Delinquency*, 1977, *23*, 1–13.

Rutherford, A., & McDermott, R. *National evaluation program Phase I Summary Report*. Washington, D.C.,: National Institute of Law Enforcement and Criminal Justice, Law Enforcement Assistance Administration, 1976.

Ryan, W. *Blaming the victim*. New York: Vintage Books, 1971.

Sagarin, E. *Deviants and deviance: An introduction to the study of disvalued people and behavior*. New York: Praeger, 1975.

Sarason, S. B. *The creation of settings and the future societies*. San Francisco: Jossey-Bass, 1972.

Scari, R., & Hassenfeld, Y. (Eds.). *Brought to justice? Juveniles, the courts and the law*. Ann Arbor, Mich.: National Assessment of Juvenile Corrections, 1976.

Scarpitti, F. R., & Stephenson, R. M. Juvenile court dispositions: Factors in the decision-making process. *Crime & Delinquency*, 1971, 142–151.

Schlesinger, S. E. The prediction of dangerousness in juveniles: A replication. *Crime & Delinquency*, 1978, *24*, 40–48.

Schlichter, K. J., & Ratliff, R. G. Discrimination learning in juvenile delinquents. *Journal of Abnormal Psychology*, 1971, *77*, 46–48.

Schur, E. M. *Radical non-intervention: Rethinking the delinquency problem*. Englewood Cliffs, N.J.: Prentice-Hall, 1973.

Seidman, E. Justice, values, and social science: Unexamined premises. In R. J. Simon (Ed.), *Research in law and sociology: An annual compilation of research* (Vol. 1). Greenwich, Conn.: Jai Press, 1978.

Seidman, E., Rappaport, J., & Davidson, W. S. *Adolescents in legal jeopardy: Initial success and replication of an alternative to the juvenile justice system*. Address presented at the meeting of the American Psychological Association, Washington, D.C., September 1976. (Reprinted in Ku, R., & Blew, C. *The adolescent diversion project: A university's approach to delinquency prevention*. Washington, D.C.: National Institute of Law Enforcement and Criminal Justice, 1977.)

Selltiz, C., Wrightsman, L. S., & Cook, S. W. *Research methods in social relations* (3rd ed.). New York: Holt, Rinehart & Winston, 1976.

Shah, S. A. The criminal justice system. In S. E. Golann & C. Eisdorfer, (Eds.), *Handbook of community mental health*. New York: Appleton-Century-Crofts, 1972.

Silver, I. (Ed.) *The challenge of crime in a free society: A report by the President's Commission on Law Enforcement and Administration of Justice*. New York: Avon Books, 1968.

Sjoberg, G. Politics, ethics and evaluation research. In M. Guttentag & E. L. Struening (Eds.), *Handbook of evaluation research* (Vol. 2). Beverly Hills, Calif.: Sage Publications, 1975.

Smart, R. G., & Jones, D. Illicit LSD users: Their personality characteristics and psychopathology. *Journal of Abnormal Psychology*, 1970, *75*, 286–292.

Smith, J., & Lanyon, R. I. Prediction of juvenile probation violators. *Journal of Consulting and Clincial Psychology*, 1968, *32*, 54–58.

Stein, K. B., Sarbin, T. R., & Kulik, J. A. Future time perspective: Its relation to the socialization process and the delinquent role. *Journal of Consulting and Clinical Psychology*, 1968, *33*, 257–264.

Stein, K. B., Sarbin, T. R., & Kulik, J. A. Further validation of antisocial personality types. *Journal of Consulting and Clinical Psychology*, 1971, *36*, 177–182.

U.S. Department of Health, Education and Welfare. *The challenge of youth service bureaus.* Washington, D.C.: Author, 1973. (ERIC Document Reproduction Service No. ED 083 526)

Vinter, R. D. (Ed.). *Time out: A national study of juvenile corrections programs.* Ann Arbor, Mich.: National Assessment of Juvenile Corrections. 1976.

Watzlawick, P., Weakland, J. H., & Fisch, R. *Change: Principles of problem formation and problem resolution.* New York: Norton, 1974.

Whitehill, M., DeMyer-Gapin, S., & Scott, T. J. Stimulation seeking in antisocial preadolescent children. *Journal of Abnormal Psychology, 1976, 85,* 101–104.

Wiggins, J. S. *Personality and prediction: Principles of personality assessment.* Reading, Mass.: Addison-Wesley, 1973.

Chapter 6: A National Study of Ethical Dilemmas of Psychologists in the Criminal Justice System

Reference Note

1. Monahan, J. Unpublished communication to the APA Task Force on the Role of Psychologists in the Criminal Justice System, 1977.

References

Bersoff, D. N. Therapists as protectors and policemen: New roles as a result of Tarasoff? *Professional Psychology, 1976, 7,* 267–273.

Brodsky, S. R. *Psychologists in the criminal justice system.* Marysville, Ohio: American Association of Correctional Psychologists, 1972.

Clark, R. *Crime in America.* New York: Simon & Schuster, 1970.

Davison, G. C., & Stuart, R. B. Behavior therapy and civil liberties. *American Psychologist, 1975, 30,* 755–763.

Ennis, B. J., & Litwack, T. R. Psychiatry and the presumption of expertise: Flipping coins in the courtroom. *California Law Review, 1974, 62,* 693–752.

Ennis, B., & Siegel, L. *The rights of mental patients.* New York: Avon, 1973.

Ethical standards of psychologists. Washington, D.C.: American Psychological Association, 1979.

Franks, C. M., & Wilson, G. T. (Eds.). *Annual review of behavior therapy: Theory and practice.* New York: Brunner/Mazel, 1976.

Friedman, P. Legal regulation of applied behavior analysis in mental institutions and prisons. *Arizona Law Review,* 1975, *17,* 75–104.

Heinz, A. M., Heinz, J. G., Senderowitz, S. J., & Vance, M. A. Sentencing by parole board: An evaluation. *Journal of Criminal Law and Criminology,* 1976, *67,* 1–31.

Irwin, J. Adaption to being corrected: Corrections from the convict's perspective. In D. Glaser (Ed.), *Handbook of criminology.* Chicago: Rand-McNally, 1974.

Kaimowitz v. Michigan Department of Mental Health, U.S.L.W, 42, 2063 (C.A. 73-19343-AW, Cir. Ct. Wayne County, Mich., July 10, 1973).

Megargee, E. The prediction of violence with psychological tests. In C. Spielberger (Ed.), *Current topics in clinical and community psychology.* New York: Academic Press, 1970.

Mischel, W. *Personality and assessment.* New York: Wiley, 1968.

Mischel, W. Toward a cognitive social learning reconceptualization of personality. *Psychological Review,* 1973, *80,* 252–283.

Mitford, J. *Kind and usual punishment: The prison business.* New York: Knopf, 1973.

Monahan, J. The prevention of violence. In J. Monahan (Ed.), *Community mental health and the criminal justice system.* New York: Pergamon Press, 1975.

Moos, R., & Insel, P. *Issues in social ecology.* Palo Alto, Calif.: National Press, 1973.

Morris, N. *The future of imprisonment.* Chicago: University of Chicago Press, 1974.

Opton, E. M. Institutional behavior modification as a fraud and a sham. *Arizona Law Review,* 1975, *17,* 20–28.

President's Commission on Law Enforcement and Administration of Justice. *The challenge of crime in a free society.* Washington, D.C.: U.S. Government Printing Office, 1967.

Reppucci, N. D. & Saunders, J. T. The social psychology of behavior modification: Problems of implementation in natural settings. *American Psychologist,* 1974, *29,* 649–660.

Robinson, D. N. Harm, offense, and nuisance: Some first steps in the establishment of an ethics of treatment. *American Psychologist,* 1974, *20,* 233–238.

Saunders, J. T., & Reppucci, N. D. The social identity of behavior modification. In M. Hersen & R. M. Eisler (Eds.), *Progress in behavior modification* (Vol. 6). New York: Academic Press, 1978.

Shah, S. Editorial. *APA Monitor,* February 1977, p. 2.

Siegel, M. Editorial *APA Monitor,* February 1977, p. 5.

Simmons, S., Monahan, J., Whiteley, R., & Whitely, J. California court ruling in dangerousness stirs controversy. *APA Monitor,* March 1975, pp. 12; 18.

Skinner, B. F. *Beyond freedom and dignity*. New York: Knopf, 1971.

Szasz, T. *Law, liberty, and psychiatry: An inquiry into the social uses of mental health practices*. New York: Macmillan, 1963.

Von Hirsch, J. Prediction of criminal conduct and preventive confinement of convicted persons. *Buffalo Law Review*, 1972, *21*, 730–740.

Watzlawick, P., Weakland, J., & Fisch, R. *Change: Principles of problem formation and problem resolution*. New York: Norton, 1974.

Wenk, E., & Emrich, R. Assaultive youth: An exploratory study of the assaultive experience and assaultive potential of California Youth Authority Wards. *Journal of Research in Crime and Delinquency*, 1972, *9*, 171–196.

Wexler, D. Token and taboo: Behavior modification, token economies and the law. *California Law Review*, 1973, *61*, 81–109.

Wexler, D. B. Reflections on the legal regulation of behavior modification in institutional settings. *Arizona Law Review*, 1975, *17*, 132–143.

Whiteley, J., & Whiteley, R. California court extends privilege debate. *APA Monitor*, February 1977, p. 5.

Ziskin, J. *Coping with psychiatric and psychological testimony*. Beverly Hills, Calif.: Law and Psychology Press, 1975.